MW01122039

Racial, ethnic, and homophobic violence: killing in the name of otherness

Hate-motivated violence is now deemed a 'serious national problem' in most Western societies. In the last decade, laws against hatred have been widely debated in Britain, Australia and the United States, as punishing hate crimes is increasingly viewed as a political and legal priority. Yet what is a hate crime?

With contributions by British, Australian, American, Canadian, Irish, Italian and French researchers, this book provides an analysis of crime related to race, ethnicity and sexual orientation. Killing the Other implies constructing the Other: whether the Australian Aborigine, the Gypsy, the immigrant, or the gay or lesbian. And, addressing how perpetrators of hate crimes have attempted to construct otherness in a way that legitimises violence, this book thus opens up an interdisciplinary perspective on hate crime, and on the ways in which certain groups or individuals are transformed into expiatory victims.

Professor Michel Prum, Professor of British History at Paris 7 University, founded the Groupe de Recherche sur l'Eugenisme et le Racisme (GRER – Research Group on Eugenics and Racism) in 1998 and he has edited six books on racism in English. **Dr Bénédicte Deschamps** is Senior Lecturer also at Paris 7 University. **Dr Marie-Claude Barbier** is Senior Lecturer and head of department at the Ecole Normale Supérieure of Cachan.

Racial, ethnic, and homophobic violence: killing in the name of otherness

Edited by Michel Prum,
Bénédicte Deschamps and
Marie-Claude Barbier

/ 6 0 2 0 1

Routledge·Cavendish
Taylor & Francis Group
a GlassHouse book

First published 2007 by Routledge-Cavendish
2 Park Square, Milton Park, Abingdon, Oxon OX14 4RN

Simultaneously published in the USA and Canada
by Routledge-Cavendish
270 Madison Ave, New York, NY 10016

A Glasshouse book

Transferred to Digital Printing 2007

*Routledge-Cavendish is an imprint of the Taylor & Francis Group, an
informa business*

© 2007 Marie-Claude Barbier, Bénédicte Deschamps and Michel
Prum

Typeset in Times New Roman by
RefineCatch Limited, Bungay, Suffolk
Printed and bound in Great Britain by
TJI Digital, Padstow, Cornwall

British Library Cataloguing in Publication Data
A catalogue record for this book is available from the British Library

Library of Congress Cataloging in Publication Data
   Racial, ethnic, and homophobic violence : killing in the name of
otherness / edited by Marie-Claude Barbier, Bénédicte Deschamps,
and Michel Prum.
      p. cm.
   ISBN-13: 978-1-904385-15-8 (hardback)
   ISBN-10: 1-904385-57-5 (hardback)
   1. Hate crimes.   2 Race relations.   3. Ethnic relations.
4. Homophobia.   I. Barbier, Marie-Claude.   II. Deschamps,
Bénédicte.   III. Prum, Michel.
   HV6773.5.R33 2007
   305.8—dc22   2006027736

ISBN10: 1-90438-557-5 (hbk)
ISBN13: 978-1-90438-557-8 (hbk)

Contents

Acknowledgements

This book could not have been written without the support of the University of Paris 7, in particular the department of Intercultural Studies and Applied Languages (EILA), and the Ecole Normale Supérieure of Cachan. We would also like to thank the Research Group on Eugenics and Racism (GRER) and the Interdisciplinary Centre on North-American Research (CIRNA) – two research units of Paris 7 University. We are similarly grateful to the Canadian Cultural Centre of Paris, particularly to Ms Orietta Doucet-Mugnier.

We are pleased to acknowledge our debt of gratitude to Professor Neil Davie for carefully reading and correcting part of this book.

Notes on contributors

Marie-Claude Barbier is a Senior Lecturer at the Ecole Normale Supérieure du Cachan. Her research is on the Commonwealth focusing on Canada and South Africa. She published *Immersion and Bilingualism in Ontario* (1992).

Stanley R. Barrett is Professor at the University of Guelph, Canada. His research has included a study of organised racism and anti-Semitism in Canada and class and ethnicity in rural Ontario. He has published *Is God a Racist: The Right Wing in Canada* (Toronto, 1987) and *Paradise: Class, Commuters and Ethnicity in Rural Ontario* (1994).

Chris Cunneen is the New South Global Professor of Criminology at the University of New South Wales, Australia. His main areas of research include hate crime, colonialism and Aboriginal contact with the criminal justice system. He has published numerous books, including *Conflict, Politics and Crime* (2001).

Neil Davie is Professor of British History at the Université Lumière Lyon 2, France. His research is mainly in the field of criminal justice history, particularly the history of British criminology and penal policy in the Victorian and Edwardian periods. He has published *Visages de la criminalité : à la recherche d'une théorie scientifique du criminel-type en Angleterre, 1860–1914* (2004) and *Tracing the Criminal: The Rise of Scientific Criminology in Britain, 1860–1918* (2005).

Bénédicte Deschamps is a Senior Lecturer at the University of Paris 7. Her research focuses on Italian-American immigration history and on the ethnic press in the United States. Her publications include *L'Immigration aux Etats-Unis, de 1607 à nos jours* (1998, with Dominique Daniel) and *La Presse italo-américaine* (forthcoming).

Bryan Fanning is a Senior Lecturer in the School of Applied Social Science at University College Dublin. He is the author of *Racism and Social Change in the Republic of Ireland* (2002) and editor of *Immigration and Social*

Change in the Republic of Ireland (Manchester, 2006). He is co-editor of *Ireland Develops: Administration and Social Policy 1953–2003* (2003), *Theorising Irish Social Policy* (2004) and *Care and Social Change in the Irish Welfare Economy* (2006).

David Fraser is Professor of Law and Social Theory at the University of Nottingham, UK. His research focuses on the role of law and the legal profession in the Holocaust, anti-Semitism and Holocaust Denial, and Roma rights. His most recent work is *Law After Auschwitz – Towards A Jurisprudence of the Holocaust* (2005).

Jack Levin is the Brudnick Professor of Sociology and Criminology at Northeastern University, where he directs its Brudnick Center on Violence and Conflict. His research has been in the areas of hate crimes and multiple murder. Levin's books include *The Violence of Hate: Confronting Racism, Anti-Semitism and Other Forms of Bigotry* (2002) and *Extreme Killing: Understanding Serial and Mass Murder* (2005 with James A. Fox).

Stefano Luconi teaches history of North America at the University of Florence, Italy, and specialises in Italian immigration to the United States. His books include *The Italian-American Vote in Providence, Rhode Island, 1916–1948* (2004) and *From Paesani to White Ethnics: The Italian Experience in Philadelphia* (2001).

Guillaume Marche is Senior Lecturer in American Studies at the University of Paris 12 – Val du Marne. He earned a PhD in 2000 with a dissertation on private and political identities in lesbian and gay mobilisation in the United States in the period 1980–2000. His current research deals with issues of community, identity, and subjectivity in lesbian and gay movements in the United States.

Lawrence McNamara is a Senior Lecturer in the Division of Law at Macquarie University, Sydney, Australia. He researches and publishes in the areas of defamation, the legal regulation of hatred and freedom of speech.

Marguerite Moritz is Professor and Associate Dean for Graduate Studies at the University of Colorado, Boulder. Her research is on media portrayals of gays. She was writer and story consultant for the award winning film *Scout's Honor*, which examines the Boy Scouts of America's anti-gay policies. Currently, she is working on a documentary on gay marriage in Colorado. She is UNESCO Chair in International Journalism Education.

Claire Parfait is a Senior Lecturer at the University of Paris 7. Her research is about African-American history and American book history. She has published a number of articles on both subjects and co-edited a special issue of *Cahiers Charles V*: 'Histoire(s) de livres: Le livre et l'édition dans le monde anglophone' (December 2002). Her book *The Publishing History* *of* Uncle Tom's Cabin, *1852–2002* is to be published by Ashgate Press in 2007.

Michel Prum is Professor of British History at the University of Paris 7. He founded the Research Group on Eugenics and Racism (GRER) in 1998. He is Director of the 'Racism and Eugenics' series for L'Harmattan Publishing House in Paris. He has also been editing the Complete Works of Charles Darwin in French with Patrick Tort and seven collective volumes of the GRER since 2000.

Gordana Rabrenovic is Associate Professor of Sociology and Education and Associate Director of the Brudnick Center on Violence and Conflict at Northeastern University. Her substantive specialties include community studies, urban education and inter group conflict and violence. She is the author of the books *Community Builders: A Tale of Neighborhood Mobilization in Two Cities* (1996) and *Why We Hate* (2004) co-authored with Jack Levin.

Introduction

Hate-motivated violence is now deemed a 'serious national problem' in most Western societies.[1] In the last decade, laws against racial hatred have been widely debated in Britain, Australia and the United States, as punishing hate crimes is being increasingly viewed as a priority on the agenda. Yet what is a hate crime? The legal definition used by the United States House of Representatives is that a hate crime is 'a crime in which the defendant intentionally selects a victim, or, in the case of property crime, the property that is the object of the crime, because of the actual or perceived race, color, religion, national origin, ethnicity, gender, disability, or sexual orientation of any person'.[2] However recent scholarship has challenged that definition, by introducing a new approach not based solely on the motivation of perpetrators, but also on the consequences such crimes may have on their victims. The additional harm to the individual victim and to society at large, in terms of tensions being created between communities, has been explored.[3] As hate crime 'constitutes a threat of more violence to minority group members', it sends out a message of terror to the members of the victim's group, what Paul Iganski calls the '*in terrorem* effect'.[4] Sociologist Kathleen M. Blee thus emphasises the limitation of a narrow intent-oriented definition which leaves 'little analytic room to consider whether violence can be about *establishing* race rather than being an *effect* of preformed racial categories.'[5] In fact, depriving a selected victim of their rights to life or property is the very act by which the injured party is constructed as Other and thus ontologised. 'Call your dog a name and drown it', the proverb goes. Naming and killing often are indeed two sides of the same coin. Naming the Other is often a way of obliterating their identity as a professional, a citizen, a member of the family, whether on the terraces at football matches or in the confines of a police custody suite.[6] This metaphorical murder of people who are marginalised by mainstream society boils down to an exclusion that can be felt by the victim as complete annihilation, and understood by other potential offenders as a call for bloodshed.

The aim of this book is to study the mechanisms that lead men and women, institutions and governments, to single out groups of individuals whom they define as Others on the basis of actual or imaginary differences for the purpose of transforming them into expiatory victims. It is not the intention of this work to provide a general survey on the development and evolution of the concept of hate crime, but rather to open up an interdisciplinary perspective, including contributions by historians, sociologists and law specialists, on the question of the murder – whether real or symbolical – of the Other in society. The articles collected in this book are concerned with racial and homophobic violence which episodically or chronically have marked the history of a number of English-speaking countries. Sadly, ethnoviolence is the monopoly of no single nation in the world. Nonetheless, the choice of a given linguistic area, arbitrary though it is, contributes to highlighting common trends not only in the rhetoric of exclusion adopted by these countries, but also in the way the concept of otherness has been used to legitimise acts of violence which would have been deemed ethically unacceptable by their very perpetrators, had the victims not been previously categorised in an attempt to deprive them of the rights granted to ordinary citizens.

Colonial governments are known to resort to classification schemes allegedly proving the inferiority of the native populations living on the territory they have conquered, so as to dispossess them of their rights. In the case of Australia, eugenics played an important part in the legitimisation of a series of racist policies victimising the Aborigines. Criminologist Chris Cunneen explains how the Australian government, drawing upon social-Darwinistic ideology, established a racial distinction between the 'so-called "full blood" aboriginal people, [who] were bound to die out because of their inferiority', and 'the apparently rapidly growing population of "mixed blood" children'. What Cunneen analyses in chapter 1 is how such classification allowed the authorities to breed the aboriginality out of 'mixed blood' children, by removing the latter from their families and forcefully integrating them into mainstream households that would 'whiten' them. Similar policies were adopted in Canada and the United States, though on a lesser scale and in a different perspective.[7] Assimilating communities by trying to wipe out differences through what could be called an ethnocide has been the common policy of the various Australian governments. While authorities have sought to achieve aboriginal conformity to a national culture modelled on white values, thus forcing the indigenous population into an uncalled-for sameness, this has meant trying to negate their historical specificity as a colonised group, and play the card of 'sameness' to reduce them to the status of 'disadvantaged minority'. Paradoxically, then, the inclusion of Aborigines into the wide spectrum of a 'diverse Australia' is a way of excluding them once more, by depriving them of a past which not only constitutes a part of their identity but also entitles them to reparations in today's society. Indigenous people are currently involved in a judicial battle, and demand compensation for the abuse of human rights they have endured. Yet, to prove they were the victims of historical injustices, they are enjoined to give scientific evidence, which is artfully exploited, distorted or ignored by politicians whenever historians are not able to reach a consensus. In such a debate where double standards are the rule, the oral tradition of aboriginal history is often discarded, leaving room for authorities to deny the claim.

Particularly striking is the Australian Conservative government's contention that the colonisers may be credited with 'beneficial intent', and that they acted according to the 'standards of the time'. Against this backdrop they feel no need to either acknowledge, apologise or compensate for the harm suffered by Aborigines. As Prime Minister John Howard declared in 1999: 'present generations of Australians cannot be held accountable . . . for the errors and misdeeds of earlier generations . . . To apply retrospectively the standards of today in relation to their behaviour does some of those people who were sincere an immense injustice.'[8] However, it is hard to sustain either that such sincerity could not be called into question, or that even if it were genuine, it would justify the actions perpetrated in its name. Chris Cunneen underlines the necessity to explore 'the connection between racist ideology and colonial practice' in order to do justice to the injured parties. Apologies and reparations are indeed central to the victims' healing process and the courts are the place where society now debates such burning issues as hate-motivated violence and the abuse of human rights. Historians are thus often summoned to court to play the dangerous role of expert witnesses in trials where assessing past events and responsibilities has a direct impact on the lives and statuses of victims and their descendants. Although soliciting historians seems inevitable in the context evoked by Cunneen, it is not necessarily a safe path, especially in the case of history wars in which, to use Richard J. Goslan's words, 'history' and 'memory' are pitted against each other.[9]

In the second chapter of this book, jurist Lawrence McNamara questions precisely the too often taken-for-granted relationship between history and law, using the double reference to Australia's colonial days and to World War Two. Portraying colonisers' atrocities or the systematic victimisation and extermination of specific groups by a dictatorship provides a mirror image which is essential not only to the understanding of the dark pages of a country's history, but also to addressing past governments' errors, abuses and misconduct. Only in this way can the malfunctions of the present be acknowledged and a just future constructed. As far as Australia is concerned, two alternative interpretations of history are at odds. On the one hand, the myth of *terra nullius* has it that the British colonisers took possession of an unclaimed territory and were therefore entitled to claim ownership of the land. On the other hand, an alternative version of Australia's colonisation depicts a bloody conquest of the continent by the British, leading to the slaughtering of roughly 20,000 indigenous people, whose heirs can consequently reclaim the property rights of the white settlers. McNamara recalls that in 1992 the *Mabo* case debunked the myth of *terra nullius*, thus crediting Aborigines with 'native title rights'. Yet some academics such as Keith Windschuttle have recently challenged this view and have gone so far as to contest the very existence of massacres, hence disqualifying Aboriginal territorial claims. In such cases, the impact of historians' expertise transcends the limited circles of academia to reach the political and social arenas in which the present relationships between Aborigines and the Australian government are at stake.

When historians are not called on by the law to give evidence as experts, they sometimes end up in the dock, as defendants or plaintiffs in defamation trials. McNamara shows that the landmark judgment against David Irving in 2000 which, by proving the Holocaust revisionists wrong, had seemed to pave the way for successful libel suits in the future, cannot be systematically taken as a model.[10] Drawing on Henry Rousso's work on history and memory which throws light on the symbolic power of legal decisions, McNamara discusses the validity of 'taking History to court' in the context of 'abuse of human rights' or 'crimes against humanity' trials.[11] He underlines that, since 'judgment can have an impact that reaches far beyond the parties to a case', one has to be cautious about initiating trials in which the court is not required to state 'its views about how things happened in the past', but only to draw 'limits within which versions of the past would be considered valid', and in which the final decision is inevitably 'vulnerable to manipulation and mis-interpretation in the media public debate.' As Antoon de Baets puts it, the crux of the problem is that 'historical truth should be settled by historians in academe, not by judges in court'.[12]

The debate on the past is not the province of historians alone, for society at large uses it as a mirror to justify its present orientation. Distorting truth and revisiting history so as to suit one's convenience is a ploy commonly adopted by the newspapers as well. Periodicals have played a significant part in the stereotyping of specific groups according to the changing political needs of the day. The media are indeed one of the various factors that contribute to the process of identity building. The representation of African Americans in the US press speaks volumes about the way the image of black people has been manipulated across decades to serve the complex purposes of a dominant white society. The fact that 'the values and behavior of both Whites and African Americans . . . were influenced powerfully by attitudes grounded in centuries old racial stereotypes' has been widely documented and reveals how essential the portrayal of the categorised Other is in shaping the relationships between ethnic communities.[13] In the third chapter, book historian Claire Parfait deals precisely with how the white readers of *Harper's Weekly* were conditioned in their perceptions of black people by the magazine's presentation of African Americans. Working on the iconography of the well-known New York-based periodical, she analyses the changes in how black people were characterised between the Antebellum and Reconstruction periods. Such 'essentialising categorisation', to use Pierre-André Taguieff's words, deprives the single black individual of their specific identity, leaving them 'no other status than that of being the epiphenomenon of [their] type'.[14] It has been established that 'media images provide a diffuse confirmation of one's own belief, promote acceptance of current social arrangements, and reassure people that things are the way they ought to be.'[15] Parfait's work corroborates such conclusions: before the Civil War, the 'social arrangements' were that African Americans should be satisfied with their condition and the imagery used by *Harper's Weekly* 'promoted acceptance' of a social order that took slavery for granted. Conversely, during the conflict the North badly needed 'courageous soldiers' and the Blacks were consequently granted the quality of 'bravery' for the purpose of the cause, as passive slaves do not qualify for feats of arms. Parfait shows how African Americans were finally demoted to their antebellum status of passive sufferers when after the war the North and the South endeavoured to reconstruct a nation.

These changing and contradicting representations of African Americans according to the nation's political agenda do not come as a surprise, as it has been shown that blackness and whiteness are but a social construct to be understood in a historical context. The French colonisers of the nineteenth century, for example, considered the Fulahs of Africa as 'Whites' because it served them to have such racial 'allies' on the 'dark continent'.[16] Similarly, Maurice Goldring has shown how the Irish Catholics in the United Kingdom of the nineteenth century were racialised in an attempt to keep them out of political power after the 1829 Catholic Emancipation Act.[17] In the United States, David Roediger has coined the notion of 'critical whiteness' and contends that:

> [t]he critical examination of whiteness, academic and not, simply involves the effort to break through the illusion that whiteness is natural, bio-logical, normal, and not crying out for explanation.[18]

In his landmark book *Wages of Whiteness*, Roediger argued that 'working-class formation and the systematic development of a sense of whiteness went hand in hand for the US white working-class.'[19] Indeed, at the turn of the century, the coming of millions of immigrants had a profound impact on the development of 'race relations' and racial perception in the United States, as the newcomers' identity was valued, defined, weighed, constructed and chal-lenged against that of Whites and Blacks. Roediger studies in his latest work how race became 'a category into which the social and intellectual structures of the United States placed new immigrants', and describes the uncomfortable social position of those who lived 'in between the stark racial binaries struc-turing US life', and the way their 'racial inbetweenness' gave way to a firmer acceptance of their position, as well as their identity, as Whites.[20] In that regard, the case of Italians is particularly relevant. As has been documented by Mathew Frye Jacobson and other scholars, Italians, like many European immigrants, were sometimes denied their status as Whites.[21] Although their condition could in no way be compared to that of African Americans, it was one of 'inbetweenness', which put them at risk in American society, socially, politically and even physically in some extreme cases. In the fourth chapter of this book, historian Stefano Luconi recalls the difficult past of Italian Americans as 'victims of ethnically motivated lynchings'. He analyses the gradual evolution of Italian-American immigrants toward whiteness, which led them to share the 'benefits of the racial identity of the wasp population'. Yet Luconi explains that such a change did not go smoothly. At the beginning of the twentieth century, although Italians were no longer threatened by lynchings, it did not mean that their victimisation was over. The *Sacco-Vanzetti* case proved that Italians had reached a stage in which the 'wages of whiteness' they had to pay 'included death within the law' but not 'a fair trial'.

The whitening process generally entails an attempt by minority groups to adopt the racial values imposed by the Whites. Sociologist Barbara Perry has underscored that it can also generate a competition between ethnic groups for 'the favours of the white majority', thus producing 'not a shared commitment to racial or gender justice, but instead shared antagonisms and hostilities directed toward one another'. As she has further explained: 'their rage at their continued disempowerment is misdirected downward or sideways toward those who are similarly victimised, rather than upward toward those who seek to exploit the cleavages'.[22] Luconi evidences the complexity of the whitening process in which, to become white, Italians crossed the line from the status of victims to that of hate crime perpetrators and concludes that 'in committing hate crimes [they] demonstrated both the integration of the offspring of the victimised late nineteenth-century immigrants within American society and the acquisition of a bigoted and racist perspective underlying white identity.' By killing 'Others', Italians were then not just revalidating the otherness of their victims. They were at the same time erasing their own.

The racist perspective underlying white culture mentioned by Luconi can also be observed in Canada, a country which is still often cited as a model multicultural society. In the fifth chapter of this book, historian Stanley Barrett challenges the 'prevailing opinion' that there is no racism there, and revisits Canada's not so quiet far-right history. Once host to slavery and segregation, Canada has not been immune to the xenophobic activities of the Ku Klux Klan in the 1920s, the fascist movement in the 1930s, the Canadian Nazi Party in the 1960s and new neofascist organisations such as the Aryan Nation since the 1970s. The impact of white supremacy on the Canadian legal system in the first half of the twentieth century has also been examined by jurist Constance Backhouse, who warns against the consequences of such [a] legacy of inequality today.[23] Yet Barrett argues that the 'Canadian radical right has not yet been as violent as its counterpart in the USA', as its attention has gradually 'turned to wider society', thus favouring the manipulation of the media and the circulation of racist literature 'rather than physical attacks on minorities'. Although the Canadian far right's approach appears less brutal, it proved quite pernicious as it helped create the image of undesirable others and planted the seeds of violence in an increasingly multicultural nation. Now, according to Barrett, it is precisely 'the racism embedded in the wider society' that has 'provided an environment hospitable to white supremacist organisations.'

In the wake of September 11, 2001, racism permeated even more deeply North American institutions. The War against Terrorism launched by the Canadian authorities resulted in the adoption of a series of preventive measures which marked a shift in the treatment of certain ethnic groups. The formation of a specific police unit aimed at identifying and deporting illegal aliens, as well as the resorting to systematic racial profiling are examples of legislation which implicitly targets the Arab and Muslim communities, at a time when Canadians are no more critical than their US or European allies of laws which profess to provide greater national security. The debate over racial profiling is fundamental because it unveils the real fragility of the Other's civil rights in western democracies in moments of crisis. The very principle of racial profiling lies in the singling out of specific racial, ethnic or national groups defined as being potentially dangerous for the rest of society, and the subsequent subjecting of these groups to scrutiny in order to prevent any criminal activity. Jurist Reem Bahdi recalls that it 'thus entails the use of race as a proxy for risk'.[24] Interestingly enough, it has been shown by jurists Deborah Ramirez, Jennifer Hoopes and Tara Lai Quinlan that there is little efficiency in a strategy which prefers racial or ethnic criteria to 'behaviour or individualised suspicion, to focus on an individual for additional investigation.'[25] The inefficacy of such a method however is deemed irrelevant compared to the psychological comfort it brings to a frightened majority. In fact, racial profiling is but a perfect illustration of institutional violence insofar as it not only reinforces the division of society along the colour/ethnic/religious line but also correlates alleged otherness with crime and peril. Barrett highlights the significant impact of the post-9/11 climate of suspicion on the revitalising of the radical right in Canada, and points to the risk that this climate might provide the latter with 'a licence to undermine multiculturalism'.

In Britain, the concept of 'institutional racism' was not officially acknowledged until 1999 when the Macpherson Report into the faulty investigation of the brutal murder of black student Stephen Lawrence in London in 1993 was finally released. Criminologist Benjamin Bowling's thorough study of violent racism in Britain makes it clear that the response of the British Police to bias-motivated crimes always proved inadequate, because it was limited to dealing with 'tightly defined *incidents*' without taking into account the 'political, historical and experiential context', thus ascribing those incidents a 'new meaning to fit the specific subjectivity of the police officer called to intervene.'[26] The Macpherson Report concluded on the police's failure to protect victims of hate crimes, exposed the impact of racist stereotypes on the institution's practices and recommended a wide-ranging reform of British policing. Crime historian Neil Davie assesses, in the sixth chapter of this book, the evolution of racism among British police forces in the years that followed the publication of the Macpherson landmark report. In February 2000, the *Birmingham Post* claimed that nearly three-quarters of people believed 'the police ha[d] learnt from the mistakes they [had] made while investigating the teenager's murder.'[27] Yet it seems that this optimistic view does not quite match reality and that the situation is more complex. As early as 1999, Jurist Lee Bridges doubted that Macpherson's recommendations would lead to a major change, for it was clear 'that the government and police's commitment to "anti-racism" [was] far from wholehearted and holistic and [was] always likely to be displaced by concerns to "tackle crime" and "speed up criminal justice" which have much wider populist appeal.'[28] Davie finds that although there has been progress in some areas such as in the proportion of racist incidents reported to the police or in the increase of minority recruitment of officers, reforming the British police's organisational culture still remains an 'uphill task'. The police are still 'more likely to perceive ethnic minorities with a degree of suspicion' and to credit Africans, Caribbeans and Asians with violent and devious behaviour. As sociologist Ellis Cashmore indicates, the policies designed to combat racism which emerged from the Macpherson Report are regarded by the most cynical observers as nothing more than 'window dressing' which gives 'the appearance of progress, while actually achieving little.'[29]

One particular ethnic minority in Britain seems to have been even more victimised. Unlike the Blacks, the South Asians or the West Indians, Gypsies can be discriminated against openly and blatantly amidst general indifference, as jurist David Fraser demonstrates in chapter 7. Indeed, categorising Gypsies as an anomaly, Leonardo Piasere remarks, 'has been a constant of European thought'.[30] Fraser analyses this specificity which makes the Gypsy more 'other' than the other 'Others' – a specificity which is corroborated by the comparative indifference of historians to the '*porajmos*' ('devouring') of Roma by the Nazi regime.[31] More generally, the absence of political representation illustrates the exceptional absence of legitimacy for Roma in Britain. Royce Turner thus remarks that 'Gypsies have been in Britain for 500 years', that there are nearly 120,0000, but that 'not since Bernadette Devlin . . . have there been any Traveller MPs.'[32] That less attention has been paid to the Gypsies' predicament is not surprising to Fraser, for whom the Gypsy epitomises otherness. The Roma is no ordinary 'trouble maker' who jeopardises public order. 'The danger here is not to the state', Fraser argues, 'but to the nation. Nomads refuse allegiance, they cross borders, they transgress.' Indeed, our sedentary societies are ill equipped to deal with nomadism. Cain the farmer slew Abel the herder.[33] In a 2001 article, Fraser used the example of the Martin trial to illustrate violence against Roma. The killing of

16-year-old Fred Barras by farmer Tony Martin as the former was trying to break into Martin's farm took on a totally different dimension when it became clear that Barras was a Gypsy. The press coverage then insisted on the 'possible jury intimidation' by the Roma community in an attempt to impose Gypsy law and threaten ordinary British citizens. Thus the actual murder receded to the background and the Gypsies came to the fore as the real threat to public order.[34]

Quashing such violence is no easy task. The solution to anti-Gypsyism was even envisioned through the creation of a new type nation-state, a Roma state which would have been a state without a territory, according to the claims of the International Roma Conference between 1998 and 2002.[35] This claim has now been abandoned and the territorial nature of state sovereignty seems to be unquestioned. Paradoxically, the territorial state does not object to infringing on its own rules concerning 'belonging and sovereignty', it does not mind trespassing national borders when that suits its own interests. Fraser illustrates this with the case of Prague airport, where British immigration officers operate in the Czech Republic in order to 'enforce the state of exception' against Czech Roma. The persecution of potential Gypsy immigrants to Britain is thus achieved through the violation of the principle of territorial sovereignty – 'a "truth" that has always hidden more than it reveals'.[36] Such violation is part of a system in which the Gypsy immigrant is 'suppressed' even before he reaches Britain. With this scenario, the Gypsy need not be killed as he has never existed, never trodden on British soil.

Nomadism has always been deemed a threat to mainstream society. In Ireland, where racism is described by many as a 'relatively new phenomenon', the Traveller community, although termed by the Irish authorities an indigenous minority, 'has always suffered disadvantage and discrimination in all fields of life'. So extreme is their marginalisation in education, employment and accommodation, that it has recently been labelled by the European Commission against Racism and Intolerance 'an issue of particular concern'.[37] Paradoxically, in recent years, Travellers have been all the more stigmatised as there have been attempts to protect their rights with 'the introduction of legislation against discrimination and social policies aimed at promoting [their] social inclusion', sociologist Bryan Fanning notes in the eighth chapter. He compares such anti-Traveller racism by mainstream Irish society to anti-Irish racism in nineteenth-century Britain. Turning the tables on another community is certainly no new phenomenon in history but it took few decades for the excluded to become excluders, or – to adopt Frantz Fanon's words as quoted by Fanning – for the 'colonised subject' to turn into the coloniser. This chapter examines how the colonised subject has internalised the dominant view about 'race and hygiene' and then applied it to the ostracised group as part of the nation-building process. Travellers are constructed as a filthy 'underclass' and are often reproached with not keeping clean while being denied the facilities they need to do so. Michelle Norris and

Nessa Winston have drawn a gloomy picture of Irish Travellers' appalling housing conditions, with 'one in four Traveller families [living] in caravans on unofficial encampments without access to running water, toilets or refuse collection'.[38] Fanning refers to the Housing (Miscellaneous Provisions) Act 2002 which made it possible for local authorities to evict Travellers and have their caravans seized even when 'their statutory accommodation entitlements' had not been met and 'no official sites' were provided.

Eviction is only one form of violence among many, and Fanning depicts the recurrent mob violence aimed at Travellers, including physical attacks and arson. Paradoxically but unsurprisingly, the potential victims are accused of disrupting law and order, thus deserving the punishments that they have allegedly sown. Such violence has been perpetrated by resident groups and vigilantes. Apart from the actual harm that vigilantism causes for the victimised group, it serves a second purpose since it brings pressure to bear on authorities to tighten official legislation against them. The threat of violence thus becomes a 'negotiating tool'. Indeed the potential threat of attacks by 'settled' citizens on Travellers, even when it is not followed by actual deeds, induces authorities into carrying out evictions, thus contributing to the physical disappearance, if not the murder, of Travellers.

Such threats – even when they seem to be 'only words' – should not be taken lightly. Fanning writes that 'verbal rejection is not a substitute for violence but a potential cause of violence.' In that regard, the fundamental role played by the media in the construction of the myth of the menacing Other – be the latter African-American, Muslim, or Traveller – is evident. The rise of new technologies has even reinforced the disseminating power of the mainstream press, radio and television, while allowing more obscure and radical movements to find online a new platform for their racist propaganda. Sociologists Phyllis Gerstenfeld, Diana Grant and Chau-Pu Chiang recall that 'extremists' groups were among the very early users of the communication network that eventually evolved into the Internet'.[39] Hate speech has therefore found its way through the cyberspace to reach an ever greater audience. Verbalising the rejection of allegedly undesirable groups is the rule on many sites, and homosexuals are the frequent targets of both subtle prejudice and open bashing. Media specialist Margaret Moritz, in the ninth chapter of this book, provides a study of the rhetoric strategies of homophobic websites which use a virtual medium to advocate real violence. The power of the Internet, she contends, lies in its capacity not only to spread hate more easily than with other traditional networks, but also to mobilise a highly organised movement, 'without having to face legal constraints'. More worrying than the extremists' sites openly labelling homosexuals 'fags' or the debate over the constitutional status of such legislation as the 1996 Decency Act regulating the distribution of 'indecent or obscene' material on the Internet, is the way messages of exclusion can be conveyed through apparently harmless pro-family sites, thus being 'naturalised, credentialed and hidden in everyday discourse', with the support of phoney experts identified as doctors or educators.

Interestingly enough, sociologist Guillaume Marche shows in the tenth chapter of the present book that unlike French homosexual activists, American gays and lesbians at the individual level do not necessarily respond to this virtual violence by using libel to have hate speech silenced. On the contrary, they argue that this attitude would be a 'confession of weakness'. Such scholars as communication specialist Marouf Hasian develop the same kind of argumentation as regards the response to revisionist theories. Defending the idea that 'citizens need to realise that our holocaust memories are not so fragile that we cannot tolerate the appearance of non mainstream views', Hasian maintains that 'counter narration [. . . rather than] restrictive libel laws provide[s] us with the most viable means of maintaining responsible memories'.[40] In other words, promoting free discussion on forums in which hate rhetoric unveils its very inconsistency while fair historical speech reveals its power of conviction would be more efficient a method than going to court. Many disagree with this approach and legitimately feel that the only way to protect the holocaust memory and/or the civil rights of victimised groups is to stop hate speech legally and make it a crime. In this context, Marche's work offers a challenging analysis of creative and innovative initiatives launched by some American gay groups which consist in 'meeting the challenge of a hate message, not with more hate, but with a message of an altogether different nature, which ultimately renders the former less visible and thus creates an alternative to it.' This strategy of 'struggle on equal terms with a clearly defined enemy' contrasts with the 'traditionally political achievements of standard gay and lesbian mobilisation', because it is directed toward 'informal rather than institutional forms of action'. Yet it fosters empowerment among online readers of such confrontational exchanges between homophobes and their gay respondents. Among the most inventive responses to homophobic virtual and real violence, Marche mentions the fund-raising campaign for a Michigan gay advocacy group organised in response to homophobe Fred Phelps's picketing of a gay bar in Ann Arbor. The idea was to call for a money donation for every minute Phelps was to spend in town. No less than 7,000 dollars were thus collected, 'turning the damage of hate back against the hater'. By 'reclaiming the offensive', the mobilisation of LGBT groups thus focuses on action which preserves the availability of positive material about homosexuality on the Internet. Furthermore, free discussion online creates an opportunity to engage in a debate over 'the cultural definition of sexual legitimacy', which is 'at the core of the gay and lesbian movement's agenda'.

Those alternative responses to hate crime exemplify an interesting shift in the way some activist groups suggest to counter the devastating effects of racism. A wider reflection over the best strategy to adopt in the struggle against bias-motivated violence obviously leads to seeking forms of action that would prevent such crimes from being committed in the first place. Macpherson concluded in his report that what is needed is an overall revision of our institutional practices. Drawing on Michael Eric Dyson's work, Barbara Perry claims that since 'hate crime involves the relational construction of identities', what is required is a series of initiatives that promote 'a culture in which we are not forced to choose an identity on the basis of reified and privileged categories', with the purpose not of 'transcending race or difference in general', but of 'transcending the biased meanings associated with differ-ence'.[41] In the final chapter of this book, criminologist Jack Levin and soci-ologist Gordana Rabrenovic address precisely this issue. They present an analysis of various American experiences of inter-group relations in order to determine the factors which have led to either racial hostility or solidarity, thus showing the complexity and fragility of the processes which can help prevent the emergence of hatred in our culture. With concrete examples such as the failed integration in South Boston schools in the 1970s, they challenge the contact theory of prejudice according to which antagonism between members of different communities would be necessarily reduced by increased interaction. Arguing that only in specific cases does this interaction have a positive impact on racial conflict, Levin and Rabrenovic explore the concept of interdependence as an efficient strategy for 'inoculating a community against inter-group hate'. The point of this strategy is to get individuals to work together toward 'the satisfaction of common objectives', by organising activities in which 'different groups come to rely on one another' in order to achieve 'their shared goals'. The positive effects of interdependence were observed, for example, during World War Two in Hawaii where the economic ties uniting Japanese Americans to the local population partially protected them from being massively deported to US internment camps like other Americans of Japanese ancestry. However, the relationship with the Other is always fragile. Indeed, although Levin and Rabrenovic emphasise that dependence on others defined as allies and friends is always beneficial, they also admit that there is little evidence to indicate that cooperative interaction between some members of a group 'will generalise their positive attitudes' to the group as a whole and thus they conclude that 'interdependence cannot be counted on to reduce racial prejudice in general, even if it contributes to affection developing between individuals'.

With all its limitations, instrumental dependence – that is to say having to work with the Other for one's living, and being part and parcel of the same enterprise – remains one of the most stimulating options to oppose ostracisa-tion and work toward a peaceful or appeased society. Needing the Other in a way provides a substitute for Killing the Other.

Addressing the issue of hate crime in a sociological, historical and legal perspective, this book raises the questions of the definition of these terms – be it in a colonial or post-colonial context – and of the need for society to respond not only in terms of acknowledgement, punishment and reparation but also in terms of prevention. Evaluating with precision the scale and nature of racist and homophobic attacks on a global scale is extremely difficult, and one should be extremely wary of subjective estimates based only on a general feeling of insecurity. Common opinion has it that this world is far more unsafe than it used to be. Yet the 2005 Human Security Report surprisingly established that the number and frequency of armed conflicts, genocides, human rights violations, military coups and international crises have all been decreasing since the 1950s.[42] This does not mean that hate crime has also been diminishing, but media coverage may be misleading and is definitely unrepresentative of the real evolution. What we do know is, for instance, that the number of 'gay-hate crime cases being dealt with by the courts almost doubled [in Britain] in the past year, to 600 investigations'.[43] Such fragmented information at least confirms that the need to address hate crime is still a burning issue, that legal responses alone are inadequate, and that the detailed analysis of race, ethnicity, and sexual orientation-related violence to which this book seeks to make a contribution is a vital part of the search for long-term solutions.

Bénédicte Deschamps and Michel Prum

NOTES

1 US House of Representatives, 109th Cong., 1st session, HR 2662 I H, 26 May 2005.
2 US House of Representatives, 106th Cong., Amendments Made in Order Under the Rule to HR 2366, The Small Business Liability Reform Act, Committee on Rules, 15 February 2000.
3 See Paul Iganski, 'Hate Crimes Hurt More', *American Behavioral Scientist*, vol. 45, 4, 626–638, 2001.
4 *Ibid* p 635.
5 Kathleen M. Blee, 'Racial Violence in the United States', *Ethnic and Racial Studies*, vol. 28, 4, July 2005, p 602.
6 See for example, Jason Brown interviewed by Glen Moore, 'Every Time I got the Ball, There were Monkey Chants, It's Wrong', *The Independent*, 13 April 2006. On violence and sports, also see for instance: Les Back, Tim Crabbe, John Solomos, 'Beyond the Racist/Hooligan Couplet: Race, Social Theory and Football Culture', *British Journal of Sociology*, vol. 50, 3, 1 September 1999.
7 See for instance: 'Killing the Indian to Save the Child', in Bonita Lawrence, *Real Indians and Others – Mixed-Blood Urban Native Peoples and Indigenous Nationhood*, 2004, pp 105–119, Lincoln: University of Nebraska Press.
8 Prime Minister John Howard, Transcript of the Prime Minister, 26 August 1999, p 3.
9 Richard J. Golsan, 'The Politics of History and Memory in France in the 1990s' in Henry Rousso (ed.) *Stalinism and Nazism: History and Memory Compared*, 2004, p ix, Lincoln, NE: University of Nebraska Press.
10 Also see 'David Irving Jailed for Holocaust Denial', *Guardian*, 20 February 2006.
11 See Henry Rousso, *The Vichy Syndrome, History and Memory in France since 1944*, 1991, Cambridge, MA: Harvard University Press.

12 Antoon de Baets, 'Defamation Cases against Historians', *History and Theory*, 41, October 2002, p 356.
13 Bonetta M. Hines-Hudson and J. Blaine Hudson, 'A Study of the Contemporary Racial Attitudes of Whites and African Americans', *The Western Journal of Black Studies*, vol. 23, 1, 1999, p 22.
14 Pierre-André Taguieff, *La Force du préjugé, Essai sur le racisme et ses doubles*, 1997, p 316, Paris, La Découverte (translated by the editors).
15 Scott Coltrane, Melina Messineo, 'The Perpetuation of Subtle Prejudice: Race and Gender Imagery in 1990s Television Advertising', *Sex Roles: A Journal of Research*, 2000, p 364.
16 See Anna Pondopoulo, *Les Noirs 'blancs' d'Afrique*, forthcoming 2007, Paris: L'Harmattan.
17 Maurice Goldring, 'Racialisation des Irlandais', in Michel Prum (ed.), *Exclure au nom de la race*, 2000, pp 97–115, Paris: Syllepse. On the same topic, but in the United States, see Noel Ignatiev, *How the Irish Became White*, 1995, London, Routledge.
18 David R. Roediger, 'Working Toward Whiteness', interview with Seth Sandronsky, *Counterpunch*, 26–27 November 2005.
19 David R. Roediger, *Wages of Whiteness, Race and the Making of the American Working-Class*, 1991, p 8, Verso: London.
20 David R. Roediger, *Working Toward Whiteness: How America's Immigrants Became White*, 2005, p 8, New York: Basic Books.
21 Mathew Frye Jacobson, *Whiteness of a Different Color: European Immigrants and the Alchemy of Race*, 1998, Cambridge, MA: Harvard University Press.
22 Barbara Perry, *In the Name of Hate: Understanding Hate Crimes*, 2001, pp 121–122, New York: Routledge.
23 Constance Backhouse, *Colour-Coded: A Legal History of Racism in Canada 1900–1950*, 1999, Toronto: University of Toronto Press.
24 Reem Bahdi, 'No Exit: Racial Profiling and Canada's War against Terrorism', 2003, *Osgoode Hall Law Journal*, vol. 41, 2–3, pp 293–316.
25 Deborah A Ramirez, Jennifer Hoopes, Tara Lai Quinlan, 'Defining Racial Profiling in a Post-September 11 World', *American Criminal Law Review*, vol. 40, 3, 2003, p 1200.
26 Benjamin Bowling, *Violent Racism: Victimization, Policing and Social Context*, Oxford: Oxford University Press, 1999, pp 286 and 290.
27 Mike Harrison, 'Scourge of Institutional Racism; Lawrence Judge Extends Criticism', *Birmingham Post*, 22 February 2000, p 10.
28 Lee Bridges, 'The Lawrence Inquiry – Incompetence, Corruption, and Institutional Racism', *Journal of Law and Society*, vol. 26, 3, September 1999, p 322.
29 Ellis Cashmore, 'Behind the Window Dressing: Ethnic Minority Police Perspectives on Cultural Diversity', *Journal of Ethnic and Migration Studies*, vol. 28, 2, 2002, p 327.
30 Leonardo Piasere, 'Introduzione: Ma gli Zingari sono "buoni da pensare" antropologicamente?', *La Ricerca folklorica*, n.22, Europa Zingara, October 1999, p 7.
31 On the persecution of Roma in Nazi Germany, see Sybil H. Milton, 'Gypsies as Social Outsiders in Nazi Germany', in Robert Gellately and Nathan Stoltzfus (ed.), *Nazi Germany*, 2001, Princeton: Princeton University Press.
32 Royce Turner, 'Gypsies and Politics in Britain', *Political Quarterly*, vol. 71, 1, January 2000, p 69.
33 See George Monbiot, quoted by Fraser, 'Acceptable Hatred', *Guardian*, 4 November 2003.
34 David Fraser, 'To Belong or not to Belong: the Roma, State Violence and the

New Europe in the House of Lords', *Legal Studies*, vol. 21, 4, November 2001, pp 578–580.

35 David Fraser, 'Les Roms, la citoyenneté et l'Europe', in Marie-Claire Hoock-Demarle (ed.), *Regards croisés sur l'Europe*, 2006, p 59, Paris, EILA.

36 John Agnew, 'Sovereignty Regimes: Territoriality and State Authority in Contemporary World Politics', *Annals of The Association of American Geographers*, 95, 2, 2005, pp 437–461.

37 European Commission against Racism and Intolerance, *Second Report on Ireland*, Council of Europe, Strasburg, 23 April 2002.

38 Michelle Norris and Nessa Winston, 'Housing and Accommodation of Irish Travellers: From Assimilationism to Multiculturalism and Back Again', *Social Policy and Administration*, vol. 39, 7, December 2005, p 802.

39 Phyllis B. Gerstenfeld, Diana R. Grant, Chau-Pu Chiang, 'Hate Online: A Content Analysis of Extremist Internet Sites', *Analyses of Social Issues and Public Policy*, vol. 3, 1, 2003, p 29.

40 Marouf Hasian, 'Holocaust Denial Debates: The Symbolic Significance of *Irving v. Penguin and Lipstadt*', *Communication Studies*, vol. 53, 2, 2002, p 144.

41 Barbara Perry, *In the Name of Hate, op cit*, pp 6 and 226.

42 Human Security Centre, 'Human Security Report, War and Peace in the 21st Century', http://www.humansecurityreport.info.

43 'Homophobic Killers Jailed as Gay-Hate Crimes Soar', *Independent*, 17 June 2006.

Chapter I

The effects of colonial policy

Genocide, racism and Aboriginal people in Australia

Chris Cunneen

INTRODUCTION

This chapter explores the issue of colonial policy, racism and the contemporary demand for reparations and compensation by indigenous people in Australia. It begins with an analysis of the key recommendations and findings of the National Inquiry into the Separation of Aboriginal and Torres Strait Islander Children from Their Families (commonly referred to as the Stolen Generations Inquiry). It then discusses the limitations of attempts to seek compensation through the courts and considers the arguments for a Reparations Tribunal. Finally, the chapter discusses significant areas of human rights abuses of Aboriginal people in Australia that should be considered within the context of reparations for historical injustices.

An underlying thread to these human rights abuses was colonial assumptions about the supposed racial inferiority of Aboriginal people. Thus this chapter argues that racism was a key component underpinning colonial policies. Constructing indigenous people as Other was critical to the entrenched discrimination found in laws, policies and practices which denied indigenous participation in the social, economic and political life of the nation.

THE STOLEN GENERATIONS INQUIRY

The Stolen Generations Inquiry was established in May 1995 and was the outcome of a long battle by indigenous people and their organisations for recognition of the effects of forced separations.[1] It is estimated that 10 per cent of indigenous children were removed from their families and communities under state-sanctioned policies and removal practices in Australia between 1910 and 1970.[2] Today, most indigenous families continue to be affected in one or more generations by the forcible removal of children during this time.[3] The removal of children has had a long-term devastating impact on indigenous family and community life.

The terms of reference of the Inquiry required that it investigate and assess the effects of past laws, practices and policies which resulted in the separation of indigenous children from their families by compulsion, duress or undue influence. The Inquiry was also required to examine the adequacy of services available for those affected by separation; to examine the principles relevant to compensation; and to examine current laws, practices and policies with respect to contemporary separations, and advise of changes required, taking into account the principle of indigenous self-determination.

The Inquiry found that basic legal safeguards which protected non-indigenous families from unnecessary state interference were cast aside when it came to indigenous children. The main components of forced removal were deprivation of liberty; deprivation of parental rights; abuses of power; breach of guardianship duties; and violation of international human rights.

Deprivation of liberty

The safeguard of court scrutiny before detention was denied to indigenous children. The Inquiry found that 'the taking of indigenous children from their homes by force and their confinement to training homes, orphanages . . . amounted to deprivation of liberty and [unlawful] imprisonment'.[4] The law permitted removal by the order of a public servant when the child was indigenous. The removal of non-indigenous children required a court order. Thus the scrutiny of official decisions was not seen as necessary when those decisions were being made about indigenous children and families.

Deprivation of parental rights

It was found that in some jurisdictions legislation stripped indigenous parents of their parental rights and made a Chief Protector the legal guardian of all indigenous children. This was contrary to the common law which safe-guarded parental rights and whereby a parent could only forfeit their parental rights if a court found misconduct, or that state guardianship was in the child's best interest.[5]

Abuses of power

Although legislation authorised the removal of indigenous children, some Protectors and Inspectors resorted to kidnapping or trickery to take the children from their parents. There are many examples of children being taken directly from school without their parents' knowledge.[6] These actions were abuses of power – actions beyond what was authorised by the legislation.

Breach of duty of care and guardianship duties

Furthermore, Protectors and Protection Boards had a duty of care and protection to those over whom they exercised control. The report identifies at least three ways in which guardianship duties and statutory duties failed with indigenous children.

First, there was a failure to provide contemporary standards of care for indigenous children to the same level as non-indigenous children. Although standards of care for non-indigenous children were far from satisfactory, indigenous children experienced appalling conditions, brutal punishments, sexual abuse, and so forth. Secondly, there was a failure to protect indigenous children from harm, abuse and exploitation. Many of the children were verbally, physically, emotionally or sexually abused. Thirdly, there was a failure to consult or involve parents in decisions about their children. Many children were falsely told their parents were dead.

Violation of international human rights standards

The main international human rights obligations imposed on Australia and breached by the policy of forced removals were prohibitions against racial discrimination and genocide. The policy of forced removal continued to be practised after Australia had voluntarily subscribed to treaties outlawing both racial discrimination and genocide, from the mid-1940s onwards.[7]

The legislative regimes created for the removal of indigenous children were different and inferior to those established for non-indigenous children. They were racially discriminatory and remained in place as late as the 1960s in South Australia, Northern Territory and Queensland. In addition, Government officials knew they were in breach of international legal obligations.[8] The Inquiry found that the policy of forcible removal of indigenous children could be properly called genocide, and breached international law.

In summary, the Inquiry found that the policy of forced removal of indigenous children was contrary to prohibitions on racial discrimination and genocide, and was contrary to accepted legal principle found in the common law. Finally, the removals had led to other forms of criminal victimisation, including widespread sexual and physical assault.[9]

RACE AND COLONIAL POLICY

The historical background to Aboriginal child removal shows clearly the link between racist ideologies and the forced removal of children. Aboriginal children were forcibly removed from their families by colonisers from the beginning of the European occupation of Australia.

However by the late nineteenth and early twentieth centuries there had developed a systematic and state-sponsored policy of removal which was far more extensive than any previous interventions. This policy rested on specific assumptions concerning racial purity and racial hygiene. Aboriginal people were divided according to the amount of European 'blood' they might possess.

According to the social Darwinist ideas, so-called 'full blood' Aboriginal people were bound to die out, because of their inferiority.[10] However, the concern for the state was the apparently rapidly growing population of 'mixed blood' children. It was these children that became the target of intervention. By permanently removing them from their families and communities, it was believed that this group of children would, over generations, eventually be biologically absorbed into the non-indigenous population. Their Aboriginality would be 'bred out'.

After the 1940s, ideas about biological absorption were replaced with notions of cultural assimilation. However the ultimate goal remained the same: the disappearance of a distinct group of people. Cultural assimilation was seen as leading to a form of 'equality' with Europeans. However, this equality was to be one defined on the assumption of the superiority of white Anglo-Australian cultural, economic and political institutions. It was to be the equality of 'sameness': where everyone could participate on a social terrain defined by the coloniser.

An irony of the process to assimilate indigenous people to be the coloniser's equal was that it authorised racial discrimination. To reach the level of equality the colonial subject required tutelage. They had to be taught and trained to be equal. As a result, in the post-1945 period, there was intensive supervision and surveillance through a range of state agencies, including child welfare and the police. Aboriginal children were still removed at high rates, but now increasingly because they are defined as being neglected, disruptive or delinquent.[11]

REPARATIONS AND RECOMMENDATIONS FROM THE STOLEN GENERATIONS INQUIRY

When developing its recommendations, the approach of the Inquiry was to consider international provisions for responding to and redressing gross violations of human rights.[12] Specifically, the Inquiry considered the UN-commissioned van Boven principles.[13] Van Boven recommended that the only appropriate response to people who have been the victims of gross violations of human rights is one of reparation, involving a range of methods of redress. Reparations are to include five components: acknowledgment and apology; guarantees against repetition; measures of restitution; measures of rehabilitation; and monetary compensation.

The Inquiry agreed with the van Boven position and recommended a broad ranging response to the stolen generations. There is insufficient space here to discuss at length either the recommendations or the Federal Government's response to those recommendations.[14] However, in summary, the main recommendations are as follows.

Acknowledgment and apology

The Inquiry recognised the need to establish the truth about the past as an essential measure of reparation for people who have been victims of gross violations of human rights. Various recommendations called for the recording of the testimonies of indigenous people affected by the forced removal policies, commemoration of the events and apologies from Australian parliaments and other state institutions, such as police forces, which played a key part in the removal.[15] The Prime Minister John Howard has refused to apologise on behalf of the nation.

Guarantee against repetition

The Inquiry recognised that guarantees against repetition were an important part of the reparation process. Recommendations in three areas deal specifically with this issue. They include educational materials. Secondly there was a recommendation that the Government legislate the Genocide Convention for effect in domestic law.[16] A further political guarantee against repetition is the recognition of the indigenous right to self-determination. There were several recommendations on the principle and practice of self-determination. All of these recommendations were responded to poorly by the Federal Government.

Measures of restitution

The purpose of restitution is to re-establish, to the extent possible, the situation that existed prior to the perpetration of gross violations of human rights. The Inquiry recognised that 'children who were removed have typically lost the use of their languages, been denied cultural knowledge and inclusion, been deprived of opportunities to take on cultural responsibilities and are often unable to assert their native title rights'.[17] The Inquiry made recommendations concerning the expansion of funding to language, culture and history centres, funding for the recording and teaching of local indigenous languages, funding for indigenous community-based family tracing and reunion services and recommendations aimed at the preservation of records, indigenous access to records, and indigenous community management over their own records. The Federal Government allocated a limited amount of money to implement these recommendations.

Measures of rehabilitation

Measures for rehabilitation are an important component of the reparations package. The Inquiry made significant recommendations in relation to mental health care and assistance in parenting and family programmes for those who had been removed. The Federal Commonwealth allocated limited funding for counsellors, research, clinical support and parenting programmes.

Monetary compensation

The Inquiry recognised that the loss, grief and trauma experienced by those who were forcibly removed can never be adequately compensated. However, the submissions to the Inquiry also demanded some form of monetary compensation for the harm that had been suffered – particularly as a form of recognition of the responsibility for the causes of that harm. The Inquiry recommended the establishment of a National Compensation Fund. Such a statutory body would provide an alternative to litigation. The Government has consistently refused to consider monetary compensation, and has trivialised the issue by arguing that current governments should not be held responsible for the actions of the past, and by arguing that no amount of compensation can make up for the mistakes of the past.[18] The Government position reflects a denial that indigenous people in Australia have suffered human rights abuses, and that these abuses arose from racially based government policies.[19]

LEGAL REMEDIES

Another strategy to respond to the historical injustices of colonialism has been to use litigation in the search for legal remedies. Claims by members of the Stolen Generations seek to establish civil liability through a variety of causes of action, including negligence, breach of fiduciary and/or statutory duties as well as wrongful imprisonment. Exceptions to the above include applications for criminal compensation and claims that specific indigenous 'protection' legislation violated constitutional rights.

The major limitations of the litigation process can be summarised as follows:

- the problems in overcoming statutory limitation periods, when the events occurred many decades ago;
- the difficulty of locating evidence, particularly when governments were lax in recording matters involving indigenous people;
- the emotional and psychological trauma experienced by claimants in the hostile environment of an adversarial court system;

- the enormous financial cost;
- the length of time involved before the outcome of litigation is finalised;
- the problem of establishing specific liability for harms that have been caused; and
- overcoming the judicial view that 'standards of the time' justified removal in the best interests of the child.

Litigation presents very particular evidential hurdles for members of the Stolen Generations. Indigenous cultures utilise rich and complex oral and artistic traditions as an essential part of the communicative process. Conversely, writing and record keeping were an essential part of the imperial culture. Indeed, record keeping is integral to the project of colonisation: it is a tool for describing, itemising and controlling the colonised. Knowledge through writing constructs 'the Other' and places the colonised within a particular relationship to colonial power. The legal process tends to construct, reinforce, prioritise and legitimise particular forms of knowledge, particularly written documentation, as evidence, while dismissing oral traditions as uncertain, unreliable, partial and impermanent. From the law's standpoint, oral traditions lack materiality and cannot be transfixed in time and place. Thus Aboriginal knowledge about the historical events affecting themselves, their families and their communities is seen by the courts as inherently unreliable.

History, beneficial intent and 'standards of the time'

For the purposes of the courts' understanding of truth and fact, the 'records' of removal and treatment are the official inscriptions, the notes and the forms of Government and Church.

> Evidentiary requirements make it difficult for people whose only records in relation to their childhood are often the records maintained by government, to prove that they were wrongly removed because of particular (unrecorded) breaches of state duties, or suffered harm because of particular (unrecorded) incidents. Government records, not surprisingly, fail to reveal the level of abuse, deprivation and racism . . .[20]

There are profound ironies in the demand for written records, when colonial power itself was satisfied with literal inscriptions of the bodies of the colonised. For example, in the *Cubillo*[21] case, the thumbprint of an Aboriginal mother was found, on the balance of probabilities, to signify her express and 'informed consent' to her son's removal and subsequent institutionalisation. The body of the colonised becomes a site of colonial record-keeping, but what meaning can we attach to a thumbprint? During the proceedings, there could be no real examination of, or challenge to, the consent of

Peter Gunner's mother in the absence of evidence.[22] By the time of the hearing, the mother was dead and there was no way of identifying the officer from the Native Affairs Branch who obtained her thumbprint – or indeed, of ascertaining whether the thumbprint truly belonged to her.

The question of consent goes directly to the heart of the context of colonial power and Aboriginal people. What can we mean by 'consent' when there are such profound imbalances of power? The powers under various Acts had been to institute legal regimes that provided for the total control of all indigenous activities and certainly not to require their consent. Indeed the idea that Aboriginal people would exercise any kind of informed decision-making was fundamentally alien to the racial ideology that underpinned 'protection' legislation.

Government records are likely to paint a picture in which the removal and subsequent treatment of indigenous children complied with 'their best interests' and met the standards of the time. Protection laws are characterised as benign in their intent, as 'beneficial' laws – even if they are discriminatory. Under these circumstances, the likelihood that the forced removal of indigenous children will be considered by the courts as constituting genocide is remote, particularly when the legislation under which these acts occurred was always written in the language of the 'best interests' of the 'native'.

The central defence of the Australian Government in the *Kruger*[23] case has been characterised as the defence of 'history':

> The Commonwealth argued that the *Aboriginals Ordinance* was made when community attitudes were different and the Ordinance should be viewed as intending the care and protection of Aboriginal people. It could not, therefore, be judged or characterised by contemporary attitudes or laws. The majority of the High Court effectively accepted this defence ... The court was unanimous in not defining the *Aboriginals Ordinance* as genocidal.[24]

The decision in *Kruger* reinforced that it is the community 'standards and perceptions of the time' which are relevant to the determination of the validity of the exercise of legislative power.

The 'defence of history' becomes, more precisely, the defence of a colonialist history: the history of the exercise of imperial power for the benefit of all. This was not the only conclusion open to the court in *Kruger*. The plaintiffs argued against the proposition that racist and discriminatory views *at any time* can determine the meaning and effect of the Constitution, suggesting that such a reading 'directly contradicts the very nature of the compact and the inherent equality of the parties to it'.[25] Alternatively, the point argued by the Stolen Generations Inquiry is that neither genocide nor discrimination were acceptable in the aftermath of the Second World War, according to the prevailing contemporary legal values of that time. Even prior to Australia's ratification of the Genocide Convention in 1949, it was widely accepted that genocide was contrary to international law.

In litigation, the onus is on members of the Stolen Generations to show that the removals, detentions or other exercises of statutory power were unlawful. In other words, claimants are placed in a position whereby they must counteract the official version of history. The indigenous task of counteracting this official portrayal is made more difficult by a number of factors:

- The events in question occurred up to 50 years ago, so that witnesses may be difficult to locate, no longer alive or fail to remember relevant facts.
- The experience of removal, institutionalisation and isolation meant that many children, understandably, never made complaints about abuse, particularly sexual abuse, and hence no records exist to substantiate their story.
- The nature of sexual abuse itself meant that many victims did not talk about it to anyone until later in life, if at all.[26]

Members of the Stolen Generations who proceed with litigation will be subjected to extensive cross-examination. Aboriginal people attempting to use the courts will be faced with attacks on their credibility, resulting in potential re-traumatisation. They will be required to disclose their experiences of suffering in a largely unsympathetic environment. All aspects of their lives will be subject to public scrutiny. It is likely they will be required to undergo psychological testing in order to prove harm. At the same time, the environment will not provide the space in which victims can tell their stories. Victim testimony will be limited to those events and experiences relevant to the legal issue under consideration.

Many legal practitioners and academics who have been involved with Stolen Generations' cases have concluded that litigation is a poor forum for dealing with historical injustices. The legal processes have served to reconstruct and obscure the experiences of Aboriginal people. In the *Williams*[27], *Cubillo* and *Kruger* cases, Aboriginal protection and welfare laws are seen as benign in their intent. The reality of entrenched racial discrimination which these laws embodied has been obscured. Legal responsibilities and obligations are defined narrowly and do not coincide with broader questions around responsibility for historical injustices.

There are profound difficulties in litigating claims that concern Aboriginal child removal policies. Acts of genocide within Australia are not prohibited by specific domestic law; and there is no legal redress for policies, practices or laws which were racially discriminatory prior to the introduction of the Racial Discrimination Act (1975). Government policies are generally nonjusticiable and attempts to have the Aboriginal Ordinance 1918–1957 struck down on the basis of constitutional invalidity failed in *Kruger*.

A REPARATIONS TRIBUNAL?

As noted above, the Stolen Generations Inquiry recommended, among other things, a national compensation tribunal. More recently, the Public Interest Advocacy Centre (PIAC), in consultation with indigenous people, has developed a proposal for an Australian Reparations Tribunal.[28] In cases where indigenous people can establish that they were forcibly removed, they should be entitled to a minimum lump sum payment. In addition people forcibly removed and their families, communities and descendants should be entitled to reparations. Reparations might include a range of remedies determined by the Tribunal. They could potentially include such things as acknowledgments and memorials, cultural and language centres, employment and training, the provision of counselling services and so on.

The Reparations Tribunal should adopt procedural principles that enable the victims of these abuses to have their matters heard in a dignified and sympathetic manner. These should include informal procedures, relaxed rules of evidence, legal representation, interpreters where required, and the capacity to determine group or representative claims. The Tribunal should have a majority of indigenous members and a life span of ten years.[29]

REPARATIONS FOR HISTORICAL INJUSTICES

This chapter has been primarily concerned with the question of reparations for the forced removal of indigenous children. The policy of forced removal was an integral part of colonial ideology and practice. However, forced removal was only one of a number of strategies used to exercise surveillance and control over indigenous peoples within Australia.

During the period of protection legislation and the post-1945 assimilation period, there were numerous legislative controls placed on indigenous peoples which were fundamental abuses of human rights. These included restrictions on movement, residence, education, health care, employment, voting, and welfare/social security entitlements. Prior to 1975 these actions were not unlawful by domestic legal standards. However, they were racially discriminatory, offended international human rights principles and there is an arguable moral obligation for reparations.

In addition to these legislative controls, there were negligent and, at times, corrupt practices which led to the withholding of moneys from Aboriginal wages that had been paid into savings accounts and trust funds. In addition to these practices there were also under-award payments to Aboriginal workers which continued after the introduction of the Racial Discrimination Act (1975) – legislation which made racial discrimination illegal. There is a direct case for compensation and reparations.

The removal of human remains and cultural artefacts from indigenous communities was an ongoing colonial practice, largely in the name of science. Arguably there is a case for reparations in situations where those remains or artefacts cannot be returned. Finally, there were a number of massacres of Aboriginal people in central Australia and the Kimberley in the early part of the twentieth century. The survivors and descendants of these atrocities also arguably have a case for reparations and compensation.

Many of the human rights abuses identified above are currently subject to litigation or negotiation with Australian state and territory governments. However, there are a number of problems with the current approach to these issues. There are inherent problems with using litigation as a way of responding to historical injustices. These problems have been briefly documented previously in this chapter in relation to the Stolen Generations litigation. Similar types of problems (for example, lack of documentary evidence) have emerged in cases relating to missing wages and trust funds.

Except for the administration by the Commonwealth Government of the Northern Territory, Aboriginal affairs in Australia were a state responsibility until the 1967 constitutional referendum. Thus, both legal and administrative attempts to seek redress have tended to be focused on each of the eight Australian states, or the Commonwealth in the case of the Northern Territory. This has led to a complex *ad hoc* and piecemeal approach to what were essentially common problems across the nation.

Current approaches seeking redress are also piecemeal in the sense that they ignore some gross violations of human rights. First there has been no attempt to seek compensation and reparations in relation to relatively recent mass killings. These include massacres in the early part of the twentieth century such as Coniston in central Australia in 1928 and Forrest River in the Kimberley region of north western Australia in 1926.

Secondly, there are significant areas of racial discrimination which, while lawful until the enactment of the Racial Discrimination Act (1975), provide a profound moral argument for reparations. Throughout most Australian jurisdictions, 'protection' legislation introduced significant restrictions on movement, residence, education, health care, employment, marriage and other civil rights. In addition the right to vote in either state or federal elections varied between states. Eligibility for social security benefits for Aboriginal people was also restricted. Commonwealth amendments to electoral laws in 1962 removed any remaining prohibitions on voting at the federal level. States began to dismantle their discriminatory laws during the same period. Restrictions on indigenous voting rights in Queensland were not removed until 1965. Discriminatory restrictions on eligibility for social security benefits for Aboriginal people were not completely lifted until 1966. State legislation which restricted the citizenship rights of indigenous people living on reserves in Queensland remained in place until the 1980s.[30]

Finally an important limitation with the current approach is that it fails to reposition these individual issues within the overall context of racism and colonial and neo-colonial policy. The forced removal of children, stolen wages and trust funds, restrictions on basic civil rights, the removal of human remains and cultural artefacts, and the massacres of indigenous people were all based on assumptions about racial inferiority. While these racialised concepts moved somewhat during the course of the twentieth century from notions of bio-logical inferiority to cultural or socio-biological inferiority, at their heart there still remained the basic justification for denying indigenous people funda-mental human rights. It is the abuse of these human rights, in their various manifestations, which is fundamental to the claim for reparations.

CONCLUSION

The political context in which the demand for a Reparations Tribunal is being conducted in Australia is not helpful to achieving a just resolution to the injustices of the past. The problems arise from a number of related issues that have come to the fore during the last decade of Conservative government. There has been a denial of indigenous rights, and, more generally, a denial of the legitimacy of the application of international human rights standards. Secondly, a conservative rewriting of history denies responsibility for the outcomes of the colonial process.

Broadly speaking the Conservative Government's approach to indigenous affairs has been to promote assimilation. Within this context, indigenous people are not seen as a people possessing specific group rights as colo-nised peoples. Within the contemporary ideology of Government, indigen-ous people are seen as a disadvantaged minority deserving of some assistance to reach the standards of the dominant society. This view has implications for the Stolen Generations and for reparations, because it represents a welfare-based approach, rather than one which acknowledges historical injustices committed against distinct peoples.

Within the assimilationist view, equality is essentially defined as 'sameness' – everyone must be treated the same. The view has a resonance within the Conservative Government as well as being a catch-cry for a range of racist and extreme right groups (like 'One Nation'). In this sense, the current Government's philosophy is much the same as the one that underpinned the removal of Aboriginal children from their families in the first place.

The Conservative re-writing of Australian history was shown clearly in the 1999 Federal Parliament's 'Motion of Reconciliation' and statement of regret by the Prime Minister. When speaking to the motion, the Prime Minister stated,

> I have frequently said . . . that present generations of Australians cannot be held accountable . . . for the errors and misdeeds of earlier generations. Nor should we ever forget that many people who were involved in some

of the practices which caused hurt and trauma felt at the time that those practices were properly based. To apply retrospectively the standards of today in relation to their behaviour does some of those people who were sincere an immense injustice.[31]

Rather than a 'statement of regret' the speech reads as a self-justification for the *refusal* to offer regret or apologise for past wrongs. Within this context there is little opportunity for a Reparations Tribunal.

Despite the current conservative political climate, there were some positive effects from the Stolen Generations Inquiry:

- It had a 'truth-telling' function
- It raised the issue of reparations
- It used international standards as a basis for developing an approach to compensation and reparations.

The next stage in responding to historical injustices involves both the establishment of some form of reparations as well as broadening the categories of harm that need to be included. Central to responding to the abuse of human rights is an understanding of the connection between racist ideology and colonial practice.

NOTES

1 National Inquiry into the Separation of Aboriginal and Torres Strait Islander Children from Their Families (NISATSIC), *Bringing Them Home*, Report of the National Inquiry into the Separation of Aboriginal and Torres Strait Islander Children from Their Families, 1997, Sydney: Human Rights and Equal Opportunity Commission, p 36.

2 *Ibid*, p 18.

3 *Ibid*, p 37.

4 *Ibid*, p 253.

5 *Ibid*, p 255.

6 *Ibid*, p 257.

7 *Ibid*, p 266.

8 *Ibid*, p 270.

9 *Ibid*, pp 277–278.

10 See McGregor, R., *Imagined Destinies: Aboriginal People and the Doomed Race Theory*, 1997, Melbourne: Melbourne University Press.

11 See Cunneen, C., *Conflict Politics and Crime*, 2001, Sydney: Allen & Unwin.

12 NISATSIC, 1997, pp 278–280.

13 Pritchard, S., 'The Stolen Generations and Reparations' (1997) 4(5) *UNSW Law Journal Forum Stolen Children: From Removal to Reconciliation*, p 28.

14 See Cunneen, C., 'Reparations, Human Rights and the Challenge of Confronting a Recalcitrant Government' (2003) 3 *Third World Legal Studies Journal*, Special Volume on Reconstruction and Reparations in International Law.

15 NISATSIC, 1997, p 285.
16 *Ibid*, p 295.
17 *Ibid*, p 296.
18 Senate Legal and Constitutional References Committee, *Healing. A Legacy of Generations*, (2000), Canberra: AGPS.
19 Manne, R., 'In Denial. The Stolen Generations and the Right' (2001) 1 *The Australian Quarterly Essay*.
20 PIAC, *Submission to the Senate Inquiry into the Stolen Generation*, (2000), Sydney: PIAC, pp 16–17.
21 *Cubillo and Another v Commonwealth* (No 2) [2000] FCA 1084.
22 O'Connor, P., 'History on Trial: *Cubillo and Gunner v The Commonwealth of Australia*' (2001) 26(1) *Alternative Law Journal* 27, pp 30–31.
23 *Kruger v The Commonwealth of Australia* (1997) 190 CLR 1
24 La Forgia, R., 'Truth But Still Waiting for Justice' (1997) 22(4) *Alternative Law Journal* 192, p 194.
25 Plaintiff's submission quoted in Blokland, J., 'A Feminist Amicus Brief in the Stolen Generations (NT) Litigation', (1997) 89(3) *Aboriginal Law Bulletin* 10, p 12.
26 PIAC, 2000, p 17.
27 *Williams v Minister*, Aboriginal Land Rights Act 1983 No 2 [1999] NSWSC 843 (26 August 1999).
28 Cornwall, A., *Restoring Identity*, (2002), Sydney: PIAC.
29 Support for a national Reparations Tribunal has been forthcoming from the Federal Senate Legal and Constitutional References Committee. The Committee recommended that the PIAC proposal be used as a general 'template' for the recommended tribunal. See Senate Legal and Constitutional References Committee (2000) *op cit.*
30 See generally, Chesterman, J. and Galligan, B., *Citizens Without Rights*, (1997), Melbourne: Cambridge University Press.
31 Prime Minister John Howard, Transcript of the Prime Minister, 26 August 1999, p 3.

Chapter 2

Taking history to court
Defamation and revisionism after the David Irving trial

Lawrence McNamara [1]

INTRODUCTION

Denial of the Holocaust is an international phenomenon. Although it has been examined and exposed over the past two decades in works such as Pierre Vidal-Naquet's *Assassins of Memory*, and combated through occasional prosecutions, it persists nonetheless.[2] Against all the evidence, there are continued attempts to assert, argue and even 'demonstrate' that the Holocaust did not occur. While more familiar in the pamphlets, newsletters and speeches on the extreme right of politics, denialist claims are also found in works that purport to have scholarly status, often under the banner of 'revisionist' history.[3] Among the most high-profile of the professed revisionists has been David Irving, a Briton whose historical research on the Third Reich has been read widely for over 30 years. In the 1990s Irving adopted a novel strategy for advancing and legitimising his claims: he took to the courts to compel his critics to either back down or try to prove him wrong.

Irving sued an American academic, Deborah Lipstadt, for defamation (or libel, as it is often called), claiming that she had unjustifiably attacked his reputation in her book, *Denying the Holocaust: The Growing Assault on Truth and Memory*. Lipstadt had accused Irving of deliberately distorting, falsifying and misstating evidence in his historical research, and argued that Irving could be appropriately labelled a 'Holocaust denier'. The publication was unquestionably defamatory and to defend it, Lipstadt and her publishers had to prove the truth of their claims. They did so comprehensively. In London in the spring of 2000, Lord Justice Gray made clear and unambiguous findings:

> [N]o objective, fair-minded historian would have serious cause to doubt that there were gas chambers at Auschwitz and that they were operated on a substantial scale to kill hundreds of thousands of Jews.
>
> [I have found] that Irving has for his own ideological reasons persistently and deliberately misrepresented and manipulated historical evidence; that for the same reasons he has portrayed Hitler in an

unwarrantedly favourable light, principally in relation to his attitude towards and responsibility for the treatment of the Jews; that he is an active Holocaust denier; that he is anti-semitic and racist . . .[4]

As the *New York Times* explained it, the finding 'put an end to the pretence that Mr Irving is anything but a self-promoting apologist for Hitler'.[5]

For those around the world who have sought to combat denial, this was a stunning victory. It prompted questions about the further promise the law might hold. In short, if legal action can deliver a victory like this on Holocaust denial, then might defamation laws also offer other possibilities for combating racism? In particular, might this kind of a legal action provide some authoritative way of determining the truth or falsity of other historical claims? These are the questions I want to examine here. They warrant attention generally as the *Irving* case forms a part of the sometimes troubling but ever-increasing 'judicialisation of the past'.[6] Specifically, they need consideration because the possibility of taking the *Irving* path in different circumstances has recently arisen in historical disputes about British colonialism in Australia. The suggestion is unsurprising because the History Wars, as they have become known, share significant parallels with the circumstances in *Irving*: it has been claimed that, driven by self-interest and political agendas, academics have variously suppressed, manipulated, distorted and fabricated the historical record. By exploring how an action might proceed; how defamation law comprehends and conveys stories about the past; and how law, history and memory interact, I hope to demonstrate in this chapter that – in contrast with the apparent simplicity of the outcome in *Irving* that is so suggestive of great promise – defamation laws are not at all an appropriate vehicle for determining what happened in the past.

THE HISTORY WARS

The British claimed sovereignty over Australia in 1788 under the international law doctrine of *terra nullius*. In spite of the presence of indigenous peoples, it was said that the land was empty and belonged to no one. Colonisation was portrayed as a peaceful process. It is only in the last 30 years that this legal and historical narrative has been successfully challenged. Historians such as Lyndall Ryan and Henry Reynolds have argued that 'settlement' involved systematic violence against and retaliation by the Aboriginal population, with a resulting death toll of some 20,000 across Australia.[7] This picture of conquest and violent dispossession underpinned the High Court's watershed judgment in the 1992 *Mabo* case, which overturned the fiction of *terra nullius*, ruling that certain indigenous rights to land had survived the British acquisition of sovereignty and could still be recognised as native title rights.[8] This has been the historical framework underpinning contemporary debates about colonialism and white–indigenous relations. The core questions have for some time been about how the nation should consider the violent events of the past; about weighing up the good against the bad, and considering whether guilt, shame, responsibility, sorrow or reparation should attach to those events. But, very recently, this has changed. In the new disputes of the History Wars it is suggested that some events have been wrongly accepted as true and, in fact, never happened at all.

In 2002, Keith Windschuttle, a former journalist and academic, published *The Fabrication of Aboriginal History, Volume 1*, in which he examined colonialism in the state of Tasmania.[9] He argued that the accepted historical picture of 'widespread mass killings on the frontiers of the pastoral industry that not only went unpunished but had covert public support' was not correct and that 'the story the historians have constructed does not have the empirical foundations they claim'.[10] Windschuttle claims the historians have been deliberately deceptive, 'only select[ing] evidence that supports their cause and [they] either omit, suppress or falsify the rest'.[11] Examples that do not support their theses are 'simply airbrushed . . . out of history.'[12] This systemic 'widespread corruption of Aboriginal history' derives from the historians' self-interest.[13] In the end, the historians' orthodoxy has intentionally misled the nation, building 'mythologies designed to create an edifice of black victimhood and white guilt'.[14]

Windschuttle does not stop at critique; he also offers a 'counter-history': 'The British colonisation of this continent was the least violent of all Europe's encounters with the new world. It did not meet any organised resistance . . . The notion of sustained "frontier warfare" is fictional.'[15] There were no great numbers of killings in Tasmania says Windschuttle. Ryan's estimate of 700[16] is wrong, as are Reynolds' claims about the inherent uncertainty in calculating the original indigenous population and the deaths from violence,[17] as also is later writing that, Windschuttle claims, 'implies the total was more than a thousand'.[18] Instead, there is little uncertainty and it is not a matter of estimation: there were, he claims, 118 'plausible killings'.[19] The indigenous population was certainly decimated, but if blame is to rest anywhere, it is with the indigenous people themselves: 'It was a tragedy the Aborigines adopted such senseless violence. Their principal victims were themselves.'[20] The aims of colonial military actions were 'to impose law and order' and 'to save the Aborigines from the consequences of their own actions'.[21] Moreover, by virtue of their 'abuse and neglect' of their women, 'we should . . . see them as active agents in their own demise'.[22]

The book drew a phenomenal response from editors, columnists and the public in the broadcast and print media. Along with his opponent historians, Windschuttle participated in numerous interviews and public debates around the country. Three books were published that addressed Windschuttle's critique in different ways.[23] In one of these, an edited collection entitled *Whitewash*, Reynolds and Ryan made contributions that were in parts arguably as vitriolic as the attack they were responding to. They alleged to various degrees that Windschuttle himself had engaged in distortion, manipulation and fabrication in his writing.[24] The status of Windschuttle's work was under challenge throughout: was this a case of genuine revisionist scholarship undertaken in good faith, and should Windschuttle be accorded the same status in the literature as Reynolds and Ryan had achieved earlier? Or was it an exercise in denialism akin to Holocaust denial?[25]

The disputes raise difficult questions regarding how one goes about establishing what happened in the past, both as it pertains to colonialism and as it concerns historical scholarship more generally. Leading Australian genocide scholar, Professor Colin Tatz, saw the *Irving* case as a precedent. In the absence of a prosecution for genocide, this relentless advocate for the recognition and redress of historical injustice has suggested that the best way to settle the disputes of the History Wars and to find out about the past is to use the laws of defamation:

> Certainly Australians should engage with their history. But they should do it in an appropriate place: if not a criminal court, then in the next best venue, a civil court, under strict but somewhat more flexible forensic rules, a la the David Irving trial.[26]

Although the outcome of *Irving* may make this seem an appealing path, an examination of how a case would proceed suggests that such an action would be unlikely to resolve the debates in question.

THE NATURE OF JUDGMENT: DEFAMATION, TRUTH AND HISTORY

A defamation action may be commenced by someone whose reputation has been disparaged, in the sense that a statement made about them has a tendency to lower them in the estimation of 'ordinary decent folk' or 'right-thinking persons' in the community. As in the *Irving* case, Windschuttle's accusations that Reynolds and Ryan have fabricated and distorted data would, given their status as historians, be defamatory of them.[27] At the same time, the responses by Reynolds and Ryan make similar allegations and would arguably provide Windschuttle with adequate grounds to commence proceedings.

Once a plaintiff has established their case – that is, that they have been defamed – then the person who wrote and published the allegations can only avoid legal liability if they can establish a defence. The most relevant defence here will be justification, which requires the publisher to prove that what they wrote is true. As such, Lipstadt had to prove that Irving had manipulated the historical record.[28] Justice Gray explained that the law required Irving's scholarship to be judged by the standards of an 'objective, fair-minded historian'.[29] That is, the court would not decide whether the past was in fact as Irving claimed it was, but, instead, it would determine whether Irving's version of events was one of any number of conclusions that an objective, fair-minded historian might have reached, given the available evidence. In the Australian context, it seems likely that a defamation action surrounding the History Wars would proceed using the same legal test.

DEFAMATION AND THE HISTORY WARS

It would appear that the History Wars present two basic possibilities for defamation actions: (a) Reynolds and Ryan could sue Windschuttle on the grounds of his allegations in *Fabrication of Aboriginal History*, and (b) Windschuttle could sue Reynolds and Ryan over their responses in *Whitewash*. The plaintiff's case having been established in each, the defence of justification would come into play as it did in *Irving*.

Scenario (a): *Reynolds and Ryan v Windschuttle*

Windschuttle (the defendant) would have to prove the truth of his allegations that Reynolds and Ryan (the plaintiffs) have falsified or distorted the historical evidence. The court would have to determine whether an objective, fair-minded historian could come to the conclusions Reynolds and Ryan reached about the colonial past in Tasmania. That is, the court would decide whether an objective, fair-minded historian considering the historical evidence could find plausible a conclusion that Tasmania was the site of systematic violence with frontier warfare, indigenous resistance and a death toll of 700, or maybe 1,000 Aboriginal people.

Scenario (b): *Windschuttle v Reynolds and Ryan*

Reynolds and Ryan (as defendants) would have to prove the truth of their allegations that Windschuttle (as plaintiff) has falsified or distorted the historical evidence. The court would have to determine whether an objective, fair-minded historian could come to the conclusions Windschuttle has reached about the colonial past in Tasmania. That is, the court would decide whether an objective, fair-minded historian considering the historical evidence could find plausible a conclusion that Tasmania was the site of relatively little or perhaps only *ad hoc* violence against Aboriginal people, with an indigenous death toll from such violence of around only 120 people.

Even with just this sketch of the positions, a degree of complexity soon emerges that may not be immediately evident from and contrasts sharply with the clear outcome of the *Irving* case.

First, a party will be in a fundamentally different position depending on whether they are a plaintiff or a defendant. In particular, it will always be the plaintiff's work which is under the microscope; one cannot put an opponent's thesis to the test by commencing legal action against them. For example, if Reynolds and Ryan commenced a defamation action, then the court would consider whether their theses are plausible. In doing so, it will consider Windschuttle's criticisms of their scholarship. The court will not, however, consider the merits of Windschuttle's counter-history. Thus, regardless of the outcome, there is no formal determination about the merits or otherwise of a defendant's version of history. The Irving trial was in this sense remarkable as it was only because Irving commenced the action that his work was subjected to scrutiny.

Secondly, a court's determination will not present a statement of what happened in the past. Rather, it is only a finding of plausibility or implausibility. Consider, for instance, the position where the court finds the defendant is unable to prove their claims. This would be a finding that the plaintiff's thesis is plausible; that is, the court thinks an objective, fair-minded historian could have reached the same conclusion the plaintiff did about the events of the past. Compare this with the opposite outcome (as happened in *Irving*) where the finding is that an objective, fair-minded historian could not have concluded as the plaintiff did; here, the plaintiff's version of the past is implausible. The former finding does not exclude any versions of the past, and the latter finding will exclude only certain versions of the past, but neither conclusion presents a finding about how things were.

The significance of the plausibility/implausibility finding can be contrasted with, for example, a war crimes prosecution. There, the court must make a factual finding about what happened in order to determine the guilt or innocence of the accused. It must present a narrative of events.[30] Similarly, in a native title action the court must make determinations about the historical connections a group of people has with an area of land. These cases require the court to state its view about how things happened in the past. A defamation action does not require this, though, as *Irving* illustrates, there may still be an element of factual determination.

In *Irving*, Justice Gray explicitly attempted to avoid providing a historical narrative of events. Although he would have to look at the historical evidence to tell whether Lipstadt's attack on the plaintiff was justified, he stressed that he was not making a finding about whether the Holocaust occurred:

> I do not regard it as being any part of my function as the trial judge to make findings of fact as to what did and what did not occur during the Nazi regime in Germany. [I]t is not for me to form, still less to express, a judgment about what happened. That is a task for historians.[31]

Of course, this is not quite accurate, because he could not completely avoid making some factual findings. In concluding that Irving's position was implausible, he necessarily had to reach a conclusion that a particular version of the past was categorically untrue. Thus, while he did not draw precise and definitive factual conclusions about what *did* happen during the Nazi regime, he was nevertheless effectively spelling out some limits within which versions of the past would be considered valid.

Thirdly, the court's finding will depend on the evidence available, and that will in turn depend on the type of historical inquiry at issue. In both of the History Wars scenarios the defendant's task would seem to be more difficult than Lipstadt's was in *Irving*, because the events occurred in the early nineteenth century. The documentary evidence associated with them – which will always be appealing to legal standards – is far less extensive than that surrounding World War II. On that basis, it might be thought that it would be more difficult to exclude some versions of the past, and hence a finding that the plaintiff's work is implausible would be more difficult for a defendant to secure.[32] The *Irving* trial presents a façade of simplicity and certainty because there were such remarkably strong empirical grounds for finding Irving's version of history to be implausible, and because the court's finding was one of implausibility (rather than plausibility).

In all, it does not seem clear that a defamation trial offers the promise of clear findings in the way that occurred in *Irving v Lipstadt*. A court would not present any factual conclusions about the past, except to the extent that it might exclude certain possible versions of events by virtue of a finding of implausibility. That finding is less likely when the era and events under consideration are not well-documented. The versions of events that are scrutinised by the court will depend on who commences the action, and thus the court will not be considering the range of possible stories posed by the parties in dispute, let alone other historical possibilities that are raised elsewhere. In the end, the nature of a defamation action makes it very unclear exactly what, if anything, a trial and judgment might tell us about the events of the past in any given circumstances. These shortcomings are troublesome in their own right and they are of even more concern when one considers the place of legal judgment in a nation's understanding of its history.

THE PERCEPTION OF JUDGMENT: LAW, HISTORY AND MEMORY

Legal judgment is inevitably vulnerable to misinterpretation and manipulation in public and media debate. The discussion surrounding a defamation action would, understandably, be unlikely to take account of the substantial imperfections of a defamation action that emerge upon a close examination of the how a case would proceed. Instead, the inherent complexity of the action would likely be belied (or perhaps compounded) by the apparent simplicity of the finding in favour of the plaintiff or the defendant.[33] As Osiel has noted, the fact of judgment is often 'mistakenly read as an authoritative endorsement' of the stories the successful parties have offered to the court.[34] The potential for distortion is especially significant where a judgment can have an impact that reaches far beyond the parties to the case. In the History Wars that potential is unmistakable because of what is at stake.

The Australian historians' disagreements concern not only the past, but also the present: the nation's view of its history is a cornerstone for evaluating contemporary legal and moral claims to political and economic justice for Aboriginal people. Implicit in Windschuttle's position is the disconnection between past and present: because there was no wrong done in the past, there can be no historical foundation for present claims to justice. This is very much the inverse of the implications in the Reynolds/Ryan position. These contemporary concerns play heavily in how history is understood. They help delineate the concept of history from that of memory. As Peter Novick has explained it, memory is about 'the ways in which present concerns determine what of the past we remember, and how we remember it'.[35] In a nation not so long ago admonished for its 'cult of disremembering' and 'forgetfulness practised on a national scale', history is important. Historians are, in Peter Burke's words, 'the guardians of awkward facts, the skeletons in the cupboard of social memory'; their task is 'to remind people of what they would have liked to forget'.[36] As the earlier discussion suggested, a defamation judgment does not address history adequately; it would not deliver the resolution of the debates that Tatz seeks and would be ill-suited to this protective role. This should be of great concern because legal judgments about history impact heavily on the nation's sense of itself and its past.

The significance of legal judgment was made clear in France during the 1980s and 1990s when there were several attempts at prosecutions for crimes against humanity committed under the Vichy regime during World War II. Henry Rousso argued that the trials were 'a ritualised interpretation of the past that is dependent upon the expectations of the present [and its] objective is to inscribe this past in collective consciousness, with the full force of the law and the symbolism of the legal apparatus'.[37] In public debate there were attempts to show how the connections should be drawn. There were differences of opinion over whether the trials were essential or appropriate ways of judging not just individuals but France as a nation (both past and present), the Vichy regime, and the genocidal complicity and activity of both nation and state. Tzvetan Todorov questioned the pedagogic value of a trial and wondered instead whether the prosecution and conviction allowed the nation to falsely reconstitute itself, allowing the contemporaneous mistreatment of immigrants to continue while forming a 'retrospective heroism [that] simply exempted us from combating [present injustices]'.[38] Rousso saw its only purpose as being to 'liberate a voice, organise it, put it into circulation, and thus to see to it that the suffering and responsibilities for this event are more widely shared within the community'.[39] Alain Finkielkraut saw in Papon's trial an event with the power to disturb individual consciousness such that it would become 'a little less easy for us, whatever we are – civil servants, but also photographers, technicians, researchers, executives or businessmen – to run from moral responsibility for our acts in the carrying out of our tasks'.[40] However disparate and conflicting these views are, Mark Osiel's analysis of legal adjudication of the catastrophic past seems to apply equally to all: the stories of the past in the trials serves to 'aid our remembrance not only of the events themselves, but also of the moral judgments we ultimately reached about them'.[41]

Similarly, Australia has already seen judgments about its colonial past used to shape its sense of history and memory, and to justify the path of present and future white–indigenous relations. Paul Keating, Labour Prime Minister during the mid-1990s, argued that the *Mabo* decision established and recognised dispossession as a fundamental historical truth and laid the basis for justice.[42] In contrast, Prime Minister Howard took the position that dispossession and its consequences had to be 'put behind us'.[43] For Keating, the court's story of the past had to become a part of the nation's very being. Recognition of dispossession was the basis for moving forward. For Howard, the past as a story of dispossession could not become a part of the nation's being and would be an obstacle to moving forward.

Judgments that engage with history will necessarily be interpreted as authorising or accepting as valid a particular version of the past. There is no way around that. A defamation action surrounding the History Wars would purport to judge the reputation of historians but it would inevitably speak directly and significantly to the nation. In so many ways, a defamation judgment is not equipped for that task.

CONCLUSION

At issue in the History Wars is the self-understanding of the nation and its past within which indigenous and non-indigenous relations will make moral sense.[44] Tatz is rightly concerned that the nation should understand and grapple with its history, and his call for judgment in the courts undoubtedly takes account of how significant legal judgment could be in that process. But the laws of defamation are not, I have argued, an appropriate way to resolve the disputes about the truth or falsity of histories. The prospect of judgment in such a case holds far too much potential for distorting the narratives of history. A defamation judgment almost certainly would not make a finding that claimed to determine the truth or falsity of the historians' theses. A defamation judgment is far too flawed to constitute an adequate foundation for the nation's memory and the moral judgments that underpin the evaluation of contemporary claims to justice. In the end, it might be that the judgment of David Irving should be prized not for the doubtful potential it appeared to promise on its surface, but for the compelling destruction of historical deception that it delivered in such depth.[45]

NOTES

1 This chapter draws in part on research undertaken for a broader project on defamation law and history. The most comprehensive publication of that research can be found in Lawrence McNamara, 'History, Memory and Judgment: Holocaust Denial, The History Wars and Law's Problems with the Past' 26 *Sydney Law Review* 353, 2004.

2 Pierre Vidal-Naquet, *Assassins of Memory: Essays on the Denial of the Holocaust*, Columbia University Press, New York, 1992; *R. v Zundel* [1992] 2 SCR 731.

3 See for example, the *Institute for Historical Review* and its *Journal of Historical Review*: <http://www.ihr.org> (20 June 2004).

4 *Irving v Penguin Books Ltd and Deborah Lipstadt* [2000] EWHC QB 115 (Gray J., 11 April 2000) ('*Irving*') at [13.91], [13.167]. The decision was upheld on appeal: *Irving v Penguin Books Ltd and Deborah Lipstadt* [2001] EWCA Civ 1197.

5 Cited in Deborah Lipstadt, '*Irving v Penguin UK, and Deborah Lipstadt*: Building a Defense Strategy', 27 *Nova Law Review* p 243, 2002.

6 Henry Rousso, *The Haunting Past: History, Memory and Justice in Contemporary France*, (trans. Ralph Schoolcraft; first published as *La Hantise du passé* 1998), University of Pennsylvania Press, Philadelphia, 2001. See also Richard Evans, 'History, Memory, and the Law: The Historian as Expert Witness', 41 *History and Theory* 326, p 344, 2002.

7 Henry Reynolds, *The Other Side of the Frontier*, Penguin, Ringwood, Vic., 1982, p 122. See also Henry Reynolds, *Fate of a Free People*, Penguin, Ringwood, Vic., 1995, and Lyndall Ryan, *The Aboriginal Tasmanians*, 1981, University of Queensland Press, St Lucia, 2nd edn, 1996.

8 *Mabo v Queensland (No 2)* (1992) 175 CLR 1.

9 Keith Windschuttle, *The Fabrication of Aboriginal History*, Macleay Press, Sydney, 2002.

10 *Ibid* pp 2–4.

11 *Ibid* p 403.

12 *Ibid* p 114; see also pp 178, 367.

13 *Ibid* pp 403, 404, 414–415.

14 *Ibid* p 10.

15 *Ibid* pp 3, 4.

16 Lyndall Ryan, *op cit*, p 174.

17 Henry Reynolds, *Fate of a Free People*, *op cit*, pp 75–76.

18 Keith Windschuttle, *op cit*, pp 351–353, 358–359.

19 *Ibid* pp 387–397. In response to some criticisms of his work, he has revised the table slightly and most recently, at 1 March 2003, he placed the figure at 120: <http://www.sydneyline.com/Table%20Ten%20revised.htm> (8 April 2004).

20 Keith Windschuttle, *op cit*, p 130.

21 *Ibid* p 195.

22 *Ibid* p 386.

23 Robert Manne (ed.), *Whitewash: On Keith Windschuttle's Fabrication of Aboriginal History*, Black Inc Agenda, Melbourne, 2003; Stuart MacIntyre and Anna Clark, *The History Wars*, Melbourne University Press, Melbourne, 2003; Bain Attwood

and S.G. Foster (eds), *Frontier Conflict: The Australian Experience*, National Museum of Australia, Canberra, 2003.

24 Henry Reynolds, '*Terra Nullius* Reborn' in Robert Manne, *op cit* pp 109, 113, 122, and arguably 127 and 133; Lyndall Ryan, 'Who is the Fabricator?' in Manne, *op cit* pp 230, 233.

25 On Windschuttle as a revisionist, see Alan Atkinson, 'Historians and Moral Disgust' in Bain Attwood and S.G. Foster, *op cit* p 113; Robert Manne 'Blind to Truth, and Blind to History' *Sydney Morning Herald* (Sydney), 16 December 2002; Mark Finnane, 'Counting the Cost of the "Nun's Picnic" ' in Robert Manne, *Whitewash* pp 299, 308; Martin Krygier and Robert Van Krieken, 'The Character of the Nation' in Manne, *Whitewash* pp 81, 83. On Reynolds and Ryan as revisionists, see the Introduction to Attwood and Foster, *op cit* p 4; Bain Attwood, 'Historiography on the Australian Frontier', in Attwood and Foster, *op cit* p 172. On Windschuttle and the question of denial, see A. Dirk Moses, 'Revisionism and Denial' in Manne, *Whitewash* p 342.

26 Colin Tatz, *With Intent to Destroy: Reflecting on Genocide*, Verso, London, 2003,-ol; p 136.

27 Note that it would defame them further to say that they have done so deliberately, and that allegation was also a key aspect of the *Irving* case. That point is not addressed here. For a more comprehensive discussion, see Lawrence McNamara, 'History, Memory and Judgment: Holocaust Denial, The History Wars and Law's Problems with the Past' 26 *Sydney Law Review*, 353, 2004.

28 Lipstadt's case was more onerous than this. In particular, she also had to prove that any manipulation of the record was intentional; she did so successfully.

29 *Irving op cit* [13.91].

30 See generally Mark Osiel, *Mass Atrocity, Collective Memory, and the Law*, Transaction Books, New Brunswick NJ, 1997. There is a substantial body of literature that examines critically how the courts are not a suitable forum for the discussion of history because of the different methodological foundations and the different purposes of legal and historical inquiries. This position is not addressed here because, as I have argued elsewhere, this type of defamation action is to some extent able to comprehend history as history, rather than requiring history to fit within the strictures of legal argument: see McNamara, *op cit*.

31 *Irving, op cit* [1.3]; see also [13.3].

32 I am not here drawing a conclusion about the merits of the positions. However, it seems most likely that the empirical responses to Windschuttle – a number of them published in *Whitewash* (Robert Manne, *op cit*) criticise Windschuttle's selection, use and interpretation of sources – would provide the basis for a finding that an objective fair-minded historian could indeed reach the same conclusions that Reynolds and Ryan have and that their theses are plausible. It is difficult to tell how a court would view those same materials in determining the plausibility of Windschuttle's position.

33 There are numerous legal and factual points that could complicate the finding. Among the most likely would be that a judgment would contain adverse comments against the successful party. The unsuccessful party would, of course, highlight these in public debate of the outcome.

34 Mark Osiel, *op cit*, p 106. The observation was made in the criminal context but there seems little doubt it applies similarly to civil outcomes.

35 Peter Novick, *The Holocaust in American Life*, Houghton Mifflin, Boston, 1999,-ol; p 3.

36 Peter Burke, 'History as Social Memory' in Thomas Butler (ed.), *Memory: History, Culture and the Mind*, Basil Blackwell, Oxford, 1989, p 110.

37 Henry Rousso, *op cit*, p 57.
38 Tzvetan Todorov, 'Letter from Paris: The Papon Trial' in Richard Golsan (ed.), *The Papon Affair: Memory and Justice on Trial*, Routledge, New York, 2000, p 222, (trans: John Anzalone; first published: 1999, 121–122 *Salmagundi* 3).
39 Henry Rousso, *op cit*, p 20.
40 Alain Finkielkraut, 'Papon: Too Late' in Richard Golsan, *op cit*, p 192, (trans: Lucy Golsan; first published as 'Papon, trop tard', 1996, *Le Monde*).
41 Mark Osiel, *op cit*, p 73. Where they are dealing with matters of significant public concern, the courts are not unaware of the way they will be viewed. Justice Gray's disclaimer in *Irving* that it was not his role 'to form, still less to express, a judgment about what happened' indicates that, even if he does not like it, his judgment 'will inevitably be viewed as *making* history': *Irving*, above note 3 at [1.3]. Justice Gray's sentiment had it parallels in, for example, Eichmann's trial in Israel and Osiel (pp. 80–81) quotes the opening parts of that judgment at some length where the court states that it does not see its purpose as being to provide 'a comprehensive and exhaustive historical account of the events' nor to cast judgments on 'questions of principle which are outside the realm of law'. A judicial disclaimer is of little effect because the court cannot control the way that judgment shapes and is used to shape memory.
42 Paul Keating, 'Australian Launch of the International Year for the World's Indigenous People', 10 December 1992, reproduced as an appendix to Native Title and Aboriginal and Torres Strait Islander Land Fund Senate Committee, *Sixteenth Report: Consistency of the Native Title Amendment Act 1998 with Australia's International Obligations under the Convention on the Elimination of all Forms of Racial Discrimination (CERD)*, 28 June 2000, p 272.
43 This point was made in numerous speeches and interviews: see for example, John Howard, 'Wik Statement – Address to the Nation, ABC Television', 30 November 1997, <www.pm.gov.au/news/speeches/1997/wikadd.htm> (1 February 2004).
44 The moral dimensions to the History Wars are noted on all sides of the debate. See, for example, Keith Windschuttle, *op cit*, p 3; Ann Curthoys, 'Constructing National Histories', in Bain Attwood and S.G. Foster, *op cit*, p 187; Martin Krygier and Robert Van Krieken, *op cit*, p 82.
45 In February 2006, Irving was sentenced to three years' imprisonment in Austria for denying the Holocaust in speeches delivered in that country in the 1980s. The trial judge cited the verdict in the English libel case when stating that Irving was 'a racist, an anti-semite, and a liar'. See Ian Traynor, *Guardian Weekly*, 24 February 2006.

Chapter 3

From heroic death to comic death

Representations of African-Americans in *Harper's Weekly* from the Civil War to the early twentieth century

Claire Parfait

In 1857, in the wake of the success of *Harper's New Monthly Magazine*, the New York publishing house of Harper and Brothers launched a new periodical, *Harper's Weekly*. The latter was largely designed, as Frank Luther Mott put it, 'as a vehicle for the political discussion which *Harper's Monthly* eschewed'.[1] In addition to a miscellany of news, fiction, essays, book reviews, humour etc., the weekly, which derived no small part of its appeal from its numerous engravings, provided its readers with political editorials. Hardly four years after it first appeared, *Harper's Weekly* could boast of a circulation of over 100,000, which made it one of the top contenders in the field of illustrated journalism, together with its closest rival, *Frank Leslie's Illustrated Newspaper*.[2] Advertised as a 'family newspaper', *Harper's Weekly* targeted the vast American middle class which was then in the process of being formed. As Mott noted, *Harper's Weekly* reads today as 'a vital illustrated history' of its times. In addition, the periodical also provides intriguing insights into the evolution of the representation of African-Americans during the Civil War, Reconstruction and post-Reconstruction periods. *Harper's Weekly*'s editorials and illustrations highlight the role of the periodical as both a reflector and a shaper of opinions. Beyond documenting the evolution of the magazine's attitude toward African-Americans, the analysis and contextualisation of representations – more particularly those linked with the death of their objects – throw light on the specific purposes such representations served. Since stereotyping, in its denial of individuality, enacts a form of metaphorical murder, this essay will also allude to the evolution of stereotyping, but only in passing since that particular topic has already been thoroughly examined by a number of scholars.

THE CIVIL WAR BREAKS OUT: FROM CONTENTED SLAVES TO VICTIMS

Between 1857, when it was launched, and the beginning of the Civil War in April 1861, *Harper's Weekly*, like its major rival *Frank Leslie's Illustrated*

Newspaper, targeted a national audience, and tried hard not to alienate its Southern readership. As a result, the magazine systematically downplayed the issue of slavery, and blamed all extremists, with a special emphasis on abolitionists. In the cartoons that were placed in the last pages of the periodical, slaves were portrayed as quite satisfied with their condition, in keeping with the paternalistic vision of slavery common to the defenders of the institution. In these drawings, the distorted physical features of the slaves, the systematic use of ridiculous-sounding names such as Caesar and Pompey,[3] as well as the dialect consistently put in the slaves' mouths, all combined to build stereotyped images of African-Americans.

As soon as the war broke out, however, the Southern reader became both undesirable (the 'Southern rebels' replaced 'our Southern friends') and unnecessary ('We have work enough to supply the Northern demand for *Harper's Weekly*').[4] The Southern reader, especially when he was a Democrat – although *Harper's Weekly* claimed to be non-partisan, the periodical would support the Republican party for most of the period, with a few rare exceptions – remained undesirable until the growing trend toward national reconciliation in the late 1870s. Significantly, the magazine then began to use inverted commas with the words 'The North' and 'The South', before stating outright, in the mid-1880s, that 'The South' should no longer be used.

Indications of an African-American readership are elusive. We know that *Harper's Weekly* was read avidly by both black and white soldiers during the Civil War. The magazine was sent to the Union officers free of charge and was passed from hand to hand until it fell to pieces.[5] During and after Reconstruction, the periodical occasionally printed letters from African-American readers, but it is impossible to know with any certainty what proportion of its readers belonged to the African-American community.[6]

The beginning of the war caused a genuine revolution in the tone of the editorials and the depiction of African-Americans. *Harper's Weekly* began to denounce slavery in no uncertain words, in a campaign that was to extend beyond the close of the war, still finding echoes as late as the 1880s. The paper exposed the horrors of slavery in much the same way as anti-slavery writers and activists had done before the war. In text and illustration, *Harper's Weekly* focused on the cruelty of punishments, on the separation of slave families, and on the sexual abuse of female slaves by their masters. In other words, in the pages of *Harper's Weekly*, the firing on Fort Sumter turned contented slaves into the victims of a horrifying system. Although demeaning stereotypes never entirely disappeared from the periodical, their number decreased sharply, revealing the change in status – both real and symbolical – of African-Americans.[7]

This evolution was not unique to *Harper's Weekly*; *Frank Leslie's Illustrated Newspaper* and the Northern illustrated press in general also produced a number of positive representations of African-Americans during the war years.[8] Yet, *Harper's Weekly* turned this trend into a genuine crusade in which the representations of the African-American dead played a significant part. The outbreak of the war and the need to support the Union can partly account for the marked change in *Harper's Weekly*, but the new militancy should also be attributed to the arrival on the weekly's payroll of two reform-minded men: George William Curtis, who acted as *Harper's Weekly*'s political editor from 1863 until his death in 1892, and the artist Thomas Nast, who provided the magazine with illustrations and cartoons between 1862 and 1887, when he retired.[9]

From the start of the war, with a number of inevitable ambiguities, contradictions and waverings, which reflect the debates of the time – over the status of fugitive slaves for example, or the wisdom of enrolling black soldiers – *Harper's Weekly* systematically celebrated individual and collective acts of courage by African-Americans, both fugitive slaves and soldiers. Death on the battlefield, the ultimate sacrifice for the Union cause, brought black and white soldiers together, in both text and illustration.

THE CIVIL WAR: HEROIC DEATH

In *Harper's Weekly*, the numerous engravings in which black soldiers were represented training, charging the enemy, or lying dead on the battlefield, were offered as evidence that black troops displayed the same courage and loyalty to the cause as their white counterparts: the battle at Milliken's Bend, for example, in the spring of 1863, or the attack on Fort Wagner, in July of the same year.[10] In both text and image, many portraits of individual African-American heroes were devoid of caricature.

The heroism of black soldiers on the battlefield was sometimes highlighted in *Harper's Weekly* by an illustrated article on the elaborate funeral of a distinguished hero. Such was the case, for example, when Captain Cailloux, of the First Louisiana Volunteers, was buried in New Orleans after dying on the battlefield ('a death the proudest might envy'). The engraving showed an orderly and dignified ceremony, while the article stressed that by his death, the captain had 'vindicated his race from the opprobrium with which it was charged'.[11] The heroism of the captain on the battlefield was thus presented as redemptive for the entire African-American community. The visibility and solemnity of the proceedings participated in an ongoing process which Gary Laderman characterises as the 'politicisation of death' during the Civil War, meant to increase support for the war by evoking 'ideas of national unity and the righteousness of the Union cause.'[12]

Some of the pictorial representations of the death of African-Americans on the battlefields are particularly striking in their attempt to define the new status of black soldiers in relation to their white comrades: companionship and brotherhood were underscored in an engraving which showed white and black soldiers lying dead side by side.[13] Another illustration depicted two Union veterans, one black, one white, each having lost a leg, shaking hands at the end of the war.[14] The caption read, 'Give me your hand, Comrade! We have each lost a LEG for the good cause; but, thank GOD, we never lost HEART.' *Harper's Weekly* thus clearly contended that equality had been won on the battlefield, by the common heroism of men fighting for the same cause.

THE CIVIL WAR: 'SENTIMENTALISED' DEATH

Long before the Civil War, the readers of *Harper's Weekly* were presented with frequent descriptions of death scenes, whether in text or image: articles on wars or rebellions abroad, reports on railroad accidents, boiler explosions on steamboats, were accompanied by dramatic engravings reminiscent of the sensational press. In a different vein, death also appeared in numerous poems, stories and serials, in the tradition of sentimental literature. Ann Douglas has described the 'fascination with death and mourning' that permeated Victorian society and which the Civil War did not cause, but which it dramatised and accelerated. That fascination was revealed in an abundance of death-related literature, as well as increasingly elaborate mourning rites.[15]

The Civil War naturally gave rise to what Alice Fahs calls 'an outpouring of sentimental literature', meant to comfort the nation by stressing the importance of the individual at a time when the death toll rose, and when the needs of the country were emphasised over individual suffering. To make anonymous death meaningful, countless poems and stories focused on the deaths of individual soldiers. Although, as Fahs notes, this type of literature rarely dealt with African-American soldiers ('The individualised sentimental soldier was coded as white in Northern popular literature'),[16] *Harper's Weekly* occasionally provided its readers with similar stories that had African-Americans as their main characters.

These stories generally played on pathos and melodrama to allow for a degree of identification on the part of the audience. In two such tales, a highly stereotyped protagonist was individualised and humanised in the course of the story. Both stories – they may have been produced by the same pen –[17] started with an address to the reader, in which this strategy was clearly laid out. Thus, the opening lines of 'Tippoo Sahib' warned the readers that 'all heroes are not *héros de roman* . . . Tippoo Sahib was neither handsome, nor accomplished, nor gently bred'. This unlikely hero was described as 'formed after the ultra type of his race, with misshapen skull, immense lips', and was depicted as 'heavy both of motion and intellect'. The author then openly challenged his readers: 'at the end of my story, deny, if you dare, that he was a hero, a *preux chevalier*, a man to be admired and revered.' Tippoo, a fugitive slave, indeed died a hero's death at Fort Wagner and the author inscribed Tippoo's death – unsung and anonymous, by contrast with that of Colonel Shaw, who led the attack on Fort Wagner and passed into 'deathless glory' – in the roll call of nameless heroes: 'But no nation mourns, no poet sings, no history, save this rude tale, will chronicle the closing scene of another life as brave, as earnest, as beautiful to those who have eyes to read the hearts of men as that of his hero-leader.'[18] The second tale, entitled 'Little Starlight', similarly presented the reader with an improbable hero, whose name might falsely evoke 'a pretty boy – a *beau*-ideal Young America' for one who was in fact 'as black as the ace of spades, when the ace of spades is excessively black and shiny'. Little Starlight, characterised as 'a sort of masculine Topsy' – he was prone to stealing and the way he spoke was reminiscent of that of his feminine counterpart in *Uncle Tom's Cabin* – was a young fugitive slave, who became the drummer and mascot of a New York regiment. Little Starlight died happy on the battlefield because he had fulfilled both of his dreams: he had killed his former master ('I seed him lick my ole mudder till de blood flew') and won his freedom. The protracted death scene – one that Victorian readers would have been familiar with, thanks to Harriet Beecher Stowe and Charles Dickens in particular – was evidently meant to call upon the reader's emotions, all the more so since the hero was a child.[19]

In *The Sacred Remains, American Attitudes toward Death*, Gary Laderman describes the sentimental literature of the Civil War as an effort to 'locate noble sacrifices in real flesh-and-blood examples of individual heroes who die illustrious, patriotic, Christian deaths'.[20] 'Tippoo Sahib', 'Little Starlight', and other stories aimed at performing a similar function for African-American soldiers, both in the eyes of the white readers and in those of the black soldiers who read the magazine and whose sacrifice was thus acknowledged.[21]

Representations of heroic and sentimentalised death during the Civil War were part of a vast campaign undertaken by *Harper's Weekly* to fight against racial prejudice.[22] Together with the frequent descriptions of the horrors of slavery, the campaign also aimed at making the North accept the presence of black troops and at preparing the post-war years. Black troops were important for the Union to win the war, and the weekly considered that refusing to enlist African-Americans would be both absurd and suicidal. Such was the message conveyed by an 1862 engraving that showed a white man who preferred drowning to being saved by a black man.[23]

RECONSTRUCTION: AFRICAN-AMERICANS AS VICTIMS

After the war, *Harper's Weekly* supported Radical Reconstruction, advocated full citizenship rights for freedmen, and continued to provide readers with positive images of African-Americans. The weekly often reminded its audience of the courage displayed by black troops during the war and would later praise their bravery in the West. In these articles, Indians were described as 'savages', whereas Blacks and Whites shared a common civilisation.[24] In addition, the magazine frequently underscored the low criminality of the black population, as well as the lack of vindictive spirit of the freedmen toward their former masters.

Taken together with the frequent reminders of the brutality of slavery, this reflects the continuation of what could be called an enlightened campaign as well as a political strategy on the part of the magazine: readers had to be convinced that the South was not to be trusted, and that the black vote was needed to avoid a return to power by the Democrats.

Images of black heroes dying on the battlefield (during the Civil War, but also in the post-war West) were gradually outnumbered by engravings of black victims of racist violence. In the accompanying texts, the brutality of the deeds – underscored in words and phrases such as 'massacre', 'murdered', 'slaughtered', 'brutal outrage', 'fierce and wanton slaughter' – was systematically opposed to the innocence and helplessness of the victims.[25] The engravings illustrated that defencelessness by showing, for example, unarmed men being shot while trying to flee, or being fired at when they were already lying on the ground. Thomas Nast's exposure of the Ku Klux Klan is well-known,[26] but many similar illustrations of racist violence are to be found in *Harper's Weekly* during the Reconstruction era and, while the pictures left no room whatsoever for a misinterpretation of the scene, the accompanying text explained to the audience just how to 'read' the drawing.[27]

Unlike its rival, *Frank Leslie's Illustrated Newspaper* presented its readers with engravings of white victims of the Ku Klux Klan, as well as with images that 'installed African-Americans as violent subjects'.[28] In the pages of *Harper's Weekly*, the representation of African-Americans as victims reflects the very real violence of the Reconstruction period. It can also be accounted for by the continued fight *Harper's Weekly* kept up against the Democrats, and in favour of the Republicans as the only party that could protect the rights of the freedmen. Nevertheless, by systematically calling upon the audience to pity the freedmen exposed to such violence and evidently without the means to defend themselves, the magazine assigned African-Americans the ambiguous and unenviable status of victims.[29] In *Blind Memory*, Marcus Wood has described the iconography of the runaway slave in anti-slavery literature as one of 'passivity and dependency'. The runaway slave was shown as pathetic, hunted by men and dogs, exposed to all kinds of dangers, in a narrative of 'disempowerment', which called upon the pity of the audience and ultimately conveyed the message that the slaves' only hope lay in the help of the North.[30] In *Harper's Weekly*, during the Reconstruction years, the freedmen and women seemed more akin to the disempowered fugitive slaves of old than to the Civil War soldiers, or to the heroes of antebellum fugitive slave narratives who, like Fredrick Douglass, had been the agents of their own freedom.

Passing evidence of the negative connotations of the victim status is to be found in an article describing a duel between two black men in Savannah, Georgia. The weekly condemned the practice as 'absurd and tragical'. Yet in that particular instance, *Harper's Weekly* deemed it a good sign, and interpreted the fight as an illustration of an 'awakening sense of manhood and even of self-respect'.[31]

From the end of the 1860s, the representation of African-Americans in *Harper's Weekly* was marked by increasing ambiguity, in both text and image. On various occasions, while still publishing portraits of distinguished African-Americans, the magazine voiced doubts as to their ability to take their fate into their own hands. Slavery, the periodical contended, might well have left its imprint on the former slaves, in the form of laziness and improvidence. 'The love of subordination is innate in the negro', noted an 1873 editorialist, presumably quoting yet another legacy from the institution.[32] At the same time, the number of stereotyped representations of African-Americans increased.

Reading *Harper's Weekly* during the Reconstruction years thus provides a motley narrative, in which African-Americans are in turn praised, pitied and stereotyped, sometimes in the same issue of the magazine.[33] Joshua Brown notes that in *Frank Leslie's Illustrated Newspaper*, although the general trend followed by the representations of African-Americans was clearly racist, a few engravings offered a different perspective, depicting illustrious characters or showing the freedmen exercising their duties as citizens in a dignified way.[34] One could argue that *Harper's Weekly* provided its readers with the exact opposite: a narrative that on the whole fought against racism, yet occasionally lapsed into stereotypes.

1877–1900: DEATH AS A COMIC SUBJECT

After the contested presidential election of 1876 and the compromise that ensured the election of Republican Rutherford B. Hayes in return for the promise to withdraw federal troops from the South, the tone of *Harper's Weekly* underwent a marked change. The paper approved of the compromise and began to describe Reconstruction governments as 'semi-barbarous and corrupt', led by the 'least intelligent and the most venal' part of the population, an 'apparent reversal of a rational order of society' – thus adopting the mainstream view of Reconstruction that was to prevail, both in history books and in popular culture, until the 1950s. The paper continued to castigate racial prejudice, to celebrate distinguished African-Americans and occasionally reverted to a more militant tone. However, the weekly also reflected the growing indifference of the North to the plight of African-Americans, and the spirit of national reconciliation obtained in its columns. The South, *Harper's Weekly* argued, had to be left alone and allowed 'to work out her own salvation'.[35] In a significant way, coverage of African-American-related news decreased sharply, while the number of stereotyped representations rose markedly. African-Americans were often caricatured in their physical features, shown as fond of stealing chickens, ignorant and lazy.

The attitude of *Harper's Weekly* towards lynching also sent mixed messages. As we know, the number of lynchings steadily increased in the 1880s and especially the 1890s.[36] In keeping with its 'progressive' tradition, the periodical vigorously exposed the practice as cowardly, brutal and revolting. Yet, in 1899, after Sam Hose was slowly burnt to death for murder and the alleged rape of a white woman, *Harper's Weekly* noted that, although the 'orgy' of violence could not be justified, it could nonetheless be explained. In similar circumstances, the weekly claimed, Northern readers would have reacted in the same way. The editor thus commented upon a letter he had received from a woman in Georgia: 'To read the story of Sam Hose's crime as our Georgia correspondent has written it begets absolute indifference to that negro's suffering or fate. It fills the mind with horror, and makes one feel that any means that is effectual to prevent such crimes is justified.' In the same issue of the paper, an article reminded readers, however, that four-fifths of the lynchings in the South in 1898 had been prompted by causes other than violence or attempted violence against white women.[37] Yet, the insistence on the fact that the lynching was after all but a human reaction to an abominable deed, and the call upon Northern readers to understand, strike one as an excuse for lynching in certain cases and a clear – although rare – departure from the magazine's usual condemnation of the practice. Added to the articles reporting on the high rate of criminality in the African-American population, this shows that *Harper's Weekly* had definitely moved toward mainstream attitudes in respect to African-Americans.

The 1890s were the worst decade for Blacks in post Civil War America: they suffered segregation, disfranchisement, economic exclusion and racial violence. At the same time, in the press and in popular culture, Americans were presented with ever more degraded representations of African-Americans. According to J. Stanley Lemons, the systematic use of stereotypes to depict African-Americans reflected the situation 'by trying to ease the tension with laughter'.[38]

In *Harper's Weekly* and many other magazines (all published in the North), the degraded status of African-Americans – once again both real and symbolic – translated into a number of pictures which hinted that their death was not to be seen as a tragic event. Thus, an 1887 cartoon by Edward W. Kemble in *Harper's Weekly* presented a caricatured African-American woman who failed to understand the news brought by one of her children: his brother had just drowned. Her only reaction was anger, and she promised to 'knock the life' out of the little rascal who was 'foreber an' etarnally gittin' killed some way er udder'.[39] Beyond hinting at the stupidity and/or indifference of the woman, the mere fact that death was taken as the subject of an illustration that was meant to amuse seemed to convey the message that the death of an African-American child was a trifling event. The idea of death as an occurrence to be laughed at rather than mourned appeared in a number of illustrations in *Harper's Weekly* and in other magazines. The caricature of a black child being threatened by an alligator was to become more widespread at the turn of the century, when it was used on greeting cards, cigar box labels, and in early movies (*The Gater and the Pickaninny*, 1903).[40] The press of the late nineteenth century emphasised black criminality as a justification for lynchings and racial violence in general. Representing African-Americans as targets of comic violence can be seen as a desire to remove African-Americans from the scene, while it 'made violence toward Blacks more acceptable by turning it into a source of amusement'.[41]

ERASURE OF CIVIL WAR HEROES

A number of scholars have demonstrated that the African-American Civil War hero became 'invisible' toward the end of the nineteenth century. In *Race and Reunion*, for example, David Blight explains that in the drive toward national reconciliation, and in spite of efforts by men like George Washington Williams, African-Americans lost the 'contest over memory'. Kirk Savage has shown how that defeat was inscribed in public monuments. In that respect, the 1876 Freedmen's Memorial by Thomas Ball, in Washington, DC, is particularly revealing: by showing a slave kneeling in gratitude at Lincoln's feet, it erases the part African-Americans played in their own liberation.[42] This finds an echo in a number of 1880s illustrations in *Harper's Weekly* which, in addition, suggest that African-Americans should be thankful for the abolition of slavery, rather than claim full citizenship.[43]

And yet, in *Harper's Weekly*, what Alessandra Lorini calls 'collective amnesia'[44] did not entirely preclude representations of African-American soldiers as heroes in the 1890s, especially during the last Indian wars and during the Spanish-American war.[45] Moreover the death of black abolitionists was commented upon abundantly. Thus, when Frederick Douglass died in 1895, *Harper's Weekly* printed laudatory portraits of the man and his career.[46] Even *The Century*, which provided its readers with many demeaning cartoons of African-Americans, occasionally offered reminders of black Civil War heroes, as was the case with a poem entitled 'With the Colored Regiment Band'.[47]

The representations of African-Americans in *Harper's Weekly* between 1857 and the end of the century naturally reflect changes in their status. Those representations, however, also have to be seen as rhetorical devices in the strategy pursued by the magazine at a particular time. Thus, the images of heroic and sentimentalised deaths were part of a vast campaign undertaken by the magazine to acknowledge the new role of African-Americans during the Civil War and force the reader to change his vision of former slaves. That crusade was carried out for humane as well as political purposes. During Reconstruction, the ambiguous image of the more or less passive victim replaced that of the heroic soldier fallen on the battlefield. Once again, the representation obeyed mixed motivations. With the move toward national reconciliation, *Harper's Weekly* tended to adopt the mainstream representations – of recent history and of African-Americans, and both are of course closely linked – that obtained in most Northern magazines, and at the end of the period began to represent the death of African-Americans as a comic subject.

This brief overview is of necessity reductive: a periodical, especially one that gives readers a voice in its columns, is by essence polyphonic. The analysis of *Harper's Weekly* reveals contradictions and ambiguities, often in the same issue of the magazine, evidence both of the numerous voices to be heard in the weekly, and of the discomfort many felt at these momentous changes. What is most striking perhaps, in the case of *Harper's Weekly*, is the fact that a magazine which is usually labelled 'conservative'[48] led a radical campaign in favour of African-Americans, at least during the Civil War and Reconstruction periods. Finally, towards the end of the century, in *Harper's Weekly* as well as in the other magazines, and in spite of the general trend toward stereotyped representations of African-Americans, it still remained possible to find traces of the new status Africans Americans had acquired during the Civil War period.

NOTES

1 Frank Luther Mott, *A History of American Magazines, vol. 2: 1850–1865*, 1938, pp 469–487, Cambridge MA: Harvard University Press. *Harper's Weekly* was launched in 1857 and disappeared – it was merged with another periodical – in 1916.
2 *Harper's Weekly* had a circulation of 115,000 in July 1861, according to an advertisement printed in the weekly (13 July 1861 p 447). *Frank Leslie's Illustrated Newspaper* announced a circulation of 164,000 just before the war: Mott, *op cit*, p 455. For a book-length study of *Frank Leslie's Illustrated Newspaper*, see Joshua Brown, *Beyond the Lines: Pictorial Reporting, Everyday Life, and the Crisis of Gilded Age America*, 2002, Berkeley: University of California Press.
3 By the 1860s, the number of such 'classic' names had greatly decreased in the slave population: see Peter Kolchin, *American Slavery*, 1995 (first edition 1993), pp 45–46, London: Penguin. Their systematic use in the magazine clearly reveals a derogatory intent.
4 *Harper's Weekly*, 25 May 1861: 'To our Southern Readers.'
5 See the publisher's note in *Harper's Weekly* dated 20 April 1861. For evidence of troops reading *Harper's Weekly*, see Brown, *op cit*, pp 49–50.
6 In *Harper's Weekly*, the most consistently undesirable readers (those most liable to be the butt of stereotyping) were the Irish: they were depicted as ignorant, drunken and uncivilised, in both text and image, until the 1880s.

7 Peter H. Wood and Karen C.C. Dalton, *Winslow Homer's Images of Blacks: The Civil War and Reconstruction Years*, 1988, p 45, The Menil Collection, Austin: The University of Texas Press.

8 Joshua Brown, *op cit*, pp 56–57. Historian Sidney Kaplan notes that 'During the conflict, the newspapers and magazines of the day printed regular reports of the recruitment and battlefield activities of the black regiments, as well as articles and interviews dealing with the individual exploits of black infantrymen, artillerymen, scouts, and guerrillas, illustrated copiously by journalist-artists at the fronts' (Sidney Kaplan, *American Studies in Black and White: Selected Essays, 1949–1989*, 1991, p 103, Amherst: the University of Massachusetts Press).

9 Fletcher Harper, who was responsible for the founding of the weekly and who kept a close watch on the periodical even if his name did not appear in it, seems to have refrained from exerting an influence over Curtis and Nast, even when he disagreed with their positions. For more on this, on Curtis and Nast and their occasional quarrels, see Eugene Exman, *The House of Harper: One Hundred and Fifty Years of Publishing*, 1967, chapter 8, New York: Harper & Row.

10 Respectively: *Harper's Weekly*, 4 July 1863 p 428, and 8 August 1863 p 509. Unless noted otherwise, all the articles and engravings are drawn from *Harper's Weekly*. Most of the engravings described in this essay will be found on the following website: http://blackhistory.harpweek.com.

11 'The Funeral of Captain Andre Cailloux', 29 August 1863 pp 549 and 551.

12 Gary Laderman, *The Sacred Remains: American Attitudes Toward Death, 1799–1883*, 1996, p 101, New Haven CT: Yale University Press.

13 'The True Defenders of the Constitution', 25 February 1865. White and black troops were also linked by the fact that they were victims of the same 'rebel inhumanity' ('Rebel Atrocities', 21 May 1864 p 334).

14 'A Man Knows a Man', 22 April 1865 p 256.

15 Ann Douglas, *The Feminization of American Culture*, 1988 (first published 1977), chapter 6, New York: Anchor Books, Doubleday. Also see Karen Halttunen, *Confidence Men and Painted Women: A Study of Middle-Class Culture in America, 1830–1870*, 1982, New Haven CT: Yale University Press, and David E. Stannard, *The Puritan Way of Death: A Study in Religion, Culture, and Social Change*, 1979 (first published 1977), Oxford: Oxford University Press.

16 Alice Fahs, 'The Sentimental Soldier in Popular Civil War Literature', *Civil War History*, vol. 46, no. 2, June 2000, pp 107–131.

17 Like most of the other contributions to *Harper's Weekly*, except serialised novels, these stories were unsigned.

18 'Tippoo Sahib', 2 April 1864, pp 214–215.

19 'Little Starlight', 29 October 1864, p 702. Both stories can be found on the following website: http://www.civilwarliterature.com

20 Laderman, *op cit*, p 130.

21 According to Fahs, the fact that both stories end on the death of their hero evidences white discomfort at the idea of Blacks killing Whites; Fahs interprets the death of Little Starlight as 'a crucial narrative device that contained the imagined violence of Blacks' (Alice Fahs, *The Imagined Civil War: Popular Literature of the North and South, 1861–1865*, 2001, pp 172–176, Chapel Hill, the University of North Carolina Press).

22 This did not preclude the continuation of a degree of stereotyping in the periodical: a close reading of the weekly reveals a mixture of stereotypes and more enlightened views, sometimes in the same issue of *Harper's Weekly*. Demeaning stereotypes usually originated with artists / correspondents rather than editors, yet there seems to have been little if any editorial pressure or censorship to remove racism from the various contributions.

23 'A Consistent Negrophobist', 16 August 1862 p 528.
24 See for example 'Our Indian Sketches', 9 September 1867 p 564.
25 See for instance, 'The Apology for the Late Massacre', 25 August 1865 p 531, 'The New Orleans Riot', 25 August 1865 pp 534–535, 'The Riot in New Orleans', by Theodore Davis, 25 August 1866 p 537.
26 'The Union as It Was', 24 October 1874 p 878.
27 The readers were told, for instance, that a scene was 'sickening' (see 'The Outrage in North Carolina', 14 September 1867 p 577). The sheer number of texts explaining images that speak for themselves hints that neither artists nor editors trusted their readers to interpret engravings correctly: the audience needed guidance (on similar practices in *Frank Leslie's Illustrated Newspaper*, see Brown, *op cit* p. 72).
28 Brown, *op cit* pp 123–124.
29 Thus, one famous cartoon by Thomas Nast, which depicts a black man being trampled upon by Democrats showed its victim, in the words of Hugh Honour, as 'an object of white prejudice and brutality to be saved by paternalistic white benevolence' (Hugh Honour, *The Image of the Black in Western Art*, vol IV: *From the American Revolution to World War I*, 1989, p 237, Houston: The Menil Foundation, distributed by Harvard University Press).
30 Marcus Wood, *Blind Memory: Visual Representations of Slavery in England and America, 1780–1865*, 2000, chapter 3, New York: Routledge.
31 'The Savannah Duel', 27 June 1868 pp 404–405.
32 'The Dismal Swamp', 26 July 1873 p 643.
33 See for example the cartoons entitled 'The Jubilee', 3 April 1875 p 288 and 'Civil Rights.(?) Waiting for a Five-Hundred-Dollar Kick', 17 April 1875 p 328. Editorials praised the passage of the Civil Rights Bill while cartoons presented the reader with caricatures of African-Americans.
34 Brown accounts for this by the need for the paper to fit new situations and satisfy a heterogeneous readership (Brown, *op cit* pp 112–130).
35 'Onion-Skin Ballots', 21 December 1878. On the growing indifference of the nation to the plight of African-Americans, see David Blight, *Race and Reunion: The Civil War in American Memory*, 2001, Cambridge, MA: The Belknap Press of Harvard University Press.
36 For figures, see Crandall Shiflett, *Victorian America, 1876 to 1913, Almanacs of American Life*, 1996, p 334, New York: Facts on File.
37 'This Busy World', 13 May 1899 p 473.
38 J. Stanley Lemons, 'Black Stereotypes as Reflected in Popular Culture, 1880–1920', *American Quarterly*, vol. 29, no. 1, Spring 1977 pp 102–116. On the way African-Americans were represented in a number of Northern dailies and monthlies at the time, see Rayford W. Logan, *The Betrayal of the Negro*, 1965, New York, Collier Books.
39 'A Spendthrift in Killing', *Harper's Weekly*, 19 February 1887 p 139.
40 One such drawing is entitled 'Great Expectations' (*Scribner's Monthly*, September 1878 p 758). On this type of representation, see Ellen Gruber Garvey, ' "Poignée de main fraternelle par dessus le corps inerte du Noir": Histoires de vaisseaux négriers après la guerre de Sécession ou la construction d'un mythe', in Michel Prum, ed., *Les Malvenus: Race et sexe dans le monde anglophone*, 2003, pp 71–94, Paris: L'Harmattan.
41 Janette Faulkner, ed., *Ethnic Notions: Black Images in the White Mind*, 2000, Berkeley Art Center; Marlon Riggs, *Ethnic Notions* (documentary movie), 1986. At the same period, toys allowed children to bash a black head or throw balls at black figures . . . (*Ethnic Notions*, J. Faulkner, ed., op cit, p 26).

42 Sidney Kaplan speaks of the 'invisibility' of black Civil War soldiers after what he calls 'the betrayal of Reconstruction' (*American Studies in Black and White, op cit*, p 103); Blight, *op cit, Race and Reunion* p 198 (George Washington Williams, one of the first African-American historians, wrote *A History of the Negro Troops in the War of Rebellion*, in 1888, after having devoted ample space to Civil War heroes in his 1883 *History of the Negro Race in America, 1619–1880*); Kirk Savage, *Standing Soldiers, Kneeling Slaves: Race, War, and Monument in Nineteenth-Century America*, 1997, Princeton: Princeton University Press.

43 'What the Colored Race Have to be Thankful For', *Harper's Weekly*, 27 November 1886 p 769.

44 Alessandra Lorini, *Rituals of Race: American Public Culture and the Search for Racial Democracy*, 1999, Charlottesville: University Press of Virginia.

45 For the heroism of black troops in the West, see *Harper's Weekly* dated 6 December 1896; for the Spanish-American war, see among others 'Forgotten Heroes' (*Harper's Weekly*, 15 October 1898 pp 1012–1013).

46 See for example the issue dated 23 February 1895.

47 'With the Colored Regiment Band', by Frank L. Stanton, *The Century Illustrated Monthly Magazine*, June 1899, p 328.

48 See for example Mott, *op cit* p 486. This essay does not pretend to revolutionise the common view of *Harper's Weekly* as conservative, except as regards the African-American community; the Irish, however, were so uniformly caricatured and ridiculed that the weekly can hardly be called 'progressive' or enlightened in that respect.

Chapter 4

Italian Americans and the racialisation of ethnic violence in the United States

Stefano Luconi

Although conventional rhetoric has generally overstressed the alleged inclusiveness of American society, the United States has actually experienced periodic tides of intolerance toward racial and ethnic minorities since colonial times.[1] These outbursts of xenophobia have often resulted in violence and hate crimes against aliens, or people who have been perceived as such. For instance, most of the roughly 3,500 people lynched in the United States between 1884 and 1927 were Southern Blacks. But a few victims were also European immigrants and their children, who fell prey to mob violence in part because of their foreign birth or descent.[2] Specifically, there were 3,220 African-American and 723 white victims of lynching between 1880 and 1930.[3]

Some ethnic groups, however, have eventually managed to win accommodation within mainstream America. As this process has taken place, their members have sometimes crossed the line from victim to persecutor, ending up perpetrating the kind of hate crimes previously aimed at people from their own ethnic background. This chapter provides a case study of such a change of roles in the perpetration of ethnic and racial violence by focusing on the Italian-American experience.

On 29 March 1886, a blood-thirsty mob broke into the county jail in Vicksburg, Mississippi, and hanged Federico Villarosa, an Italian immigrant who had been charged with attempting to rape the 13-year-old white daughter of the local postmaster.[4] Roughly a century later, on 23 August 1989, a gang of Italian Americans from the Bensonhurst section of Brooklyn, New York City, killed Yusuf Hawkins, a 16-year-old black youth who had been mistaken for the new African-American boyfriend of the former Italian-American fiancée of one of the hoodlums.[5] These two events epitomise the transformation that this chapter will outline.

A growing number of studies have suggested that Italian immigrants to the United States and their offspring long held a racial middle ground between Whites and Blacks before fully developing an ethnic identity as European Americans.[6] The hate crimes that people of Italian ancestry had to face or committed similarly reflected this inbetweenness. In due time, while

Italian Americans progressively shifted from a black to a white identity, they also moved from the position of casualties to that of persecutors.

In the late nineteenth century and early twentieth century, Italian Americans were often victims of ethnically motivated lynchings. In other words, they were brutally killed in retribution for actual or supposed offences by angry mobs of private individuals who resorted to extralegal punishment because of the supposed perpetrators' foreign descent.

The dark complexion that characterised immigrants from southern Italy, the intentional intermingling with African Americans at the workplace and in everyday life, along with the worship of black Madonnas and saints such as Benedict the Moor made Italian newcomers and their offspring look more similar to African Americans than to other white European ethnic groups in the eyes of their adoptive society, especially in the former Confederate states.[7] Their skin tone and behaviour not only stressed that Italian immigrants and their children were aliens in a prevailing Anglo-Saxon environment where a white identity and a Protestant faith were means of accommodation and integration; such conduct and complexion also made Italian Americans subject to the same racially motivated violence as Blacks.

The most notorious lynching occurred in New Orleans in 1891. Following the assassination of the local police superintendent, David Hennessey, during a war between rival Sicilian crime organisations, a mob broke into the city jail and killed eleven of the alleged Italian perpetrators of the homicide, who were still being held in prison on related charges, although they had just been cleared of murder in court. While local police remained idle, the acquitted men were dragged out of the jail building and shot. A few corpses and half-dead bodies were later hanged from the lampposts of the square on which the jail overlooked. Asked on his death-bed who had shot him, Hennessey had answered 'Dagoes', a notorious epithet to refer to Italians, and the native citizens of New Orleans intended to take revenge on this immigrant group regardless of the court verdict.[8]

This incident, however, was not an isolated case. Besides Villarosa in Vicksburg in 1886, there were three Italian victims of lynching in Hahnville, Louisiana, in 1896, five in Tallulah, Louisiana, in 1899, and two in Tampa, Florida, in 1910. Italians were lynched even outside the former Confederation, as happened to six of them in Croton Lake, New York, in 1912, to a Joseph Strando in Johnston City, Illinois, in 1915 and to others in the state of Colorado, respectively in Gunnison in 1890, in Denver in 1893, and in Walsenburg in 1895. Additional lynchings of Italian Americans occurred in north-eastern states in Altoona, Pennsylvania, in 1894 and in Erwin, Massachusetts, in 1901. Overall, a total of at least thirty-four people of Italian descent were lynched in the United States between the mid-1880s and the early 1910s.[9]

In all these incidents, it was the national origin of the victims – regardless of whether they were guilty or innocent of any crime – which caused the anger of the crowd. As in the case of Daniel Arata, who was shot and strung up on a telegraph pole in Detroit in 1943 after he had murdered a patron of his saloon, such bigoted shouts as 'Kill the Dago' or 'Hang the Dago' were the war cries of the mob.[10]

The alleged association with organised crime – a hackneyed and enduring anti-Italian prejudice in the United States[11] – fuelled the flames of the xenophobic violence in New Orleans in 1891. Many newspaper reports of this episode stressed the connections of the victims to the Mafia, an Italian criminal organisation which supposedly operated in the United States as well.[12] Furthermore, in response to protests from the Italian government, Senator Henry Cabot Lodge (R-MA) advocated immigration restriction in order to prevent alien criminals from entering the United States, thereby igniting the natives' supposedly legitimate retaliatory violence.[13] New Orleans' local daily, the *Times-Picayune*, praised the action of the mob against organised crime, stating that 'desperate diseases require desperate measures'.[14] Reflecting what Richard Hofstadter has called the 'mystique' of white Anglo-Saxon superiority over southern – and eastern – European immigrant groups, even the more reputable *New York Times* contended that, with reference to the Italian immigrants, 'our rattlesnakes are as good citizens as they; our own murderers are men of feeling and nobility compared to them'.[15]

Yet the crusade against the alleged presence of the Mafia in New Orleans was also exploited to intimidate Italian-Americans in order to wrestle control of the New Orleans French Market from their hands and to hamper their rise in local politics. Italian-Americans' economic success and involvement in civic affairs had aroused envy and fear among numerous native residents. It is hardly by chance that the defendants included such a prominent leader of the Italian-American community as Joseph Macheca. A wealthy Sicilian businessman with large interests in the importation of South American fruit as well as in the fishing and oyster industries, Macheca had also organised many of his fellow ethnics into an association that opposed Mayor Joseph A. Shakespeare's political machine.[16]

In the late nineteenth century, other xenophobia-related factors contributed to the carnage of Italian Americans. The supposed involvement of the latter in criminal activities and the legacy of African-American slavery in the antebellum period involved similar kinds of social stigmatisation, a shared experience that led both ethnic groups to develop ties with each other. In addition, Sicilians – who made up the great bulk of Italian newcomers to Louisiana in general and to New Orleans in particular – were tolerant of Blacks and even friendly to them, in part as a consequence of the roughly two centuries of Arab domination over their native island. Furthermore, most Italian Americans – both Sicilians and non-Sicilians – usually dealt with African Americans on equal terms and did not demonstrate bigotry against them.[17] What specifically enraged most white Southerners about the behaviour of Italian Americans was that the latter did not refrain from living with

African-American women 'in sin' or even from marrying them, in the states where such interracial marriages were legal.[18]

Such social intimacy generally led Italian immigrants, even unconsciously, to challenge the segregationist and discriminatory practices of white supremacists toward African Americans. Significantly enough for Italian–Black relations, the five 1899 victims in Tallulah were storekeepers who were held up to public scorn because they had given their white and non-white employees equal pay.[19] Therefore, as historian George E. Cunningham has suggested, Italian Americans became 'a hindrance to white solidarity' in the South and ended up challenging the racial order of a society that not only was unprepared for interracial relations but even opposed them.[20]

Grace Elizabeth Hale has argued that, besides a means of intimidating Blacks, lynchings were also a way to draw racial lines and to consolidate whiteness in postbellum Southern society.[21] In other words, since lynchers were white and the lynched were those considered 'non-white', interaction with black people could expose individuals of dubious complexion like Italian immigrants to the same lack of police protection resulting in lynchings which usually characterised African-American lives. Given that Italian Americans were somehow associated with Blacks in the public mind, they often met with the same kind of brutality that affected African Americans. Against this backdrop, Italian Americans no longer felt safe in defying the racial order and befriending African Americans. Thus in Louisiana, for example, Italian immigrants became so eager to distance themselves from Blacks in the wake of the 1891 New Orleans lynching that they even decided to give up working in the cane fields in order to avoid being associated with the state's black labour force.[22]

However, that kind of expediency was not always enough to shield Italian Americans from xenophobic violence. In the northern United States, according to Thomas Guglielmo, Italian newcomers had been perceived by native Americans as having a white identity since the very beginning of mass immigration in the late nineteenth century.[23] But, despite their more clear-cut racial affiliation, Italian Americans were still perceived as aliens, because they were Catholics of foreign descent. For this reason, in the interwar years, they became the target of the Ku Klux Klan, at a time when this organisation added non-Protestant immigrant minorities to its previous African-American victims.[24] On 4 April 1924, for instance, a group of Klansmen shot and seriously wounded two Italian Americans, Francesco Apollucci and Francesco Miasco in Lilly, Pennsylvania.[25]

Drawing on ethnic prejudice and biases, the Klan also put pressure upon courts to have Italian Americans killed by legal means. This kind of influence, for instance, led to the conviction and subsequent execution of Joseph Rini and five other men of Italian descent who had been charged with assassinating a businessman in Independence, Louisiana, in May 1921. The evidence against the defendants was rather flimsy, but they had been arrested on their way to a robbery. Although no witness was able to identify the six individuals, Klan disturbances and fears of the Mafia were enough to associate Rini and his companions with the murderers. Their national origin made them the designated culprits because, as a local newspaper put it, 'Italy has dumped a most undesirable element into the United States'.[26]

Unlike their fellow ethnics in 1891 New Orleans, Rini and his co-defendants went to the gallows in 1924. Their execution, as opposed to the lynchings of the pre-war decades, showed that the Italian-American wages of whiteness, namely the benefits of sharing the racial identity of the Wasp population, as David R. Roediger has put it, included death within the law, but not yet a fair trial.[27]

While the Rini case remains quite an obscure episode in US judicial history, the notorious conviction and subsequent death by electric chair of anarchists Nicola Sacco and Bartolomeo Vanzetti in 1927 for a murder committed during a robbery seven years previously offers the best-known example of how ethnic prejudices contributed to the legal killing of Italian Americans. In the face of a lack of conclusive evidence against the defendants, it was the national origin of Sacco and Vanzetti, rather than their commitment to anarchist violence, which sealed their fate. Although the issue of their guilt or innocence is still controversial, it is clear that ethnic bigotry and intolerance denied them a fair trial in court and in the subsequent appeals.[28] In the wake of the 'Red Scare' of the years 1919–1920 against radical groups and movements in the United States, the involvement of a handful of Italian anarchists in a series of terrorist attacks added the shameful mark of political subversion to the stigma of crime in the public perception of Italian Americans.[29] As immigrants from Italy, therefore, Sacco and Vanzetti matched perfectly the stereotypical picture of murder-prone radicals and they could not escape capital punishment.[30]

On 20 September 1910, Italian immigrants Angelo Albano and Costanzo Ficarotta were lynched in Tampa.[31] They had been arrested for the murder of a bookkeeper, James F. Easterling, and were hanged even prior to coming before the court.[32] The bookkeeper was an employee of Bustillo Brothers & Diaz Company, a local cigar factory, and became the target of threats from labour unions in the last few days of his life because he was most active in hiring 'scabs' following a walk-out. Rather than retribution for homicide, the lynching of Albano and Ficarotta was an instrument to intimidate the dark-skinned Cuban and Italian cigar makers who had been on strike for roughly three months, and to stifle their attempt at resorting to what was perceived as an alien and radical measure in labour disputes. Italian Americans' alleged taste for crime, therefore, offered a pretext to sanction their participation in a walkout that was seriously damaging Tampa's economy. As Gaetano Moroni, the Italian vice consul in New Orleans, pointed out, 'the lynching itself was not the outcome of a temporary outburst of popular anger'. The intention of the mob was 'teaching an awful lesson to the strikers of the cigar factories who had passed from quiet protest to acts of violence against the manufacturers'.[33]

It has also been suggested that the role of Italian Americans as labour agitators contributed to the lynching of five immigrants in connection with the killing of a saloon-keeper in Walsenburg at the time of a 1895 strike in the Colorado coal fields.[34] In the 1920s, however, the outcome of the Sacco-Vanzetti case demonstrated that summary justice was no longer an adequate alternative in order to pressure Italian Americans into giving up the radicalism that had become associated with their ethnic identity.[35]

An episode during a 1934 riot in Harlem, New York City, offers further evidence that lynching was no longer a viable means of killing Italian Americans, once they had acquired a white identity in the eyes of US society. In February of that year, a black mob wrecked Tonelli's, a bakery in the district, after a woman had accused the Italian-American owner of short-changing her. The crowd also began beating the baker before the police managed to save him. One may easily suggest that African Americans overreacted to the woman's claim. Yet the incident was the spark that started off the growing ethnic tensions between Italian Americans and Blacks as the latter charged the former with discriminating against African-American applicants in employment with local stores. More than the police's timely intervention to rescue the baker, it was a comment in an African-American newspaper which demonstrated that, for Italian Americans, whiteness had eventually become a sort of warranty against lynchings even within the context of ethnic conflicts. As the *Amsterdam News* remarked in amazement, it was 'unbelievable that Negroes should threaten to lynch a white man'.[36]

Tonelli's narrow escape from death, however, revealed that a light complexion was counterproductive for Italian Americans when it was a non-white minority which triggered off racial disturbances and resorted to mob violence. In wartime Detroit, Joseph De Horatiis, a physician of Italian descent, was less lucky that his fellow-ethnic baker in 1934 Harlem. On 20 June 1943, unaware that an African-American riot had just broken out, he drove to a black neighbourhood on a house call. A group of local residents spotted De Horatiis, dragged him out of his car, and stoned him to death.[37]

Whiteness, however, entitled Detroiters of Italian descent to strike back. A number of De Horatiis's fellow ethnics joined the melee to avenge his death and participated in the racial riot that pitted white Detroiters against black Detroiters. According to Ambrogio Donini, co-editor of the New York City-based Communist organ *L'Unità del Popolo* and an eyewitness to the events, the Ku Klux Klan had begun to make inroads into the Italian-American community and had turned many of its members into 'ferocious beasts in human form, drunk with race hatred, such as those I saw fling themselves on the Negroes, one hundred against one in the streets of Detroit'.[38] A few Italian Americans went to Detroit even from nearby communities in order to, as one of them put it, 'kill us a nigger'.[39] The unrest lasted for a day and a half, and eventually claimed thirty-four lives.[40] Most casualties were African Americans, which led *La Voce del Popolo* – a local Italian-language weekly – to remark in racist overtones that 'even if one wanted to blame Negroes for conduct unbecoming a civilised people, we think that the number of their dead is such to make them reflect and correct their faults'.[41]

Reproaching African Americans for the outbreak of the disturbance was not enough for Italian Americans.[42] To them, it was as if resorting to anti-black violence had become a component of their white identity. The recollections of Pisicano, an architect of Sicilian descent, about race unrest in New York City in 1943 highlight this point:

> I remember standing on a corner, a guy would throw the door open and say, 'Come on down'. They were goin' to Harlem to get in the riot. They'd say, 'Let's beat up some niggers'. It was wonderful. It was new. The Italo-Americans stopped being Italo and started becoming Americans. We joined the group. Now we're like you guys, right?[43]

For a handful of Italian-American Fascist sympathisers in the late 1930s and early 1940s, anti-Semitism was a sort of dress rehearsal for attacks on African Americans in the war and post-war years. Jewish-Italian conflicts over political patronage and recognition, the control of labour unions, and access to cheap housing units and shrinking job opportunities in the wake of the economic crisis of the 1930s saw Benito Mussolini's anti-Jewish propaganda, after the enactment in Italy in 1938 of Fascist racial legislation, make inroads into the 'Little Italys' of the United States.[44] A few Italian-American supporters of the *Duce* even outdid their own leader in embracing the Fascist anti-Jewish campaign. Mussolini's regime claimed that, unlike its Nazi ally, the Italian government confined itself to discriminating against Jews without persecuting them.[45] Yet several American Fascists of Italian ancestry began to extol the murder of Jews not only in Germany but in the United States as well. For instance, Joseph Ferri, the leader of the Black Shirts in Los Angeles, urged his fellow ethnics to declare 'war on Jewry'.[46] Even more explicitly, speaking at a rally of the anti-Semitic Christian Front, Ralph Ninfo argued that, 'if I had my way, I would hang all Jews in this country'.[47] Notwithstanding this kind of instigation, Italian Americans' attacks on Jews did not go beyond verbal and physical assaults.[48] No Italian American actually murdered any Jew out of ethnic prejudice and the round-up of Mussolini's sympathisers in the aftermath of Italy's declaration of war on the United States on 11 December 1941 put an end to Fascist anti-Semitic propaganda in the 'Little Italys'.[49]

In early August 1920, some natives of West Frankfort, a mining town in southern Illinois, repeatedly raided the local Italian district, beat its residents, and set the immigrants' houses on fire in an attempt to drive the foreign-born population and their offspring out of the town. Louis Carrari, who tried to protect his own home from the looters, was shot dead and his body was mutilated after his wife had rushed out of their dwelling to ask for help. A number of bank robberies as well as the kidnapping and murder of two young boys, which had been attributed to a supposedly Italian-led criminal organisation by the name of the Black Hand, had triggered off this wave of hysteria targeting Italian Americans and the campaign to protect the native New Frankforters' turf against the aliens.[50]

If ethnic bigotry identifying Italian immigrants with gangsterism and racketeering provoked the bloodshed of Italian-Americans before World War II, the apparent association of Blacks with urban blight and felonious behaviour turned some Italian Americans into perpetrators of racially motivated hate crimes in the post-war years. Racial tension between African Americans and Italian Americans antedated the outbreak of World War II especially outside southern states.[51] Animosities between these two minorities reached a climax in the aftermath of Italy's invasion of Ethiopia in 1935, as most Italian Americans backed the colonial venture of their ancestral land and African Americans mobilised to defend the independence of the African country.[52]

While the elaboration of Italian Americans' identity as white people was still in the pipeline, however, such strains hardly ignited homicidal sentiments on racial grounds before the wartime riots like the 1943 disturbances in Detroit. Conversely, protest against school desegregation and the racial integration of neighbourhoods often resulted in harsh confrontations between Blacks and Italian Americans in the 1960s and 1970s.[53] These conflicts sometimes degenerated into violent confrontation. Cries of 'kill the niggers' were not uncommon among Italian Americans, as was reported, for instance, on the occasion of a skirmish outside Canarsie High School, in New York City, in the fall of 1976. In addition, a few residents of Italian ancestry in the Canarsie district did not refrain from fire-bombing houses owned by African Americans in order to keep Blacks off their patch.[54]

Resistance to neighbourhood change on the part of a group with a remarkable tendency toward residential stability placed Italian Americans at the forefront of Whites' struggles against the growing African-American presence in inner city districts.[55] Perceived as aliens in areas previously settled almost exclusively by people of European descent, Blacks became a scapegoat for falling standards of provision in housing, jobs, public services, and welfare benefits that were still available to the working-class and lower middle-class Italian Americans who had not yet joined the flight toward the suburbs by the late 1980s. Informal networks – by which word of mouth, rather than public notices, advertised housing for rent or sale and community volunteers supplemented the police in patrolling their own neighbourhoods – developed to prevent African Americans and other outsiders from moving in.[56]

Yet violence was sometimes resorted to in order to confront these so-called trespassers. This was Yusuf Hawkins's fate when he entered Bensonhurst with three African-American friends to check out a used car on 23 August 1989. Some thirty primarily Italian-American hoodlums assaulted the group of Blacks and one of the former, Joseph Fama, shot Hawkins dead. An African American in a white neighbourhood, this young man was the epitome of the external threat to the Italian-American community and its cohesiveness. Not only was he the alleged black date of a white girl, who might have come with fellow ethnics to cause trouble in the district and attack local people,[57] he was also one of the members of the racial group that had been benefiting from affirmative action programmes, to the detriment of local Italian-American residents, who blamed such policies for the shrinking job opportunities of their own younger generations.[58]

There is, though, evidence of community co-operation between Italian Americans and African Americans in the nearby Greenpoint-Williamsburg area of New York City in the years before Hawkins's assassination through the Coalition of Community Organisations, an umbrella association bringing together roughly one hundred groups that promoted neighbourhood unity and activism across racial lines in education, sport, and civic affairs.[59] Furthermore, a few Italian Americans did distance themselves from the murder of Hawkins, expressed their outrage at that act of racial hatred, and took steps toward the reconciliation between the two minorities involved in the incident.[60] Politics did not help this process. The killing occurred during a most divisive mayoral election campaign that polarised New York City along racial lines, with African-American Democrat David N. Dinkins, pitted against Italian-American Republican Rudolph Giuliani, for City Hall.[61] Nor did Italian-American leaders make a significant contribution to debates during the campaign, because they were concerned less with the denunciation of racism *per se* than with countering the slur that all people of Italian descent were racists.[62] In addition, an exculpatory attitude prevailed in the Bensonhurst community. As a resident stated to the *New York Times*, with reference to Fama and his fellow gangsters, 'these were good boys ... they were defending the neighbourhood'.[63] None of the Italian-American witnesses made any public statement that might incriminate Fama or his confederates. One even argued: 'I didn't see nothing, and even if I did see something, I didn't see nothing'.[64]

On 27 August 1989, when Reverend Al Sharpton, a flamboyant and controversial African-American minister and civil rights activist, staged a march through the streets of Bensonhurst to condemn Hawkins's murder and to provoke the racists in the district into coming into the open, many Italian-American residents organised a counter-demonstration. They hurled resentful insults and abuse at the marchers and made such illogical statements as 'I'm not a racist, I just hate niggers' even in front of reporters and television crews.[65]

The persistence of homicidal feelings toward African Americans was revealed again on 12 January 1991. While Sharpton was marching once more through Bensonhurst, this time to protest against the light sentence Hawkins's killer had received, a local Italian-American resident, Michael Ricciardi, stabbed the civil rights activist with a four-inch blade and injured him in the chest.[66]

However, deadly assaults on minorities by Bensonhurst's Italian Americans were not confined to African Americans. In October 1994, four teenagers of Italian ancestry attacked a group of Ecuadorian immigrants with lead pipes and baseball bats in Dyker Beach Park. They killed one of them, Manuel Aucaquizphi, an inebriated homeless man who – unlike his companions – was not quick enough to find a way out. The hooligans resented the fact that the immigrants were using what the Italian Americans considered as their own park. But, in fact, Aucaquizphi fell victim to hostility arising from growing complaints among workers of Italian descent in the district that newcomers from South and Central America were 'stealing their jobs'. Two Italian-American brothers tried to kill an immigrant from Central America and another from Asia the following year.[67]

In addition, the incidents in Bensonhurst were similar to cases in other Italian-American neighbourhoods. After all, the murder of Hawkins was one of the 577 hate crimes that were committed in New York City in 1989, although Italian-Americans were not involved in them all.[68] However, on 19 December 1986, Italian Americans were in a gang of Whites who chased three young African Americans and beat them with baseball bats and golf clubs in the streets of Howard Beach, in New York City's Queens borough. One of the black youths, 23-year-old Michael Griffith, rushed to Belt Parkway in search of sanctuary and was killed by a passing car.[69] The reaction of the local Italian-American residents was similar to that of many of their fellow ethnics in Bensonhurst. As one Michelle Napolitano contended, 'We're a strictly white neighborhood. They had to be starting trouble'.[70] Yet Griffith and his friends ended up in Howard Beach because the car in which they were riding had broken down there.[71] Like Hawkins, in the eyes of local residents, Griffith became a scapegoat for the racial animosity infused by muggings and other crimes ascribed to African Americans.[72]

Four years earlier, on 22 June 1982, 18-year-old Gino Bova led a gang of about 20 Italian Americans in assaulting Willie Turks, a black transit worker. Turks and two co-workers had stopped at a bagel shop in Gravesend, a district adjoining Bensonhurst, when the Italian-American hoodlums appeared shouting, 'Nigger, get out of here', pulled him out of his car, and beat him to death.[73]

Similarly, on 21 March 1997, Italian-American 17-year-old Frank Caruso and two other teenagers – Polish-American Michael Kwidzinski and Hispanic Victor Jasas – beat Leonard Clark, a thirteen-year-old African-American boy, almost to death as he rode his bicycle along the outskirts of Bridgeport, a working-class district in Chicago.[74]

The co-operation between Italian Americans and members of other immigrant groups from European backgrounds in committing hate crimes demonstrates both the integration of the offspring of victimised late-nineteenth-century immigrants within American society, and their acquisition of a bigoted and racist perspective underlying a white identity and accompanying mainstream status in the United States. To the early Italian Americans who had moved to Long Island, New York, despite ethnic intolerance *circa* World War II, it would have been inconceivable that a member of their nationality group, Frank DeStefano, should have become the local Grand Dragon of the Ku Klux Klan by 1997.[75] Likewise, the Italian Americans who were lynched because of their social interaction with African Americans in the late nineteenth century would hardly have credited that some of their offspring would engage in fatal attacks on Blacks just a few decades later.

NOTES

1 Higham, John, *Strangers in the Land: Patterns of American Nativism 1860–1925*, 1955, New Brunswick: Rutgers University Press.
2 Shapiro, Herbert, 'Lynching', in Roller, David C. and Twyman, Robert W. (eds), *The Encyclopedia of Southern History*, 1979, Baton Rouge: Louisiana State University Press, pp 762–3; Guzman, Jesse P. and Hughes, W.H., 'Lynching crime', in Guzman, Jesse P. (ed.), *Negro Year Book: A Review of Events Affecting Negro Life 1941–1946*, 1947, Tuskagee: Tuskagee Institute, p 307.
3 Brundage, William F., *Lynching in the New South*, 1993, Urbana: University of Illinois Press, p 259.
4 (1886) *New York Times*, 30 March, p 5.
5 DeSantis, John, *For the Color of His Skin: The Murder of Yusuf Hawkins and the Trial of Bensonhurst*, 1991, New York: Pharos.
6 Roediger, David R., *Colored White*, 2002, Berkeley: University of California Press, pp 34–7, 142–4, 163, 167; Guglielmo, Jennifer and Salerno Salvatore (eds), *Are Italians White? How Race Is Made in America*, 2003, London: Routledge.
7 Mayor des Planches, Edmondo, *Attraverso gli Stati Uniti*, 1913, Turin: Utet, p 144; Daniel, Peter, *The Shadow of Slavery: Peonage in the South, 1901–1969*, 1972, Urbana: University of Illinois Press, pp 94, 103, 152; Birbaum, Lucia C, *Black Madonnas: Feminism, Religion and Politics in Italy*, 1993, Boston: Northeastern University Press; D'Angelo, Anthony, 'Italian Harlem's Saint Benedict the Moor', in Bona, Mary Jo and Tamburri, Anthony Julian (eds), *Through the Looking Glass: Italian & Italian/American Images in the Media*, 1996, Staten Island: American Italian Historical Association (hereafter AIHA), pp 235–40.
8 Kendall, John S, 'Who killa de chief?' (1939) 22(2) *Louisiana Historical Quarterly* 492–530; Gambino, Richard, *Vendetta*, 1977, New York: Doubleday.
9 Stella, Gian Antonio, *L'orda*, 2003, Milan: Rizzoli, pp 17–25; Salvetti, Patrizia, *Corda e sapone*, 2003, Rome: Donzelli.
10 Worrall, Janet E., 'Adjustment and integration: The Italian experience in Colorado', in Juliani, Richard N. and Juliani, Sandra (eds), *New Explorations in Italian-American Studies*, 1994, Staten Island: AIHA, pp 195–208 (here at pp 205–6).

11 For anti-Italian biases in the United States, see Deschamps, Bénédicte, 'Le racisme anti-italien aux Etats-Unis (1880–1940)', in Prum, Michel (ed.), *Exclure au nom de la race (Etats-Unis, Irlande, Grande-Bretagne)*, 2000, Paris: Syllepse, pp 59–81.

12 Marr, Robert H., 'The New Orleans Mafia case' (1891) 25(3) *American Law Review* 414–31.

13 Cabot Lodge, Henry, 'Lynch law and unrestricted immigration' (1891) 152(414) *North American Review* 602–12.

14 As quoted in Rolle, Andrew F., *The Immigrant Upraised*, 1968, Norman: University of Oklahoma Press, p 103.

15 Hofstadter, Richard, *Social Darwinism in American Thought*, 1959, New York: Braziller, p 172; *New York Times* as quoted in Rolle, Andrew F., *The Italian Americans: Troubled Roots*, 1980, Norman: University of Oklahoma Press, p 83.

16 Boiten, Barbara, 'The Hennessy case: An episode in anti-Italian nativism' (1979) 20(3) *Louisiana History* 261–79.

17 Martellone, Anna Maria, 'Italian mass emigration to the United States, 1876–1930: A historical survey', (1984) 1 *Perspectives in American History* 379–423 (here at 415–18); Cinel, Dino, 'Sicilians in the deep south: The ironic outcome of isolation' (1990) 27(97) *Studi Emigrazione* 55–86.

18 Scala, Luigi, 'Poche considerazioni giuridiche e sociali su l'emigrazione italiana negli Stati Uniti e particolarmente in Louisiana', in *Atti del Congresso degli italiani all'estero*, 1913, Rome: Tipografia Editrice Nazionale, pp 17–23 (here at p 19).

19 Haas, Edward F., 'Guns, goats, and Italians: The Tallulah lynching of 1899', (1982) 13(2–3) *North Louisiana Historical Association Journal* 45–58.

20 Cunningham, George E., 'The Italian: A hindrance to white solidarity in Louisiana 1890–1898' (1965) 50(1) *Journal of Negro History* 22–36.

21 Hale, Grace Elizabeth, *Making Whiteness: The Culture of Segregation in the South, 1890–1940*, 1998, New York: Pantheon, pp 199–239.

22 Scarpaci, Vincenza J., 'Italians in Louisiana's sugar parish 1880–1910', in Assante, F. (ed.), *Il movimento migratorio italiano dall'Unità ai giorni nostri*, vol 2, 1978, Geneva: Droz, pp 197–216.

23 Guglielmo, Thomas A., *White on Arrival: Italians, Race, Color, and Power in Chicago 1890–1945*, 2003, New York: Oxford University Press.

24 Chalmers, David M., *Hooded Americanism: The First Century of the Ku Klux Klan*, 1965, New York: Doubleday, pp 236–42.

25 (1924) *Trinacria*, 11 April, p 3; (1924) *Il Patriota*, 30 May, p 5; (1924) *Trinacria*, 15 June, p 3.

26 Baiamone, Jr, John V., *Spirit of Vengeance: Nativism and Louisiana Justice, 1921–1924*, 1986, Baton Rouge: Louisiana University Press. The quotation from the Hammond *Louisiana Sun* is in Baiamone, Jr, *op cit*, p 114.

27 Roediger, David R., *The Wages of Whiteness: Race and the Making of the American Working Class*, 1991, London: Verso.

28 Innumerable studies have dealt with this *cause célèbre*. Those sympathetic with Sacco and Vanzetti include Fraenkel, Osmond K., *The Sacco-Vanzetti Case*, 1931, New York: Knopf; Joughlin, Louis G. and Morgan, Edmund M., *The Legacy of Sacco and Vanzetti*, 1948, New York: Harcourt, Brace; Ehrmann, Herbert B., *The Case That Will Not Die: Commonwealth vs. Sacco and Vanzetti*, 1969, Boston: Little, Brown; Feuerlicht, Roberta S., *Justice Crucified: The Story of Sacco and Vanzetti*, 1977, New York: McGraw-Hill; D'Alessandro, Frank M., *The Verdict of History on Sacco and Vanzetti*, 1997, New York: Jay Street Publishers. The opposite interpretation comprises Montgomery, Robert H., *Sacco-Vanzetti: The Murder and the Myth*, 1960, New York: Devin-Adair; Felix, David, *Protest: Sacco-Vanzetti and the Intellectuals*, 1965, Bloomington: Indiana University Press. It has also

been suggested that Sacco was guilty but Vanzetti innocent. See Russell, Francis, *Sacco and Vanzetti: The Case Resolved*, 1960, New York: Harper & Row.

29 Murray, Robert K., *Red Scare: A Study in National Hysteria 1919–1920*, 1955, Minneapolis: University of Minnesota Press; Preston, Jr, William, *Aliens and Dissenters: Federal Suppression of Radicals, 1903–1933*, 1994, Cambridge, MA: Harvard University Press, pp 181–237; Goldstein, Robert J., *Political Repression in Modern America*, 1978, Cambridge, MA: Schenkman, pp 93–191; Pernicone, Nunzio, 'Luigi Galleani and Italian anarchist terrorism in the United States' (1993) 30(111) *Studi Emigrazione* 469–89.

30 Frankfurter, Felix, *The Case of Sacco and Vanzetti*, 1927, Boston: Little, Brown.

31 Ingalls, Robert P., *Urban Vigilantes in the New South: Tampa 1882–1936*, 1988, Nashville: University of Tennessee Press, pp 96–9.

32 Mormino, Gary R., 'Italians in Florida', in Mormino, Gary R. and Serra, Ilaria, *Italian Americans & Florida*, 2003, Boca Raton: Dorothy F. Schmidt College, pp 1–25 (here at p 14).

33 As quoted in Mormino, Gary R. and Pozzetta, George E., *The Immigrant World of Ybor City: Italians and Their Latin Neighbors in Tampa 1885–1985*, 1987, Urbana: University of Illinois Press, p 120. See also, Salvetti, *op cit*, pp 101–9. For a broader perspective on the 1910 strike, see Pozzetta, George E., 'Italians and the Tampa general strike of 1910', in Pozzetta, George E. (ed.), *Pane e Lavoro: The Italian-American Working Class*, 1980, Toronto: Multicultural History Society of Ontario, pp 29–46.

34 Parillo, Vincent N., *Strangers to These Shores: Race and Ethnic Relations in the United States*, 1985, New York: Wiley, pp 98–9; Gambino, Richard, *Blood of My Blood*, 2000, Toronto: Guernica, p 118. This interpretation has been rejected by Woodall, Conrad, 'The Italian massacre at Walsenburg, Colorado, 1895', in Candeloro, Dominic, Gardaphe, Fred and Giordano, Paolo A. (eds) *Italian Ethnics: Their Languages, Literature and Lives*, 1990, Staten Island: AIHA, pp 297–317 (here at pp 311–12).

35 Vecoli, Rudolph J., 'The search for an Italian-American identity', in Tomasi, Lydio F. (ed.), *Italian Americans: New Perspectives in Italian Immigration and Ethnicity*, 1985, Staten Island: Center for Migration Studies, pp 88–112 (here at p 94).

36 Price, Isabel B., 'Black response to anti-Semitism: Negroes and Jews in New York 1880 to World War II', unpublished PhD dissertation, 1973, University of New Mexico, pp 253–4.

37 (1943) *La Tribuna Italiana d'America*, 25 June, p 1.

38 As quoted in Venturini, Nadia, 'African-American riots during World War II: Reactions in the Italian-American Communist press' (1997–98) 6 *Italian-American Review* 80–97 (here at p 89).

39 Capeci, Jr, Dominic J. and Wilkerson, Martha, *Layered Violence: The Detroit Rioters of 1943*, 1991, Jackson: University Press of Mississippi, p 156.

40 Shogan, Robert and Craig, Tom, *The Detroit Race Riot: A Study in Violence*, 1964, Philadelphia: Chilton; McClung Lee, Alfred and Humphrey, Norman D., *Race Riot: Detroit, 1943*, 1968, New York: Octagon.

41 As quoted in Venturini, *op cit*, p 89.

42 (1943) *La Tribuna Italiana d'America*, 30 July, p 1.

43 As quoted in Terkel, Studs, *'The Good War': An Oral History of World War II*, 1984, New York: Pantheon, pp 141–2.

44 Luconi, Stefano, 'The response of Italian Americans to Fascist antisemitism', (2001) 35(3) *Patterns of Prejudice* 3–23.

45 Sarfatti, Michele, *Mussolini contro gli ebrei: Cronaca dell'elaborazione delle leggi del 1938*, 1994, Turin: Zamorani.

46 *Fifth Column Facts: A Handbook of Information on Nazi, Fascist, and Communist Activities in the United States*, 1940, Kansas City: Veterans of Foreign Wars of the United States, pp 21–2, pamphlet in William Vanderbilt Papers, box 35, folder 32, University of Rhode Island Library, Kingston, RI.

47 Curran, Henry H., 'Jail riot inciters', (1939) 1(7) *Equality* 8–9, 24.

48 (1938) *Philadelphia Record*, 15 October, p 3; Kramer, Dale, 'The American Fascists', (1940) 181 *Harper's Magazine* 378–88 (here at 380, 384, 386).

49 DiStasi, Lawrence (ed.), *Una Storia Segreta: The Secret History of Italian-American Evacuation and Internment during World War II*, 2001, Berkeley: Heyday.

50 (1920) *New York Times*, 8 August, p 8.

51 Merithew, Caroline W., 'Making the Italian other: Blacks, Whites, and the inbetween in the 1895 Spring Valley, Illinois, race riot', in Guglielmo and Salerno (eds), *op cit*, pp 79–97.

52 Diggins, John P., *Mussolini and Fascism: The View from America*, 1972, Princeton: Princeton University Press, pp 302–12; Venturini, Nadia, *Neri e italiani a Harlem: Gli anni Trenta e la guerra d'Etiopia*, 1990, Rome: Lavoro; Harris, Joseph E., *African-American Reactions to War in Ethiopia, 1936–1941*, 1994, Baton Rouge: Louisiana State University Press, pp 34–103.

53 Formisano, Robert P., *Boston Against Busing: Race, Class, and Ethnicity in the 1960s and 1970s*, 1991, Chapel Hill: University of North Carolina Press; Sugrue, Thomas P., *The Origins of the Urban Crisis: Race and Inequality in Postwar Detroit*, 1996, Princeton: Princeton University Press; Luconi, Stefano, *From Paesani to White Ethnics: The Italian Experience in Philadelphia*, 2001, Albany: State University of New York Press, pp 125–46.

54 Rieder, Jonathan, *Canarsie: The Jews and Italians of Brooklyn Against Liberalism*, 1985, Cambridge, MA: Harvard University Press, p 185.

55 Freeman, Robert C., 'The development and maintenance of New York City's Italian-American neighborhoods', in Krase, Jerome and Egelman, William (eds), *The Melting Pot and Beyond: Italian Americans in the Year 2000*, 1987, Staten Island: AIHA, pp 223–35.

56 De Sena, Judith N., *Protecting One's Turf*, 1990, Lanham: University Press of America.

57 DeSena, Judith N., 'Defending our neighborhood at any cost? The case of Bensonhurst', in Landry, Harral (ed.), *To See the Past More Clearly: The Enrichment of the Italian Heritage 1890–1990*, 1994, Austin: Nortex, pp 177–90.

58 Krase, Jerome, 'Yusuf Hawkins and the closing of the American mind', in Sorrentino, Frank and Krase, Jerome (eds), *The Review of Italian-American Studies*, 2000, Lanham: Lexington, pp 236–40 (here at p 238).

59 DeSena, Judith N., 'Community co-operation and activism: Italians and African Americans in Williamsburg, Brooklyn', in Cavaioli, Frank J., Danzi, Angela and LaGumina, Salvatore J. (eds), *Italian Americans and Their Public and Private Life*, 1993, Staten Island: AIHA, pp 116–24.

60 (1991) *Newsday*, 11 September, p 87; Sciorra, Joseph, 'Italians against racism: The murder of Yusuf Hawkins (RIP) and my march on Bensonhurst', in Guglielmo and Salerno (eds), *op cit*, pp 192–209 (here at pp 192–4, 204–5).

61 Barrett, Wayne with Fifield, Adam, *Rudy: An Investigative Biography of Rudolph Giuliani*, 2000, New York: Basic Books, pp 199–200, 221, 223; Kirtzman, Andrew, *Rudy Giuliani: Emperor of the City*, 2000, New York: Morrow, pp 21–22.

62 Krase, Jerome, 'Lest we forget: Racism will make victims of us all', in Sorrentino and Krase (eds), *op cit*, pp 240–44; Tricarico, Donald, 'Read all about it! Representations of Italian Americans in the print media in response to the Bensonhurst racial killing', in Aguirre, Jr, Adalberto and Baker, David V. (eds), *Sources:*

Notable Selections in Race and Ethnicity, 2001, New York: McGraw-Hill, pp 291–319; Guglielmo, Jennifer, 'Introduction', in Guglielmo and Salerno (eds), *op cit*, pp 1–14 (here pp 6–7).

63 (1989) *New York Times*, 1 September, p B4.
64 (1989) *Village Voice*, 5 September, pp 34–8.
65 Laurino, Maria, *Were You Always an Italian?*, 2000, New York: Norton, pp 123–4; Sciorra, *op cit*, pp 193–4, 203 (quote p 203).
66 (1991) *Newsday*, 14 January, p 3; (1991) *Washington Post*, 14 January, p A12.
67 (1994) *New York Times*, 16 October, p 39; (1994) *Newsday*, 27 November, p A84; Laurino, *op cit*, pp 129–31 (quote p 130).
68 (1990) *New York Times*, 26 January, p B5.
69 (1986) *Newsday*, 21 December, p 3.
70 (1986) *New York Times*, 23 December, p B4.
71 (1986) *Newsday*, 22 December, p 2.
72 (1986) *Newsday*, 23 December, p 45.
73 (1982) *New York Times*, 23 June, p A1; Laurino, *op cit*, p 122.
74 (1997) *New York Times*, 27 March, p A18.
75 (1997) *Newsday*, 19 July, p A22. For Italian Americans in Long Island, see LaGumina, Salvatore J., *From Steerage to Suburbs: The Long Island Experience*, 1988, Staten Island: Center for Migration Studies, pp 1, 57, 66–79, 235.

Chapter 5

The role of violence in the far right in Canada

Stanley Barrett

INTRODUCTION

The prevalent opinion among Canadians of British origin[1] is that there is almost no racism in the country, especially the organised variety like the Ku Klux Klan. Admittedly, there may be a handful of neo-Nazis, but they are poorly-educated, half-crazy thugs clinging to the periphery of society, unconnected to the mainstream. To the extent that racism exists at all in Canada, it can be dismissed as an American virus which has unfortunately breached the border.

These, of course, are myths, and they go a long way in explaining how Canadians are able to continue to believe that they dwell in an exceptionally tolerant nation, and why the study of racism remains somewhat of a taboo subject even today. My purpose is to puncture these myths by providing an overview of organised racism and anti-Semitism in Canada, and analysing the nature of violence connected to them. The chapter will conclude with an examination of why there has been less violence associated with the radical right in Canada compared to the USA, what the impact of 9/11 has had on the far right in Canada, and what overlap, if any, exists between white supremacists and anti-Semites and the wider Canadian society.

OVERVIEW OF THE FAR RIGHT

There have been four distinct periods of organised far-right activity in Canada. In the 1920s, the Ku Klux Klan took root in several provinces, including Saskatchewan, where it assisted the Conservatives in their success- ful attempt to overthrow the ruling Liberals.[2] At that time the Klan was not only anti-Asian and anti-African, but also strongly opposed to French Canadians and Catholics. In the 1930s, fascism made its appearance on Canadian soil, led by Adrian Arcand in Quebec,[3] who described Hitler as the greatest man except Jesus Christ who had ever existed, and John Ross Taylor in Ontario, who during an interview in the early 1980s remarked: 'Hitler was a softy on the Jew question.' The main organisations were the National Social Christian Party, the Canadian Nationalist Party, the Canadian Union of Fascists, plus a Brownshirt Party and several swastika clubs. The outbreak of World War II put an end to the fascist era, with Arcand and Taylor interned in a camp for the duration of hostilities.

The late 1940s and 1950s have been labelled the sanitary decades.[4] Fascism, racism, and anti-Semitism were taboo topics, and those attracted to them were forced to keep a low profile. But by the 1960s, there were signs of a resurgent right wing, or what I have referred to as incipient neo-fascism. This was the third phase, the two main organisations being the Canadian Nazi Party and the Edmund Burke Society. The first organisation brought Taylor back into the spotlight. The Edmund Burke Society actually began as a highly conservative, anti-communist movement; not until later, by which time its name had changed to the Western Guard (which eventually mutated into today's Nationalist Party), did it openly embrace racism and anti-Semitism. This occurred during the 1970s, coinciding with the fourth phase of the Canadian radical right or full-blown neo-fascism, marked by a virtual flood of new organisations, including the Ku Klux Klan again, the Nationalist Party, and the Aryan Nations. During the 1990s, and continuing into the new century, the internet emerged as a forum for far-right expression,[5] and could well be regarded as a fifth phase.

VARIETIES OF VIOLENCE

Although the Canadian radical right has been bellicose in ideology, advocating the forceful overthrow of 'the Jewish controlled, liberal-left establishment', it has not been as violent as its counterpart in the USA. A great deal of its activity has been directed internally, holding regular meetings and preaching to new recruits and the already converted. The assumption has been that most Canadians are incapable of understanding its message because of the liberal-left propaganda that they have been fed. When the far right's attention has turned to the wider society, it has usually taken the form of trying to manipulate the media and dispersing racist literature rather than physical attacks on minorities. Confrontations that have occurred more often than not have involved its enemies on the far left. In fact, it could be argued that there has been more violence within the radical right than with its targeted populations, especially among those members vying for the position of top dog. Of course, the definition of violence arguably should be stretched to embrace the mere message that people of colour are inferior and Jews are dangerous. From the victim's perspective, racist ideology and propaganda may be regarded as only minutely less painful than a punch to the face.

Let it be clear that numerous cases of physical violence have been documented over the decades. An early example occurred in the 1920s in Ontario, when a Catholic church in the small town of Barrie, north of Toronto, was bombed by the Ku Klux Klan. Oakville and Hamilton at that time were the sites of cross-burnings. In the 1930s, after fascism took root, a pitched battle broke out between the Balmy Beach Swastika Club in Toronto and Jewish students and factory workers. The confrontation, which became known as the Christie Pits incident,[6] spilled over onto nearby streets where Jews were randomly assaulted and Jewish-owned shops were vandalised.

The Canadian Nazi Party's outdoor rallies in Toronto's Allan Gardens during the 1960s, led by John Beattie, gave birth to counter-demonstration, as thousands of protesters gathered to shout down the Nazis. While more than a dozen organisations sprang up, the most prominent was N3 Fighters against Racial Hatred, named after Newton's Third Law saying that for every action there is an opposite and equal reaction. N3 was clearly out for blood. As its members kicked and punched Beattie and his followers, it soon gained a reputation as being just as violent as the Nazis it opposed, drawing criticism from more moderate elements in the anti-racist movement.

Counter-demonstration was not restricted to the opponents of the right wing. It became the speciality of the Edmund Burke Society. In 1968, a bloody brawl broke out when EBS members attacked hundreds of people who had gathered in front of the American Consulate in Toronto to protest against the Vietnam War. On another occasion, the Edmund Burke Society showed up at a celebration of Lenin's 100th birthday. Tables were turned over, glass doors were shattered, a smoke bomb was thrown, and one of the Burkers suffered a stab wound. Curiously, the Edmund Burke Society, albeit primarily an anti-communist rather than a racist and anti-Semitic organisation, and therefore belonging to the fringe rather than the far right,[7] often displayed a greater willingness to engage in violent confrontations than did organisations such as the Ku Klux Klan. But this merely reflected the Edmund Burke Society's slogan, 'militant conservative activism', and its description of itself as a political movement rather than a political party, devoted to action rather than talk. Besides, from the point of view of the radical right, the time for fighting on the street was premature. It would come when racial wars across the globe erupted, setting the stage for the glorious battle in which the forces of fascism finally would demolish their rivals on the left and gain dominion over the world.

'Violence is the last resort of the incompetent.' These were the words of James Alexander McQuirter, the man who led the Ku Klux Klan in Canada during the early 1980s. According to McQuirter, the modern Klan is nothing like its predecessor. Its members dress in business suits, not white robes, and they don't hate anyone or advocate violence. McQuirter declared that if a prospective member expressed hatred towards people of colour or Jews, he or she would be shown the door. Nevertheless, under McQuirter's reign cross-burnings were held in different parts of the country, and training camps were organised (at least on paper) for young people in the use of firearms and explosives. Ironically, in view of his statement about violence and incompetence, McQuirter was soon serving a prison sentence for the attempted murder of a fellow Klansman who had fallen out of favour, for participating in an attempt to overthrow the country of Dominica, which was to become a haven and base for the far right, as well as for various charges linked to fraud.

Arguably even more pernicious than the physical violence the far right has perpetrated has been its discourse and its tactics to manipulate public opinion. Black people, according to the white supremacists, are genetically inferior. Often scientific studies were cited such as Jensen's work on IQ (1969) or Coon's contention (1962) that Blacks evolved into *Homo sapiens* 200,000 years later than Whites, which supposedly accounts for their purported incapacity for civilisation. Inter-racial breeding was said to be more dangerous than the atomic bomb. Race-mixing was portrayed as unnatural – literally against nature, bound to fail. Race riots, rather than being deplorable, were seen as occasions to rejoice; they were merely natural manifestations of the antagonism between different species, and may be a sign that white people are finally waking up.

The right-wing members I interviewed repeatedly dismissed the Holocaust as a hoax, arguing that Jews were actually safer inside the Nazi concentration camps than outside them. The media, financial institutions and the courts were supposedly controlled by Jews, with ZOG (Zionist Occupation Government) just around the corner. Communism and capitalism were said to be in cahoots, twin programmes directed by Jews en route to fulfilling their long-established international conspiracy to dominate the world. Race riots were seen as products of that conspiracy, as black and Whites, manipulated by Jews, killed each other off.

In summary, unlike the extreme right in the USA, which has a long history of intimidation and murder, the far right in Canada has only occasionally crossed the line between talk and action to physically attacking its victims. The vast bulk of its activities have centred around the production and promotion of racist ideology.

One might wonder why the radical right in Canada has been less violent than its counterpart in the USA. Of course, American society in general, not just its far right, appears to be more violent than Canadian society, reflected, for example, in the number of people killed by firearms. I suppose the most obvious explanation concerns culture. The central Canadian values are said to include obedience, order and respect for authority. Then, too, although this may be fading in the wake of NAFTA, Canadians have placed less emphasis on individualism than have Americans. Ernst Zundel, the Canadian-based anti-Semite who became infamous for dispersing masses of anti-Holocaust literature around the globe,[8] once remarked to me that because of Canada's culture, he posed no danger to the country; however, he declared, if he lived in the United States, with its rampant individualism and taste for confrontation, he would set that nation on fire.

Another difference, although it too may have been modified by NAFTA, is that Canadians have assigned a greater value to social and economic equality, or at least have been less comfortable with wide gaps between rich and poor. Class stratification, in fact, may constitute a more powerful explanation of the different degrees of violence in Canada and the United States than does culture, because violence below the border is concentrated in the social and economic underclass, and therefore conditioned as well by race. Nevertheless, the contention that culture is the key has been promoted in scholarly circles for at least half a century, notably in the writings of the sociologist, S.D. Clark (1954). Quite a different perspective has been offered by an historian, McNaught.[9] Not only does he contend that Canada's non-violent image is belied by its history, but he also identifies the peculiar nature of violence in Canada: the much greater degree, in comparison to the United States, to which violence has been linked to the state, masked, presumably, by the values of obedience, order, and respect for authority. What this might mean is that there has been a relative absence of violence connected to the Canadian radical right because if the state has not 'owned' the violence, it has not allowed it.

It is pertinent to assess the impact of 9/11 on organised racism and anti-Semitism in North America.

Obviously, there is much about the transformed world in the wake of the terrorist attack on America in 2001 that has been to the liking of the radical right: an increase in racial profiling by government agencies, a renewed suspicion of non-European immigrants, a more hospitable climate in which to express racist and anti-Semitic bigotry, and a hardening of political and ideological positions in relation to long-existing trouble spots such as the Middle East. There also has been a vigorous repudiation of the philosophical position of relativism, as the world has increasingly been divided into good people and bad people, and rationality, objectivity and balanced viewpoints have given way to emotional commitment to one's cause, neatly captured by the slogan that you're either with us or against us. From the far right's perspective, the potential clash of civilisations between the Islamic and Christian worlds, with its undertone of racism, is certain proof that an inevitable global racial war is drawing ever closer.

If it is a mistake to think that the radical right lamented 9/11, it is equally erroneous to assume that the terrorist attack has rendered the threat of the far right irrelevant. According to the Canadian Jewish Congress,[10] the radical right has become bolder in the wake of 9/11, which it blames on American support for Israel. In turn, representatives of Canadian Arabs and Muslims have pointed out that 9/11 has provided the far right with a licence to undermine multiculturalism and encourage antipathy between Muslims and Christians.[11] Of course, the radical right's contention is that it is the Jews who have manipulated Christians and Muslims to do battle with each other, just one version of the conspiracy theories connected to the far right that have sprung up in the wake of 9/11. Another version envisages the radical right joining forces with Muslim terrorists to attack Jews. A more convoluted theory portrays the radical right beating up Jews, but blaming it on Muslims, who are then targeted by the same radical right in supposed retaliation for anti-Semitic acts.

No doubt the most odious version of conspiracy, once again with a far-right connection, is the one that identifies Israel and Jews as the architects of 9/11. David Duke (see The Freedom-Site May 7, 2002), a prominent white supremacist and anti-Semite in the United States who had a major influence on Canada's McQuirter, claims that Israel's spy agency, the Mossad, had penetrated al-Qaeda networks in America well before 9/11. It then either manipulated al-Qaeda to carry out the terrorist assault, or at the very minimum had precise knowledge about the impending attack but did not inform the American government. This was because it believed that the attack would be entirely to Israel's benefit. It would turn America against the Muslim world, especially Iraq and Iran, would scuttle any plans for a Palestinian state, and would give Israeli Prime Minister Sharon a free hand to crack down on the Palestinians and accelerate Israel's colonisation of Palestinian territory. As proof of Israel's culpability, Duke claims that although nearly 4,000 Jews worked in the World Trade Center and vicinity, hardly any of them were killed in the terrorist attack. Duke's explanation is that a couple of hours before the attack, the Mossad sent coded messages to Israeli firms and Jewish employees warning them about the imminent catastrophe. Of course, Duke's charge is merely a variation on the ancient conspiracy theory that Jews are bent on world domination, supposedly revealed in *The Protocols of the Elders of Zion*, a notorious forgery that continues to circulate in far-right circles today, and apparently in parts of the Arab/Muslim world as well.[12]

THE RADICAL RIGHT AND THE WIDER CANADIAN SOCIETY

As Hughes and Kallen[13] have observed, racism in Canada has been as deeply rooted as in the United States. When Canada emerged from the experience of colonisation, the major victims were the native peoples. Valentine[14] has pointed out that as a result of successive government strategies to dominate and control native peoples, today they 'have the lowest incomes, the poorest health, and the highest rates of unemployment of any single group in the country'. They are also over-represented in jails and under-represented in the educational system. In some cases, such as that of the now extinct Beothuk of Newfoundland in the eighteenth century, native peoples were the victims of outright slaughter.[15] Many Canadians probably are not aware that their country once was host to slavery. The first slaves were Indian captives sold to traders.[16] Eventually black slaves were brought to Canada, and in Nova Scotia there were slave sales and newspaper advertisements for runaways.[17] Indeed slavery lasted longer in Canada than in the northern United States, and many fugitive slaves actually escaped from Canada to New England.[18]

In 1849, racial segregation was legalised in schools in Ontario.[19] As late as the 1930s, in Alberta, an Indian student who had won a prize for obtaining the highest academic standing in Grade 12 was told that she did not qualify. In the same decade, a black student was refused a scholarship that she had won, on the assumption that no opportunities to use it would be offered to her. In British Columbia classrooms in the 1950s and 1960s, Grade 4 students still used a workbook called *Ten Little Niggers*.

The first Jewish settlers in Toronto were apparently treated with respect, partly because of their small numbers (only twelve in 1846 and 350 in 1875) and partly because most of them had emigrated from Britain and the USA.[20] But there was a dramatic change in the early 1900s with the arrival of East European Jews. In terms of culture and language they no longer were invisible, and according to Wrong[21] even the established Jewish community saw them as a threat to harmonious relations with the gentile majority. By the end of the 1920s, Jews were barred from some college fraternities and golf and tennis clubs, and from professions such as teaching and nursing. It was during the 1920s that swastika clubs began to emerge in the country, and although fascists like Arcand and Taylor were interned in concentration camps for the duration of World War II, that was also the period when Canadian government officials shut the country's doors to Jewish refugees.[22]

In a House of Commons speech in 1882, Sir John A. Macdonald, Canada's first prime minister, remarked that 'a Mongolian or Chinese population in our country . . . would not be a wholesome element for this country'.[23] Echoing Macdonald's words in an article in the popular magazine *Saturday Night* in 1911, Canada's noted humorist, Stephen Leacock, observed that non-Anglo Saxon immigrants were 'fit objects for philanthropic pity, but indifferent material from which to build the Commonwealth of the future'. No doubt such statements today would evoke a robust reaction from the media, politicians and ordinary citizens. Yet in a study in the 1980s of employment opportunities, Henry and Ginzberg[24] found that Whites had three job prospects to every one for Blacks. In that same decade, a survey of employment agencies in four cities found that 17 of 25 of them were willing to provide employers with Whites only, and a golf club on the edge of Toronto decided to refuse Jewish members in order to elevate its status. In my own study of race and ethnicity in rural Ontario in the 1990s,[25] I was surprised to learn that the natives, most of them descendants of Protestant immigrants from Northern Ireland in the late 1800s, who had had hardly any contact with people of colour, readily offered racial classifications of the world's population, and held strong views about racial superiority and inferiority based mainly on skin colour. The implication is that the racism embedded in the wider society has provided an environment hospitable to white supremacist organisations. As Sher[26] has observed: 'Far from being an aberration in a supposedly just and equal society, the Klan arguably is more of a reflection – however exaggerated – of the racism endemic in that society.' And referring to the fascist parties in Canada in the 1920s, Wrong[27] has stated: 'anti-Semitic violence and political demagoguery are nearly always the outward and visible signs of milder antipathies that have deep roots in the population.'

CONCLUSION

Although the radical right in Canada has not been as violent as its counterpart in the USA, in terms of the sheer number of far-right organisations and their persistence over time, Canada has been decidedly unexceptional in the English-speaking world. It cannot be plausibly argued that the racist and anti-Semitic ideology of the radical right is totally incompatible with the wider society. Nor can it be concluded that momentous events in recent history, notably 9/11, have rendered the far right obsolete. To the contrary, 9/11 has enhanced the environment in which the far right operates, and has provided it with renewed conviction that a global racial war is imminent.

NOTES

1 Barrett, Stanley R., *Paradise: Class, Commuters and Ethnicity in Rural Ontario*, 1994, Toronto, University of Toronto Press.
2 Kyba, Patrick, 'The Saskatchewan General Election of 1929', unpublished MA thesis, 1964, Department of Economics and Political Science, University of Saskatchewan.
3 Betcherman, Lita-Rose, *The Swastika and the Maple Leaf: Fascist Movements in Canada in the Thirties*, 1975, Toronto, Fitzhenry and Whiteside.
4 Raab, Earl, 'Anti-Semitism in the 1980s', 1983, pp 11–18, *Midstream* 32.
5 Hier, Sean P., 'The Contemporary Structure of Canadian Racial Supremacism: Networks, Strategies and New Technologies' (2000) *Canadian Journal of Sociology* 25, pp 1–24.
6 Levitt, Cyril H. and Shaffir, William, *The Riot at Christie Pits*, 1987, Toronto, Lester and Orpen Dennys.
7 The radical right is anti-black, anti-Semitic, anti-communist, anti-egalitarian, anti-homosexual, anti-feminism, anti-abortion, anti-Third World immigration, anti-peace movement, and anti-world government; it also advocates violence. The fringe right shares many of these elements, but denies that it is racist, anti-Semitic or fascist, or that it encourages or condones violence.
8 Barrett, Stanley R., *Is God a Racist? The Right Wing in Canada*, 1987, Toronto, University of Toronto Press.

9 McNaught, Kenneth, 'Violence in Canadian History', in Moir, John (ed.), *Character and Circumstance*, 1970, pp 66–84, Toronto, Macmillan of Canada.

10 Prutschi, Manuel, 'Resurgent anti-Semitism and Jewish community strategies to combat it', *DAIS*, Canadian Jewish Congress, vol 8 (no. 1), Summer 2003, pp 1–12.

11 Gibson, Will, 'The Far-Right Fallout', *Maclean's*, December 3, 2001.

12 Yet another conspiracy theory suggests that the number of official deaths at the World Trade Center was greatly underestimated, and advances the argument that the American government itself may have employed advanced technology to force the two passenger jets to strike the twin towers, the purpose being to rally Americans behind their government's military adventures abroad. See the Heritage Front's *Upfront*, Issue 22, December 2002.

13 Hughes, David and Kallen, Evelyn, *The Anatomy of Racism*, 1974, Montreal, Harvest House.

14 Valentine, Victor, 'Native Peoples and Canadian Society', in Breton, Raymond, Reitz, Jeffrey, Valentine, Victor (eds), *Cultural Boundaries and the Cohesion of Canada*, 1980, pp 45–135, Montreal, The Institute for Research on Public Policy.

15 Hill, Daniel, *Human Rights in Canada: A Focus on Racism*, Canadian Labour Congress, 1977.

16 Greaves, Ida, *The Negro in Canada*, 1930, Montreal, McGill University.

17 Jones, B., 'Nova Scotia Blacks: A Quest for a Place in the Canadian Mosaic', in D'Oyley, Vincent (ed.), *Black Presence in Multi-Ethnic Canada*, 1978, pp 81–96, Vancouver, Faculty of Education, University of British Columbia.

18 Winks, Robin W., 'The Canadian Negro: A Historical Assessment – Part I', *Negro History* 53, 4, October 1968, pp 283–300.

19 Head, William, The Black Presence in the Canadian Mosaic: A Study of Perception and the Practice of Discrimination against Blacks in Metropolitan Toronto, 1975, Ontario Human Rights Commission.

20 Speisman, Stephen A., *The Jew of Toronto: A History to 1937*, 1979, Toronto, McClelland and Stewart Ltd.

21 Wrong, Dennis H., 'Ontario's Jews in the Larger Community', in Rose, Albert (ed.), *A People and Its Faith*, 1959, pp 45–59, Toronto, University of Toronto Press.

22 Abella, Irving and Troper, Harold, *None Is Too Many*, 1982, Toronto, Lester and Orpen Dennys.

23 Sher, Julian, *White Hoods: Canada's Ku Klux Klan*, 1983, Vancouver, New Star Books.

24 Henry, Frances and Ginzberg, Effie, *Who Gets the Work: A Test of Racial Discrimination in Employment*, 1985, The Urban Alliance on Race Relations and the Social Planning Council of Metropolitan Toronto.

25 Barrett, Stanley R, *Paradise: Class, Commuters and Ethnicity in Rural Ontario*, 1994, Toronto, University of Toronto Press.

26 Sher, Julian, *op cit*, p 83.

27 Wrong, *op cit*, p 53.

Chapter 6

A 'bolt-on extra to the police's work'?[1]

Racism and policing in the UK since the Macpherson Report

Neil Davie

> It is by outcome that the [Police] will be judged, not by the expenditure of energy on good intentions.
> Alan Marlow and Barry Loveday, *After Macpherson: Policing after the Stephen Lawrence Inquiry* (2000), p 1.[2]

INTRODUCTION

In February 1999, Sir William Macpherson issued the findings of his investigation into the death of London teenager Stephen Lawrence, killed in what was evidently a racist attack as he waited at a bus stop one evening in April 1993. Controversially, Sir William found that the initial murder inquiry, conducted by the Metropolitan Police Service (MPS), had been marred not only by incompetence and management failure[3] – serious enough in themselves – but by what he termed 'institutional racism'. The report provided the following definition:

> The collective failure of an organisation to provide an appropriate and professional service to people because of their colour, culture, or ethnic origin. It can be seen or detected in processes, attitudes and behaviour which amount to discrimination through unwitting prejudice, ignorance, thoughtlessness and racist stereotyping which disadvantage minority ethnic people.[4]

Such racism persists, the report went on,

> . . . because of the failure of the organisation openly and adequately to recognise and address its existence and causes by policy, example and leadership. Without recognition and action to eliminate such racism it can prevail as part of the ethos or culture of the organisation. It is a corrosive disease.[5]

The intention of this chapter is to examine to what extent such 'recognition' and 'action' have actually characterised official responses to Macpherson, both within the Police and at government level, and to reach some conclusions about the state of police–ethnic minority relations in the UK nearly eleven years after Stephen Lawrence's death.

'INSTITUTIONAL RACISM' AND POLICE ORGANISATIONAL CULTURE

The Macpherson Report made it clear that it did not consider the MPS to be *consciously* racist; on the contrary, the London Police was praised for such anti-racist initiatives as the Racial and Violent Crime Task Force, set up while the Stephen Lawrence inquiry was in progress.[6] The kind of racism highlighted by the report was unwitting, unconscious and unintentional:

> Unwitting racism can arise because of a lack of understanding, ignorance or mistaken beliefs, . . . from well-intentioned but patronising words or actions, . . . from unfamiliarity with the behaviour or cultural traditions of people from ethnic minorities, . . . from racist stereotyping, . . . out of uncritical self-understanding born out of an inflexible police ethos of the 'traditional' way of doing things. Furthermore, such attitudes can thrive in a tightly-knit community, so that there can be a collective failure to detect and outlaw this breed of racism. The police canteen can easily be its breeding ground.[7]

The concept of 'institutional racism' was not new of course – its history goes back to the late 1960s[8] – but this was the first time that its presence had been affirmed in an official inquiry into UK policing. It is interesting in this context to compare Sir William's findings with those of the last major inquiry into race and policing, that of Lord Scarman (1981). His report, commissioned in the wake of the Brixton Riots of that year, rejected the relevance of the term 'institutional racism'.[9] He conceded that 'racial prejudice does manifest itself occasionally in the behaviour of a few officers on the street', but declared that 'the direction and policies of the Metropolitan Police are not racist'. There had been, he noted, 'errors of judgement, . . . a lack of imagination and flexibility', but he did not see the need for new legislation or indeed a general rethink of policing priorities or methods.[10]

In many ways the opportunity afforded by the Scarman Report for the police to 'take a courageous and revealing look in its attitudinal mirror', as a later internal police report put it, was lost. Instead, much of the post-Scarman progress, noted the same report, 'was allowed to ebb away on the tide of changing fashion'.[11] Without any apparent need for the root-and-branch reform of the police's organisational culture and with no targets set for the implementation of the report's more specific recommendations, progress was slow and uneven. It was with reference to this view that Home Secretary Jack Straw, speaking in the House of Commons in March 1999 expressed his view that 'the changes required by the Lawrence inquiry will only work if they are systemic – embraced by the culture of the police force as well as in its practice'. To simply 'bolt on' reforms to existing practice, as had been tried following the Scarman Report, would not do.[12]

POLICE AND RACISM ON THE EVE OF THE MACPHERSON REPORT

An inspection carried out on the eve of the Lawrence Inquiry by Her Majesty's Inspectorate of Constabulary (HMIC), called *Winning the Race*, found 'continuing evidence ... of inappropriate [racist] language and behaviour by police officers' – language and behaviour apparently widely tolerated by sergeants and inspectors. Ethnic minority officers were found to feel 'unsupported by management'; 'some supervisors displayed little awareness or understanding of harassment or discrimination issues' and there was 'a lack of faith in the grievance procedure by many individuals'. The kind of leadership called for by Scarman remained, it seems, elusive.[13]

A follow-up study, *Winning the Race – Revisited*, conducted in 1999, and published shortly after the Macpherson Report, found little progress, a state of affairs it described as 'surprising', especially given the context of widespread media attention and public concern regarding police interaction with ethnic minorities.[14] There were signs of good practice, HMIC found, but these were 'sporadic, uncoordinated and often under-resourced'. Action on race relations issues from senior police officers was described diplomatically as 'diffuse'. A detailed analysis of these two HMIC inspections by Barry Loveday in 2000 concluded: 'Irrespective of the good intentions of senior officers, the failure of operational line managers on the ground to abandon established prejudice runs like a fault line through the police service.'[15] For its part, HMIC concluded darkly that without 'tangible' change, there was a real danger that 'the consent of part of the population' could be 'withdrawn'.[16]

WHITHER MACPHERSON?

This was the state of play when the Macpherson Report was published in February 1999. Publicly, the Police closed ranks behind their senior officers, and the Home Office. Metropolitan Police Commissioner Sir Paul Condon spoke of his commitment to 'lead[ing] in taking things forward so that the new standard can be applied in practical ways', while Fred Broughton, chairman of the Police Federation, Britain's largest police union, described the Macpherson Report as 'a watershed of opportunity', declaring his union's intention to 'look to the future' and address its own 'agenda, structure and culture'.[17] The Government, for its part, welcomed the 'clear and sensible' conclusions of the report. Speaking in the House of Commons, Home Secretary Jack Straw expressed his hope that the Stephen Lawrence inquiry would 'serve as a watershed in our attitudes to racism', emphasising that 'it must mark the beginning of a process of making racial equality a reality, not the end'.[18]

There was then, in February 1999, an apparent consensus among senior police officers and government ministers about why Scarman had failed, and about what needed to be done this time; namely to launch a wholesale attack on the organisational culture of Britain's police forces; to

> confront, [as Alan Marlow has put it] the more insidious aspects of police culture that tend to categorise social groups by the attributes of the worst of their members or, at the very least, to prevent those assumptions being made manifest in behaviour.[19]

If such a sea change were to be effected, it would need the unbending support of the junior ranks of the Police; those inspectors, sergeants and constables at the sharp end of British policing. This support could by no means be taken for granted. Without calling into question the sincerity of the Police's public commitment to rooting out racism, there is strong evidence to suggest that many rank and file police officers resented the way the Stephen Lawrence Inquiry had been carried out, and in particular the label of 'institutional racism' with which they had been collectively stamped at its end. There was a widespread perception within the Police that the Macpherson Inquiry had not respected the rules of fairness and objectivity appropriate for a judicial inquiry.[20] Significantly, one of those sharing this view was Deputy Chief Constable Robert Ayling of Kent Police, whose Police Complaints Authority investigation into the Stephen Lawrence case had formed the kernel of Macpherson's substantive criticisms of the original MPS murder investigation. Writing in the *Police Review* in March 1999, Ayling observed that:

> [Police officers giving evidence to the inquiry] were in a 'no-win situation', often being asked questions such as 'Have you ever heard a racist remark made by a colleague?' If they said 'Yes', I believe it was taken as proof of institutional racism; if they said 'No', in my view it was taken as proof that they must be lying and covering up institutional racism.[21]

The author of these words went on to note that in his judgement, 'the principal shortcomings of the Stephen Lawrence murder investigation can be put down to management failures and lack of effective leadership.' Evidence for 'institutional racism' was, he concluded, 'flimsy'.[22]

If the methods employed by Sir William Macpherson and his team brought rumblings of discontent from within the police, this was nothing compared with the reaction prompted by the Inquiry's conclusion that the British police was collectively 'institutionally racist'. In tarring the whole Police Service with the 'institutionally racist' brush, many felt that it was being made a scapegoat for what was in reality a much wider social problem. As the chairman of the Police Federation put it, 'Ordinary officers in London and across the country are feeling bruised, battered and bewildered by the blame that is being laid at their door, blame that is shared by the whole of society.'[23] The Association of Chief Police Officers equally emphasised that 'Police forces have 200,000 staff, all with roots in a wider society that is itself often racist.'[24]

The danger of such statements is that they are used to justify inaction; with the police as the 'mirror' of society-wide racism, it is powerless to do anything more than weed out the (rare) cases of police malpractice. As Professor P.A.J. Waddington has pointed out:

> This oft-used defence that the police merely reflect the racism of the society from which they are drawn is not only morally bankrupt, it is ridiculous. Do first-class police drivers only aspire to achieve the same level of driving skill as ordinary motorists? Do specialist firearms officers seek only the marksmanship expected of anyone? Of course not. Professionalism means achieving levels of exemplary performance.[25]

How was this 'exemplary performance' to be achieved? According to criminologist John Lea, the strategy adopted by the Macpherson Report can be characterised as one of 'rule-tightening', seen for example in its recommendations regarding the definition and investigation of racist crimes and the police use of its powers under the 1984 Police and Criminal Evidence Act (PACE) to 'stop and search' individuals either on foot or in a car suspected of carrying stolen property or prohibited articles.[26] Both areas of police procedure were identified by Macpherson as contributing to what he called the 'climate of mistrust' which existed between police and Britain's minority ethnic communities.[27]

However, as Lea points out, the insistence on 'rule-tightening' fails to take into account a feature of the organisational structure of the British police noted by many researchers,[28] namely the substantial autonomy accorded to junior officers in the construction of cases for the prosecution. Lea observes:

> The existence of rules in no way guarantees their application in the face of incompetence, racial prejudice or both . . . It is well established in other

areas of policing, for example domestic violence and sexual assault, that the existence of a set of rules in no way ensures equal treatment nor that the police will take a particular incident seriously as a criminal offence and deal with it competently.

'The argument', Lea concludes, 'is ultimately circular. Rule tightening will only eliminate the effect of racism where police culture is already committed to the rigorous application of rules as a matter of substantive policy.'[29]

'Rule-tightening' was not the only avenue pursued by the Home Office in the wake of the Macpherson Report, but it could be argued that it constituted the main thrust of the government response. In an ambitious 'Action Plan' launched in March 1999, a whole raft of procedural reforms was announced. These included a new definition of a 'racist incident' based on the victim's (and not the Police's) perception of the crime; new procedures for recording and monitoring 'Stops and Searches'; race equality training for all serving police officers; improved disciplinary procedures for rooting out racist behaviour in the service; a new, independent complaints body; and a democratically-elected 'Metropolitan Police Authority'. In addition, the Government also promised a new Race Relations Act, bringing the Police for the first time under the aegis of the existing anti-racism legislation.[30] The Police would hitherto have a statutory duty to promote racial equality at the level of policy making, implementation and service delivery.[31]

A new 'Lawrence Steering Group' was set up to pilot these changes. Chaired by the Home Secretary, and drawing its membership from community leaders as well as criminal justice professionals, the Steering Group would publish an annual report, detailing progress on each of Macpherson's recommendations. The sixth such report was published in October 2005.[32]

POLICING THE ETHNIC MINORITIES TODAY

Given our earlier point about the extent of discretion accorded to front-line police officers, it is difficult to assess the extent to which these initiatives have been translated into real changes in the organisational culture of the British Police. The 2000 HMIC inspection of the MPS, carried out in accordance with Recommendation 4 of the Macpherson Report, recognised the difficulty of penetrating all levels of the police organisational structure:

> Whilst those working within the specialist units [like the Racial and Violent Crime Task Force] are beginning to see positive results, there is more to be done in securing the professional hearts and minds of non-specialist police officers. A pervasive feeling exists among some staff that what is seen as special treatment for the victims of racist attacks can only be delivered by prejudicing services to the wider community.[33]

The report also found, as in 1999, that ethnic minority police officers lacked support from their immediate superiors and had little faith in the grievance procedure.[34] A nationwide inspection, carried out the same year, also drew attention to 'residual resistance' in some quarters to the new definition of a racist incident; 'complacency' in some forces concerning the issue of the disproportionate representation of the ethnic minority population in police stops and searches; and 'an inconsistent picture' with respect to anti-racism training.[35] The last conclusion received confirmation from a more recent HMIC inspection, published in 2003. Significantly, the report concluded that 'training in race and diversity was reasonably efficient in terms of *meeting targets*, but not totally effective in delivering *organisational change* . . . Ineffective or inadequate supervision/line management undermines any message that is contained within training . . .'.[36]

The failings identified by the various inspections carried out since the publication of the Macpherson Report reveal with striking clarity the uphill task facing those seeking the reform of the British police's organisational culture. Although there has been progress in the proportion of racist incidents reported to the Police;[37] in the higher level of lay participation in both police decision-making and Home Office policy-making; and in the improved ethnic minority recruitment figures for the Police,[38] there remain other areas of concern. New grievance procedures are in place, but those police officers likely to suffer from racist abuse or behaviour appear to have little confidence in them.[39] Indeed, the Commission for Racial Equality has drawn attention to the growing number of reported racial incidents at the police's own training schools; one of three factors underlying its decision in October 2003 to undertake an official inquiry into police racism, under the auspices of the Race Relations (Amendment) Act 2000.[40] The other two factors mentioned were the doubling in the number of racism complaints from serving police officers in the previous five years, and a worrying HMIC report on the Manchester Police, which revealed 'a lack of sensitivity' in its officers' dealings with minority races and cultures; 'unnecessary reference to the racial origin of suspect offenders during briefings' and 'low' awareness of the new race relations legislation.[41]

A further area of concern in police–ethnic minority relations is that of stops and searches; an issue which has been described as 'the "litmus test" of equality in policing'.[42] Referred to in the Macpherson Report as the subject of 'universal' complaint,[43] it remains the case, despite new procedures and Home Office monitoring, that police stops and searches are disproportionately aimed at the ethnic minority population. Indeed, the disproportion is even greater today than it was at the time of the Macpherson Report.[44] Even though there may be sound operational reasons for targeting high-crime areas which also have a high minority ethnic population, independent research has pointed to the presence of 'racist stereotyping on the part of the police, who are more likely to perceive ethnic minorities with a degree of suspicion and specifically portray African/Caribbean people as violent offenders, and to consider Asians as devious liars'.[45] It was just this kind of racist stereotyping which led to an initial police assumption that Stephen Lawrence's death was the result of a fight between rival gangs, and to a view that Stephen's friend, Duwayne Brooks, present at the scene, was a protagonist rather than the victim of an unprovoked attack.[46]

There remains a widespread perception in Britain's minority ethnic population, as Liberal-Democrat peer Lord Dholakia has observed, that:

> [The Police] are still sending out mixed messages about their attitudes to black and Asian people. They might be setting up community safety units or anti-victimisation units up and down the country, and they might be recording more racist incidents than before, but still black people are five times more likely than Whites to be stopped and searched.[47]

CONCLUSION

Significantly, the CRE announcement in October 2003 to set up an inquiry into police racism came just a week after the screening of a BBC documentary, 'The Secret Policeman', in which an undercover reporter, posing as a police trainee, had witnessed – and filmed – explicitly racist language and behaviour in the Police. The documentary provoked – rightly – very strong reactions, and was followed by a series of official apologies and resignations, together with a promise from the Police to review its diversity strategy and selection procedures.[48]

On the tenth anniversary of Stephen Lawrence's death earlier that year, a number of commentators, including former CRE chairman Lord Ouseley, and specialist on racial violence Dr Ben Bowling of King's College London, had noted that, compared with the immediate post-Macpherson era, there had been a loss of momentum in the drive towards stamping out racism in the police.[49] The conviction in November 2005 of the murderers of Liverpool schoolboy Anthony Walker – killed, like Stephen Lawrence, in a racist attack as he waited for a bus – may, ironically, have served to reinforce this loss of momentum. The rapidity with which the suspects were arrested and charged,[50] and the apparently cordial relations between Anthony's family and the Merseyside Police, would tend to reinforce the view expressed by Mrs Walker herself that '[It] was 13 years ago, when Stephen Lawrence was killed, and times have changed. The police made mistakes then, but they learned their lesson and they've not made the same mistake twice.'[51]

The conclusions of the CRE inquiry into Britain's Police Service published in March 2005,[52] together with those reached by Home Office-sponsored research on the long-term impact of the Stephen Lawrence Inquiry in

October,[53] provide only partial confirmation for such an optimistic assessment. Certainly, in presenting his report, CRE inquiry chairman Sir David Calvert-Smith QC was able to point to 'significant progress in the area of race equality in recent years' and welcome 'the improvements that have already been made and the strong leadership shown by the Association of Chief Police Officers.'[54] In similar fashion, the team of researchers from the London School of Economics found 'substantial changes in policing in the past five years, not least the general excision of racist language, together with other positive developments in relation to the reporting, recording and investigation of hate crimes, murder investigation, family liaison, and community consultation'.[55]

It would appear, however, as the LSE team put it, that there remain 'a number of important caveats to this picture'. It should come as no surprise, given our preceding discussion, to learn that 'positive developments . . . are not uniformly visible across police forces', that 'changes in the general climate of policing' are often seen as 'cosmetic' by minority officers, or that 'willingness to change at the top is not translating into action lower down, particularly in middle-management'.[56] Indeed, Calvert-Smith, a former head of the Crown Prosecution Service, went as far as describing Britain's police force as 'like a perma-frost – thawing on the top, but still frozen solid at the core'. He added that 'unless more is done, it won't melt any time soon'. For the moment at least, there would appear little sign on the horizon of a speed-up in that thawing process.

NOTES

1 'I believe that the crucial failing was the implementation of the Scarman agenda treated race and the whole issue of community relations as a bolt-on extra to the police's work. That is why, in my judgement, the changes required by the Lawrence inquiry will only work if they are systemic – embraced by the culture of the police force as well as in its practice. That must mean that they are implemented in the mainstream of the police service at every level and do not become an add-on extra' (Straw, Jack, *Hansard, House of Commons*, 29 March 1999, col 769).
2 Marlow, Alan and Loveday, Barry, 'Race, Policing and the Need for Leadership', in *idem*, eds., *After Macpherson: Policing after the Stephen Lawrence Inquiry*, 2000, p 1, Lyme Regis: Russell House Publishing.
3 Macpherson, Sir William, *The Stephen Lawrence Inquiry: Report by Sir William Macpherson of Cluny*, (Cm 4262), Feb 1999, §46.1, London: The Stationery Office. On the events leading up to the inquiry, see Cathcart, Brian, *The Case of Stephen Lawrence*, 1999, London: Viking; Younge, Gary, 'The Death of Stephen Lawrence: The Macpherson Report', *The Political Quarterly* (July-September 1999) vol. 70, no. 3, pp 329–334; McLauglin, J. Eugene and Murji, Karim, 'After the Stephen Lawrence Report', *Critical Social Policy* (August 1999) vol. 19, no. 3, pp 371–385; Bridges, Lee, 'The Lawrence Inquiry – Incompetence, Corruption and Institutional Racism', *Journal of Law and Society* (September 1999) vol. 26, no. 3, pp 298–322; Davie, Neil, 'Racisme, police et l'affaire Stephen Lawrence', in Prum, Michel, ed., *La Peau de l'autre*, 2001, pp 73–88, Paris: Syllepse.

4 Macpherson, *op cit*, § 6.34.
5 *Ibid.*
6 *Ibid*, § 6.24. On these initiatives, see 'Building an Anti-Racist Metropolitan Police Service', MPS Press Release, 1 October 1998; Grieve, John G.D. and French, Julie, 'Does Institutional Racism Exist in the Metropolitan Police Service?', in Green, David G., ed., *Institutional Racism and the Police: Fact or Fiction?*, 2000, pp 7–19, London: Institute for the Study of Civil Society.
7 Macpherson, *op cit*, §6.17. Cf. Hall, S., 'From Scarman to Lawrence', *Connections* [Commission for Racial Equality Newsletter] (Spring 2000), p 16: 'It is perfectly possible for young [police] officers to love reggae, eat vindaloo curry every Saturday night, have a few black friends, and still think that "good policing" requires them to act on the assumption that a young black man carrying a holdall at a bus stop has almost certainly committed a robbery and should be "sussed".'
8 On the history of the concept, see Singh, Gurchand, 'The Concept and Context of Institutional Racism', in Marlow and Loveday, *After Macpherson*, *op cit*, ch 3; Lea, John, 'The Macpherson Report and the Question of Institutional Racism', *The Howard Journal* (August 2000) vol. 39, no. 3, pp 219–233.
9 Scarman, Lord, *The Brixton Disorders 10–12 April 1981, Report of an Inquiry by the Rt Hon Lord Scarman, OBE*, 1981, § 2.22, London: HMSO. The disorders in the south London suburb of Brixton, described by Benjamin Bowling as 'the culmination of a deteriorating relationship between the police and black communities in Britain over the previous three decades' (*Violent Racism: Victimisation, Policing and Social Context*, Oxford University Press, 1999, p 79), were triggered by a heavy-handed police stop-and-search operation in the district known as 'Operation Swamp 81'. Some 350 individuals were injured in three days of rioting, and there was widespread damage to property. There were 82 arrests.
10 *Ibid*, § 4.62 – 4.63. See O'Byrne, Michael, 'Can Macpherson Succeed Where Scarman Failed?', in Marlow and Loveday, *op cit*, ch 10.
11 Her Majesty's Inspectorate of Constabulary, *Winning the Race: Embracing Diversity*, 2000, p 6, London: HMIC/Home Office.
12 See n.1 for full text and reference.
13 Her Majesty's Inspectorate of Constabulary, *Winning the Race: Policing Plural Communities*, 1997, London: HMIC/Home Office.
14 Her Majesty's Inspectorate of Constabulary, *Winning the Race: Policing Plural Communities – Revisited*, 1999, § 8.1, London: HMIC/Home Office. See also 'Winning the Race?', *Police Review* (March 1999) 5, pp 26–27.
15 Loveday, Barry, 'Must Do Better: The State of Police Race Relations', in Marlow and Loveday, *After Macpherson*, *op cit*, p 26.
16 HMIC, *op cit*, §§ 7.4.1, 8.7.
17 'Condon Admits New Race Definition', *The Daily Telegraph* (25 February 1999); 'We Will Change, Insists Condon', *Guardian* (25 February 1999).
18 *Hansard, House of Commons*, 24 February 1999, col 389–393.
19 Marlow, Alan, 'Policing in the Pillory: Macpherson and its Aftermath', in Marlow and Loveday, *After Macpherson*, *op cit*, p 13.
20 Cf. the remarks by the Police Federation, quoted in Marlow, 'Policing in the Pillory', *op cit*, p 11, comparing the Stephen Lawrence Inquiry to '. . . the show trials in Eastern Europe fifty years ago, and the treatment of the victims of Mao's cultural revolution'.
21 Ayling, Robert. 'Challenging Macpherson', *Police Review* (12 March 1999) p 17. See also Crompton, Dan, 'Unreasonable Terms', *Police Review* (30 October 1998).
22 Ayling, *op cit*, p 18.
23 Quoted in 'We Will Change, Insists Condon', *Guardian* (25 February 1999).

24 *Ibid*. See also Davie, 'Racisme, police et l'affaire Stephen Lawrence', *op.cit.*, p 83.
25 Waddington, Peter A.J., 'Think Tank', *Police Review* (26 February 1999).
26 Lea, 'The Macpherson Report', *op cit*, pp 222–223, 228.
27 Macpherson, *Stephen Lawrence Inquiry*, §45.8–45.12. See Davie, *op cit*, p 87.
28 See Waddington, Peter A.J., *Policing Citizens*, 1999, ch 8, London: UCL Press.
29 Lea, *op cit*, p 223.
30 *The Stephen Lawrence Inquiry: The Home Secretary's Action Plan*, March 1999, London: Home Office. See Davie, *op cit*, pp 86–87.
31 O'Brien, Mike MP, 'Institutional Racism and the Police', in Green, *Institutional Racism and the Police, op cit*, p 35.
32 Home Office, *Lawrence Steering Group: 6th Annual Report 2005*, October 2005, London: Home Office.
33 HMIC, *Policing London: Winning Consent : A Review of Murder Investigation in the Metropolitan Police Service*, 2000, p 6, London: Home Office/HMIC.
34 *Ibid*, p 9.
35 HMIC, *Winning the Race – Embracing Diversity*, pp 4–6.
36 HMIC, *Diversity Matters*, 2003, pp 27–28 (my emphasis), London: HMIC/Home Office.
37 Phillips, Coretta, and Bowling, Ben, 'Racism, Ethnicity, Crime and Criminal Justice', in Maguire, Mike *et al.*, eds, *The Oxford Handbook of Criminology*, 2002, p 583, Oxford: Oxford University Press. For the year 2003/4, the total number is 52,694, compared with 23,049 for the year 1998/9 (Home Office, *Statistics on Race and the Criminal Justice System, 2002*, 2003, Table 9.1, p 65, London: Home Office; Home Office, *Race and the Criminal Justice System: An Overview to the Complete Statistics 2003–2004*, pv, London: Home Office, February 2005).
38 The latest figures (2003/4) show that 3.3% of police staff are from ethnic minorities., compared with 2% in 1999 (Home Office, *Race and the Criminal Justice System*, p 16).
39 HMIC's conclusions are supported by a 2002 survey of the experiences of ethnic minority officers in Scotland. The survey found that 69% of the police officers interviewed had experienced racism from their colleagues, but that only 17% had made a formal complaint. Of those who had made a complaint, all, without exception, had experienced negative reactions from their line managers and colleagues. According to the survey, many of those interviewed 'believed that much of the effort put into fighting racism over the last few years was geared towards the public and . . . appeared tokenistic' (Scottish Executive Central Research Unit, *The Experience of Black/Minority Ethnic Police Officers, Support Staff, Special Constables and Resigners in Scotland*, 2002, Edinburgh: The Scottish Executive).
40 Phillips, Trevor [CRE Chairman], Speech to Metropolitan Black Police Association AGM (31 October 2003); 'New Racism Investigation into Police', *The Guardian* (31 October 2003).
41 HMIC, *Inspection of South Manchester BCU, Greater Manchester Police*, May 2003, §1.55, London: Home Office/HMIC. See also 'Manchester Police Labelled Sexist and Racist', *Guardian* (27 August 2003).
42 Kennison, Peter, 'Being Realistic About Stop and Search', in Marlow and Loveday, *After Macpherson, op cit*, p 61.
43 Macpherson, *op cit*, §45.8–45.10. See also Kennison, *op cit*, pp 64–65.
44 For the year 2003/4, black people were 6.4 times more likely to be stopped and searched than white people. This compares with five times more likely for the year 1999/2000 (Home Office, *Stephen Lawrence Inquiry . . . Fourth Annual Report*, p 4; Home Office, *Race and the Criminal Justice System*, p 9).
45 Phillips and Bowling, 'Racism, Ethnicity, Crime', *op cit*, p 584.

46 *Ibid*, p 585.
47 Dholakia, Lord, 'Stephen Lawrence – What Next?', Criminal Justice Conference: 'Stephen Lawrence Two Years On: What Have We Achieved?', Tring, 22–23 March 2001.
48 'Senior Officers Agree Plan to Tackle Racism', *Guardian* (24 October 2003).
49 'Momentum in Fight Against Racism "Wanes" ', *Guardian* (18 April 2003).
50 Anthony Walker was murdered at the end of July 2005; the two suspects who would subsequently be convicted were arrested at the beginning of November. Both were sentenced to terms of life imprisonment.
51 Quoted in 'They've Not Made the Same Mistake Twice', *Guardian* (30 November 2005).
52 Commission for Racial Equality, *The Police Service in England and Wales*, London: CRE, March 2005.
53 Foster, Janet, Newman, Tim and Souhami, Anna, *Assessing the Impact of the Stephen Lawrence Inquiry*, Home Office Research Study 294, London: Home Office, October 2005.
54 CRE Press Release: 'CRE investigation finds "ice in the heart" of the police service' (8 March 2005).
55 Foster *et al.*, *Assessing the Impact*, p 97.
56 *Ibid*, pp 97, 95; CRE Press Release, *op cit*.

Chapter 7

Roma sacer

Constructing the 'Gypsy other' in British political and legal discourse

David Fraser

INTRODUCTION

Bonfire Night, or Guy Fawkes Day, 5 November, marks the anniversary of the failed plan to blow up the English Parliament in 1605. Guy Fawkes was discovered in the cellar below the Houses of Parliament with enough gunpowder to blow the legislature and the King to smithereens. Bonfire Night celebrates the saving of the King and Parliament from the plotters. Bonfire societies plan, organise and carry out local celebrations which are attended by tens of thousands of ordinary British men, women and children who cheer the lighting of the traditional Bonfires. Across the country, Bonfires are lighted to commemorate the 'joyful day of deliverance'. On the surface, 5 November marks the triumph of English Parliamentary democracy over what would now be called 'terrorism'. As such, the Bonfires and parties which surround them can be seen to mark popular support for the traditions of British democracy.

As is always the case with accepted accounts of history and tradition, there is another story; one which is not so clearly and unambiguously that of the triumph of democracy over terror. Guy Fawkes and his co-conspirators were Roman Catholics who plotted to destroy and overthrow not a democratic Parliament, but a legislative and executive system of government which oppressed, expropriated, tortured and murdered citizens who continued to practice 'the old religion'. At the most well-known Bonfire at Lewes in Sussex, the effigy, 'the Guy' which has featured most commonly is that of Pope Pius IX who re-established the Roman Catholic hierarchy in England with the 1850 bull, *Universalis Ecclesiae*. In fact then, Bonfire Night does not simply mark the triumph of Parliamentary democracy over terror, but instead also gives vent to the strong tradition of anti-Catholic bigotry which marks English history.

At the village of Firle in Sussex, in the autumn of 2003, the local Bonfire Society carried out the tradition of burning a figure of local scorn and popular hatred. The effigy in question was a 'Gypsy caravan'. The caravan bore the registration plate 'P1KEY', 'pikey' being a popular slang expression for

Gypsies and travellers. In addition, the window of the trailer was filled with
pictures of a woman and several small children, portrayed as a Gypsy family.[1]
The caravan also carried a portrait of a bed and a family car contrasted with
a picture of a van and a trailer with the caption 'Fair?'[2] The effigy was
marched through the village to the shouts and admiration of the local population, to be set alight to traditional cheers of 'burn it, burn it' as the Bonfire
celebration reached its apogee.

A member of the local community, who had Romani heritage, filed a formal complaint with the local police. The Commission for Racial Equality, the
body charged with ensuring compliance with Britain's anti-racist legislation,
intervened in support of the Roma, traveller and Gypsy communities.[3] These
events in the village of Firle illustrate in microcosm many of the issues of
anti-Gypsyism which continue in England. Violence against Gypsies exists
not just at the level of violent attacks against individuals and property, but is
also constituted by official bureaucratic and judicial practices and discourses,
as well as through the ways in which such acts and discourses are reported
in the media.

BURNING ISSUES OF NATIONAL IDENTITY: ANTI-GYPSY VIOLENCE AND THE SEMIOTICS OF THE FIRLE BONFIRE

The decision to incinerate a Gypsy caravan with its depiction of a Roma family
and the juxtaposition of traditional English family values (the bed and family
car) did not arise out of a general feeling of anti-Gypsyism, although such
sentiments no doubt exist. The context was much more specific, localised and
real. During the summer of 2003, a family of Gypsies had established an
'illegal' camp on a local property. The perceived failure of local police and
government authorities to intervene and remove the family caused much con-
sternation in the local community. Following the outcry over the Firle effigy,
the local Bonfire Society issued a press release apologising to anyone who had
been offended by the effigy. They sought to explain the Bonfire subject as
an attack not on a racial or ethnic minority but on the politicians and police
who had failed to act against the illegal camping activity.[4] The MP for
Lewes, Norman Baker (Liberal Democrat) wrote that the media coverage had
misinterpreted, if not the actions, then the intentions of the actors.

> In the tradition of the bonfire, societies have for generations burned
> effigies of a topical nature. They have included world leaders from Blair
> and Bush to Bin Laden, and local politicians – I was burned about
> 10 years ago. So while I believe the Firle tableau crossed a line, it needs
> to be seen in the context [sic] a vigorous history of social context and
> lampooning.

Second, Firle, a small village, suffered much damage from the gratuitous actions of some itinerants who camped there this year and which the
police were slow to deal with.[5]

There is the tradition of local democratic debate about political controversy.
Bonfire Night serves as a reaffirmation of the political vibrancy of English
village life, as lampoon and parody are introduced and deployed as essential
elements of liberal political discourse. This is reinforced by the semiotics of
concrete local political events. Indeed, according to the most broadly held
hermeneutic position locally, the victims are at least partly to blame as the
'gratuitous actions of some itinerants' raised the hackles of local residents.

At this level, the story of anti-Gypsy violence at Firle is explained and regulated within the standard discourses of liberal democratic values. However,
things are more complicated than such a simple exercise of rights balancing
between free speech and anti-discrimination paradigms. First, it must be noted
that the police were present at the parade and Bonfire. Under pressure from
the Commission for Racial Equality (CRE) and the media, Sussex police
launched an investigation and arrested the leaders of the Bonfire Society for
inciting racial hatred.[6] They took no action to intervene until political and
media pressures were brought to bear by a complaint by a resident and by the
public and publicised intervention from the CRE. The idea of proactive
policing in the case of hate crimes and instances of public hate speech is not
embodied in the (in)actions of the Sussex police.

Discourses about democracy, race and law which underpin the events of the
autumn of 2003 in Firle provide key insights into debates about anti-Gypsy
violence in England. The central element of the debate and conflict is precisely that which underpins Bonfire Night specifically and the Firle case more
generally, i.e. that a certain historical and continuing view and understanding of 'Englishness' is grounded in an experience and ideology of exclusion and
violence against the Other. The conflict at Firle is a microcosmic example and
embodiment of these interconnected feelings of belonging and exclusion
which define 'Englishness'. Anti-Gypsy violence can only be understood as a
particular example of the broader policies and practices of racist exclusions
which for many constitute 'England'.

In his discussion of the events at Firle, columnist George Monbiot articulates part of the problem as concisely as possible. 'Racism against Gypsies
is acceptable in public life in Britain.'[7] Anti-Gypsy hatred manifests itself
throughout English legal and political discourse.[8] What is of immediate interest are the apparent contradictions and conflicts which surround anti-Gypsy
hatred in England and which serve to highlight not just the complexities of
the Firle Bonfire case.

Monbiot asserts that anti-Gypsy discursive practices are acceptable and
accepted in England because of a complex socio-psychological set of signifiers
about nomadism and settled society. The deep-seated resentments towards,

and hatred of, Gypsies stem, according to Monbiot, from a collective frustration felt by those who live sedentary lives against the freedom of the travellers. The historically and socially close connections between the phenomena of anti-Semitism and philo-Semitism, find their echo here in the ways in which the Gypsy life is at once romanticised in film, music and popular culture[9] and vilified by those who detest the Gypsy's apparent lack of respect for the distinction between public and private space. They condemn and exclude all those who flaunt private property rights and refuse to accept the English way of life and settle down.[10] The illustrations on the Firle effigy, contrasting the signifier of a sedentary English way of life (the bed) and the sign of a transient Gypsy lifestyle (the caravan), point to a strong antipathy to travelling communities and their nomadism. Indeed, the level of acceptability of anti-Gypsy sentiment can be in part attributed to an attitude of the state about the idea and ideal of Gypsy nomadism.

Travelling communities violate the state's sense of discipline and control over its citizenry and population. The lack of a permanent address runs counter to the state's desire to establish a relationship with and knowledge of its citizens' or residents' place of abode. Homelessness and nomadic communities require greater policing and greater state resources precisely because they tend to slip under the radar of surveillance. It is not surprising that the Hitler regime classified nomadic Gypsies as 'asocials' or that the Vichy government released interned Gypsies only if they could prove that they would go to a fixed abode.[11] But the nomadic lifestyle of Gypsies and travellers poses an even greater threat to the state than the policing difficulties and bureaucratic problems of administrative surveillance. The danger here is not to the state, but to the nation. Nomads refuse allegiance, they cross borders, they transgress, in both the literal and figurative sense. They violate borders between nations, between public and private spaces, and between members of the nation itself.[12] They quite simply do not belong.

Giorgio Agamben argues that the essence of nomadism, of those without a clearly established territorial, spatial loyalty, goes to the very heart of all that underpins our understandings of sovereignty and thence the rule of law:

> What the State cannot tolerate in any way, however, is that the singularities form a community without affirming an identity, that humans co-belong without any representable condition of belonging (even in the form of simple presupposition).[13]

This insight allows us to situate the case of Firle in a more nuanced sociopolitical and legal context. State and members of the nation will be hostile to those who attempt by the very nature of their existence to escape from these normative boundaries, and the state will attempt to re-incorporate these dangerous elements. In this particular context, the intervention of the CRE and the Sussex police in 'favour' of the Gypsy community, can, and should, be read as an act of constitutive legal violence through which Gypsies are constructed not just, or primarily, as victims, but more centrally, as subjects of law, as citizens of the nation, covered by the protective legality of the patriarchal state.[14]

Both the Bonfire Society and its defenders, including the local Member of Parliament, assert democratic values of free speech and community in urging a more contextualised understanding of events preceding and surrounding the Bonfire itself. They also refer to the historicity of Guy Fawkes celebrations. How can what happened at Firle in the autumn of 2003 be understood in context?

What must be underlined here is that the tradition of Bonfire Night is centrally important to the construction of national identity in England, particularly in the south east, but elsewhere as well. This key role of 5 November in constructing Englishness highlights what is at stake in the expression of anti-Gypsy feeling at Firle. Hatred of the Other, Catholic or Gypsy, is vital to the manifestations of national identity which accompany Bonfire Night. Guy Fawkes was a deadly enemy of the English nation, of its embodied sovereign, the King, of the body politic, of the Parliament. Most importantly perhaps, he was the deadly enemy of the nation because he was a Catholic. His loyalty lay not with the Protestant English nation, but with Rome, with the Papacy, with an exterior sovereign. He must be destroyed symbolically every year in order to ensure a public remembrance of the defining characteristics of Englishness, both by what it is – Protestant and loyal – and by what it is not – Catholic and traitorous. The Gypsy caravan and family which were symbolically destroyed by the Bonfire at Firle posed a similar threat to an embodied Englishness. Gypsies are Other; they are disloyal because they infringe on the boundaries of English life and law by the very nature of their existence, which brings with it criminality and filth and an attack on the very central basis of the sovereign nation.

The emerging role of rights discourse, the Human Rights Act, and the part played by the CRE, also raise intriguing questions about English national identity. Carl Stychin, for example, carefully deconstructs and analyses the intersections of identity, nation and rights in his study of the conflict arising out of the desire by gay, lesbian and bisexual persons to participate in the St Patrick's Day Parade in Boston.[15] He creates a complex and intriguing argument about the centrality of the parade as a public spectacle in which a particular minority identity (Irish-American) negotiates its place in an American multicultural society and the manner in which rights discourse can be invoked to protect and defend at one and the same time the minority and hegemonic majority ideal of an American identity while excluding sexual minorities from the identity framework. The English example of the Firle Bonfire is at once simpler and more complex. The two parties to the debate (neither of which is Roma) manifest what Davina Cooper has described as the 'reconstruction of public space'. She argues that a fuller understanding of what is at stake in these political and legal struggles over sovereign space requires an analysis which

> treats public space as a process rather than as an object, one that involves the development and materialisation of a spatial imagery in which those who use the space are constituted as a 'public'.[16]

The question here is who belongs in the space defined as public and who gets to operate the taxonomical authority between public and private, between inside and outside, between identity and rights? The 'majority' portrays itself as endangered by the Other, the *demos* is under attack. At the same time and place the rhetoric of public identity, rights discourse, the new *nomos*, is deployed by a competing public 'nation', the nation of a multi-ethnic Britain/England in which 'human rights' and 'human rights bureaucracies' play an important and definitional role. The battle here is between a state of law and a state of democratic exception.

The police stood by at Firle on the night of the Bonfire because English national identity manifests itself both inside and outside the law. Bonfires are carnivalesque. They are moments of collective identity where the nation defines itself, outside or without the law. While this carnivalesque state of anomie is perhaps marked by a freedom, it is still always marked by a sense of obligation, a sense of being in the community of the nation. It is also always marked in space and time. The carnival here owes its sense of meaning, indeed, its very existence to a shared understanding of the lawlessness itself. The lawlessness defines the nation as a state of exception from which the Other is excluded. The Bonfire unites the nation against its sworn enemies. The lawlessness of the state of exception serves a purpose which is not necessarily opposed to the hegemonic function of human rights discourses and practices. It decides who belongs and how. The force of the law of human rights discourse and the practices of government and police bureaucratic instrumentalities and the force of lawlessness of the Bonfire must both, if they are to make any sense, be grounded in a sense of what it means to be 'English'. Both seek to define not just a concept of the citizen as 'English' or as 'rights bearer', but they seek to inscribe a space and an event, as 'English'.

The multicultural impulse which informs human rights legislation and laws which criminalise racist incitement and the English identity of the Guy Fawkes carnival both contain elements of English identity politics. One invokes a *volkisch* community of values and belonging, and the other on the surface calls for an inclusive multicultural Englishness.[17] Yet both serve to enforce a form of violence against Gypsies. The former seeks to exclude them through the symbolic violence of the Bonfire celebration. The latter seeks to include them as legal subjects, to keep them from escaping the letter and application of the law of the nation.

There is, in this context, a 'valid' democratic expression of community values at stake in Firle. The people do feel ignored by local authorities and by the police and they do resent incomers and nomads. Indeed, the participants clearly manifest a self-understanding, an existential politics, which posits an authenticity of community belonging, which they explain as a form of self-expression against a political and legal regime which does not serve or meet their interest and needs as English men and women.

> 'The Firle display was Sussex bonfire at its best. Don't forget the pikey contingent did a lot of damage', said one member of the East Sussex Association of Bonfire and Carnival Societies.[18]
>
> Men, women and children of the local community cheered as the effigy passed through the streets of the village and when it was set alight. Local children had been chosen to paint the figures of the Gypsy family which was burned. A simple and simplistic rejection of these feelings and even of their manifestation as 'racist' and 'bad' will do little to either understand the issues and actions of those involved or to serve as any basis for change. This was, in simple terms, a manifestation of democracy and of democratic feelings. To speak here of the evil nature of the display is to speak of the inauthenticity of the feelings expressed. Any possible critique and engaged political analysis must somehow find a way to go beyond these outdated notions of existential authenticity and the bad faith of evil.[19]

Apprentice parades on 12 July in Northern Ireland, Bonfire Night in England, football hooliganism in Istanbul or Bratislava, or Nice, or anywhere else, are complex manifestations of identity, history, fear and pride. They cannot be easily appropriated in any way which allows for a deconstruction or reversal of the potent racist imagery which is at their core.[20] That does not mean that a collective duty to a careful contextualisation and thence to an ethical deconstruction of the phenomena of racist behaviour is removed or alleviated. It does mean however that authentic manifestations of democratic will do not in and of themselves offer any way around the facticity of racism, or as Stychin amply demonstrates, the hegemonic construction of heterosex, as an essential part of national identity. What must be confronted, as Jean-Luc Nancy argues, is ourselves, our own conceptions, often contradictory, of what we understand by community.[21] The essential connections between current understandings of community and the lawful and political construction of the Nazi *Volksgemeinschaft* cannot be ignored or elided.[22] The 'fascist', 'populist' uprising in Firle, the symbolic, and therefore real, destruction of the Gypsy family and its caravan, are part of English identity, part of the politics of violence and law which construct Englishness and the residents' belief in the village way of life. Only if this contradiction is confronted as inherent in collective experiences of community and therefore of the legal forms which permit and encourage this process of belonging and exclusion, can an understanding of the true complexity and the high stakes in the field of the legalised violence against Roma in English, British and European culture and politics begin. All communitarianisms must be subjected, in terms which are not themselves unproblematic in current political and legal struggles about nation, state, identity and exclusion, to a form of republican autocritique. The Firle Bonfire Night celebration of community may well be 'democratic' but it is not 'republican'. Its violent and categorical destruction of the Other for no other reason than the alterity of the subject is at once unjust and unethical.

That the law might intervene as it has at Firle with police action and anti-racist bureaucratic discourses in no way undermines the democratic nature of the events. Crude democracy is not a necessary condition for anti-racism. Conversely, in this confrontation between racism and virtue, for want of a better term, the state of exception, the interstices of law and a state of not law, can offer intriguing examples for our deeper understandings of the nature of legalised anti-racism. Law circulates all around the Firle Bonfire case, yet its very presence and authority are undermined by the will of the people and by its own institutional failures.

DOMESTICATING THE *ROMA SACER*: SOVEREIGN SPACE AND ANTI-GYPSY VIOLENCE

What unites the anti-Gypsy violence of the Firle Bonfire and other instances of hate crime against Roma is the intimate political, sociological and legal nexus which surrounds current conceptions of nation, citizenship, belonging and sovereignty, all of which in turn revolve around and implicate collective understandings of the subject of law and territory. The centrality of this embodied spatial idea of the citizen/subject limits, explains and produces the various acts of violence and exclusion against Roma. Yet there is one other space, at the margins of law and extra-legality, between the norm and the exception, between public and private, between sovereignty and anarchy, which defines the situation of permissible violence against the *Roma sacer par excellence*. That space, that state of exception, is the Gypsy camp.[23]

The citizens and residents of Firle had no trouble in analysing and situating the Gypsy camp within their understanding of the modern nation state. It was an outlaw place, a place to be excluded by the power and lawful violence of the police and of the sovereign state. It was a space from which the normal rules of law and sovereign power had been excluded.

> Travellers arrived on the Firle estate last August. Soon afterwards 200 pheasants were killed in a field belonging to the estate, home to Henry Gage, the eighth Viscount Gage. Later, human excrement was found on the front doorstep of the estate's gamekeeper.

> The travellers were evicted last September. Photographs taken by residents reveal mounds of rubbish including bathtubs and abandoned cars. They were blighting the area.[24]

The very basis of English rule of law, the rules of land tenancy, 'the Englishman's [or Viscount's] home is his castle', is in this instance defied by the establishment of this illegal encampment. The public health of the body politic is threatened as excrement and filth blight the surroundings. Intriguingly and tellingly, no counter-narrative about Englishness is invoked. The idea of the gentleman poacher, of outlawry as democratic rebellion against the landed aristocracy and tyrannical law versus democratic, popular law, could arguably have been cited here to explain the death of the game birds and the symbolic act of defiance against the gamekeeper, but they are nowhere to be found. The gentleman poacher, of myth, legend and jurisprudence, is part of the *demos*, he is one of 'us'. Gypsies are Other.

When lawful power in the form of the police failed to operate, the good citizens of Firle invoked a sovereignty of their own, a popular democracy which, outside the law, imposed the state of exception and reconstituted the Gypsy camp as beyond the pale of citizenship and deserving of death. The *Roma sacer* becomes at Firle Bonfire Night, and on their campsite, the *homo sacer*. One becomes a citizen by an act of sovereign will and one can lose that citizenship at the will of the sovereign. The democratic sentiments of the villagers of Firle operate to place the Gypsy inhabitants of the camp outside and beyond the bounds of law, belonging and Englishness. The Gypsy is someone who lives in the state of exception as the outlaw subject of the law.

LAW, VIOLENCE, GYPSIES: CONCLUSION

The violent exclusion of the Gypsies from English civil society also tends to hide their status as victims of real hate-inspired violence. In addition to crimes of state and semiotic hatred, Gypsies in Britain are targeted for physical attacks, abuse and violence on a regular basis. In June of 2003, the Gypsy teenager Johnny Delaney was attacked and brutally beaten to death by five youths. Two 16-year-olds were charged with his murder in Cheshire.[25] Johnny Delaney's death was for him and his family the culmination of a lifetime of suspicion, racist taunts and physical attacks. It was, on the day, the consequence of a racial taunt, hurled at Johnny by one of the youths who called him a 'Gypsy bastard'. According to counsel prosecuting the case, 'as the youth lay dying, one of the defendants attempted to justify what he had done by saying he deserved it because he was a Gypsy'.[26] In fact, what the accused said was that Delaney deserved it because 'he was only a fucking Gypsy'.[27] Johnny Delaney's 'crime' was not just that he was a Gypsy but that he was a Gypsy who was walking on the streets and footpaths of the town on his way home. His mere presence was a violation of a sacred, non-Gypsy space. His existence as a Gypsy boy constituted a territorial violation of English space and he was punished for it. In the eyes of his attackers, he could be killed for his transgression. And for the judge, apparently, his killing could not be murder, because after all Johnny Delaney was only a 'Gypsy bastard'. He was assaulted by a group of boys as he lay helpless on the ground. He was kicked repeatedly in the head with a force which one eyewitness described as being a nine on a scale of ten.[28] Yet the Honourable Mr Justice Richards felt that the attack was not one which evidenced an intention to kill or to inflict grievous bodily harm. He found the boys guilty of manslaughter and not murder. To increase the violence of the law against the victim and his family, the judge found that, despite the evidence of the statements of the original insult – 'Gypsy bastard' – which instigated the attack and the subsequent declaration that Delaney was 'only a fucking Gypsy', the attack was not racially motivated. Johnny Delaney was killed and his memory was killed by the judge and by the law of homicide but he was not murdered, nor was he the victim of race hate. The *Roma sacer* can be killed but he cannot be murdered. Homicide here becomes *Romicide.*

While incidents of racial killing are not common in England, other forms of physical violence against Gypsies are. In Sussex, the centre of Bonfire Night, violent arson attacks against Gypsy caravans have seen an upsurge. In the village of Peacehaven, a petrol bomb attack was reported to police. In Crawley, Margaret Murphy lost her van and the family dog when a petrol soaked firework was ignited. Near Brighton, other similar attacks have been reported and some local Gypsies have discovered caches of petrol and fire-works hidden near their camp. Bricks are hurled through caravan windows with regularity and verbal abuse is common. In Hove, a 'No Travellers' sign appeared outside a local laundrette and in Lewes, home of the predominant anti-Catholic Guy Fawkes Bonfire in the country, a similar sign could be found outside a local pub.[29] Throughout the country, local councils and police forces continue to force Gypsy families to move on whenever they attempt to establish themselves.

The real context of the Firle Bonfire case remains the legitimate expression of illegal, unlawful, outside the law, public hatred of Gypsies. The creation of the Gypsy camp as a space where lawful and unlawful violence share domin-ion marks British legal and political discourse as essentially operating against Gypsies/Roma in a way which signifies and exceeds the limits of lawful, sovereign territorialised violence. The Firle Bonfire, the streets of Cheshire and Gypsy encampments throughout the country mark this exceptional state of public and private violence targeting the *Roma sacer.*

> If this is true, if the essence of the camp consists in the materialisation of the state of exception and in the subsequent creation of a space in which bare life and the juridical rule enter into a threshold of indistinction, then

we must admit that we find ourselves in the presence of a camp every time such a structure is created, independent of the kinds of crime that are committed there and whatever its denomination or specific topography.[30]

The problem in combating anti-Gypsy racism returns to this point of the indeterminacy of law and democracy, of the instance and emplacement of law and not law in the grey zone of legalised killings and exclusion. Explorations of the zone of the deterritorialisation of the interstices of the non-law of the democratised, populist extra- or supra-legal violence of the Firle Bonfire, return us to the necessity of finding a space in which we might re-situate a state of pure politics.

Such a politics demands not just an active re-imagination of law and sovereign power, of the fate of the *homo/Roma sacer*, but a re-territorialisation of the space of the counter-camp. The plea for the creation of so called 'cities of refuge' (*villes-refuges*) in the late 1990s as a democratic (republican) counter-weight to populist, democratic(?) anti-refugee policies in France resonates clearly here. Not only would such spaces serve an urgent political and social, ethical need, but they, in order to exist, and by their very existence, demand a radical reconstruction of our ideas and understandings of law and community. They are, as conceived and imagined, spaces outside the law of the camps, counter-hegemonic spaces which insist on an ethical de/re/construction of public political space on the edges, at the margins, in the interstices of law.

NOTES

1 'Gypsy effigies burnt on bonfire', *BBC News*, 30 October 2003, http://news.bbc. co.uk/go/pr/fr/_england/southern counties/3222321.stm. Rebecca Ellinor, 'Gypsy Caravan Burned in Village Bonfire', *Guardian*, 31 October 2003.
2 http://www.parklife.me.uk/Firle2003/images/ThumbnailFrame.htm, 21 November 2003.
3 'CRE Backs Gypsies', *Guardian*, 8 November 2003.
4 Firle Bonfire Society, 'Press Statement', 28 October 2003.
5 Letter, *Guardian*, 8 November 2003.
6 Helen Carter, 'Arrests for Burning of "Gypsy Caravan" ', *Guardian*, 12 November 2003; 'Firle Bonfire Celebrations – Arrests Made', www.sussex.police.uk/news-feed/ index.asp?uniqueid=8343, 23 November 2003.
7 'Acceptable Hatred', *Guardian*, 4 November 2003.
8 See David Fraser, 'To Belong or not to Belong: the Roma, State Violence and the New Europe in the House of Lords', 21 *Legal Studies* 569, (2001).
9 See Ralph Sandland's, 'The Real, the Simulacrum and the Construction of the "Gypsy" in Law', 23 *J. Law & Society* 383, (1996); W. Willems, *In Search of the True Gypsy: From Enlightenment to Final Solution*, (London: Frank Cass Publishers, 1997); Gilad Margalit, 'Antigypsyism in the Political Culture of the Federal Republic of Germany: A Parallel with Antisemitism?', 9 *Analysis of Current Trends in Antisemitism*, (Jerusalem, 1996); Gilad Margalit *Germany and*

Its Gypsies: A Post-Auschwitz Ordeal, (Madison: University of Wisconsin Press, 2002), especially Chapter 1.

10 David Fraser, *op cit*, and works cited.

11 See Margalit, *Germany and Its Gypsies*, *op cit* and Guenter Lewy, *The Nazi Persecution of the Gypsies*, (New York and Oxford: Oxford University Press, 2000); Denis Peschanski, *Les Tsiganes en France, 1939–1946*, (Paris: CNRS Editions, 1994).

12 See David Fraser, *op cit*.

13 Giorgio Agamben, *The Coming Community*, (Minneapolis and London: University of Minnesota Press, 1993) p 86.

14 See the fascinating analysis of Carl Stychin in another context, 'A Stranger to Its Laws: Sovereign Bodies, Global Sexualities and Transnational Citizens', 22 *J. Law & Society* 601, (2000).

15 See Carl Stychin, 'The Nation's Rights and National Rites', in *A Nation by Rights*, (Philadelphia: Temple University Press, 1998), pp 21–51. More recently, one could point to the controversy surrounding the Macy's Thanksgiving Parade and gay rights activist Harvey Fierstein who attempted to enter the parade dressed as Mrs Claus in order to underline the struggle for gay marriage rights. See Michael Brick, 'Macy's Informs "Mrs. Claus": It's a Parade; It's Not a Pulpit', *New York Times*, 27 November 2003.

16 Davina Cooper, 'Regard between Strangers: Diversity, Equality and the Reconstruction of Public Space', 57 *Critical Social Policy* 465 p 466.

17 See Clive Harris, 'Beyond multiculturalism? Difference, recognition and social justice', 35 *Patterns of Prejudice* 13, (2001).

18 'A Burning Issue in the Village', *Observer*, 16 November 2003.

19 See e.g. Jean-Luc Nancy, *The Experience of Freedom*, (Stanford: Stanford University Press, 1993), especially at Chapter 12, for an examination of the problematic of freedom and evil.

20 See in another context, R. Amy Elman, 'Triangles and Tribulations: The Politics of Nazi Symbols' 30 *J of Homosexuality* 1, (1996).

21 Jean-Luc Nancy, *La Communauté affrontée* (Paris: Galilée, 2001).

22 *Ibid* p 26.

23 See David Fraser, 'To Belong or not to Belong', *op cit* pp 581–593.

24 'A Burning Issue in the Village', *op cit*. A similar eviction controversy erupted in Bulkington, Warwickshire, in January 2004. See, 'Eviction Stand off at Traveller Site', *BBC News*, 12 January 2004; Steven Morris, 'Traveller Camp Drives away Bailiffs', *Guardian*, 13 January 2004. The interesting fact about this particular case is that the Gypsies here are the legal owners of the land. That land, however, is designated 'green belt' land and no permission has been given by local council for occupation. The broader and more generalised problem is that little if any land is actually set aside for purchase/use by travellers in Britain. See, Heaven Crawley, 'Safe as Houses', *Guardian*, 20 January 2004.

25 Audrey Gillan, 'Brutal Death of a Travelling Child', *Guardian*, 10 June 2003.

26 David Ward, 'Murder of Gypsy "Racial" ', *Guardian*, 18 November 2003.

27 David Ward and Helen Carter, 'Youths Guilty of Killing Traveller', *Guardian*, 29 November 2003.

28 *Ibid*

29 'A Burning Issue in the Village', *Observer*, 16 November 2003.

30 Giorgio Agamben, *Homo Sacer; Sovereign Power and Bare Life* (Stanford: Stanford University Press, 1998) p 174.

Chapter 8

Anti-Traveller racism in Ireland

Violence and incitement to hatred

Bryan Fanning

> The sooner the shotguns are at the ready and these travelling people are put out of our county the better. They are not our people, they aren't natives.[1]

INTRODUCTION

Hostility towards Travellers is frequently uncritically reported in the local and national press, yet has rarely been the subject of academic research. Media coverage generally relates to opposition by residents and politicians to the provision of accommodation for Travellers, to court cases against Travellers and to pejorative accounts of deviance amongst Travellers. Claims that Travellers are intrinsically violent have become central to a politics of ethnic exclusion in Ireland. This has been reflected in media accounts of Travellers.[2] These have focused, in particular, upon accounts of feuds between Traveller families and unruly behaviour at weddings and funerals. It is arguably the case that the racialisation of Travellers as a violent out-group in Irish society has intensified in recent years, in response to the introduction of legislation against discrimination and social policies aimed at promoting the social inclusion of Travellers.[3] There is a profound disjuncture between official policies promoting the integration of Travellers, which to some extent acknowledge Traveller ethnicity, and a trenchant opposition by many residents' groups and local politicians to the very presence of Travellers in their communities. For example, in 2002, the Vintner's Federation of Ireland marshalled accusations of Traveller violence to campaign for the exemption of Travellers from the Equal Status Act (2000).[4] This Act specifically outlawed discrimination against Travellers in the provision of goods and services. As a result of this campaign, the state's Equality Authority lost its powers to directly investigate allegations of discrimination against Travellers by owners of hotels and public houses.

The case study addressed in this chapter focuses on anti-Traveller racism in County Clare between the beginning of 2000 and the end of 2002. It develops a previous analysis of the politics of Traveller exclusion in Clare from the 1960s to the end of 1999.[5] From the 1960s, opposition to the provision of halting sites for Travellers and discrimination against Travellers in the provision of public housing was frequently justified by claims that the dominant community lived in fear of Travellers. Anti-Traveller hostility was sometimes expressed in terms of alleged claims about Traveller violence. Opposition to Traveller accommodation was justified on an ongoing basis by allegations of violence by Travellers against settled people. Emotionally charged, hyperbolic or even apocalyptic language was a feature of most discussions on Travellers at local authority meetings from the 1960s. Newspaper accounts of discussions about Travellers frequently described residents and councillors as angry. In such accounts residents were often described as living in fear of Travellers, of being 'terrorised' by Travellers or of being harassed, abused and assaulted by Travellers. However, allegations of this kind were always vague. No specific instances of violence or harassment by a Traveller against any member of the settled community was identified by councillors, local authority officials or residents' groups from 1963 to 1999 in Clare to support the various allegations which were made.[6]

Travellers in Clare lived under a microscope where any real or imaginary transgressions were subject to intense scrutiny. The general lack of evidence of Traveller violence against settled people did not prevent such allegations from acquiring the status of truth. Over the last two decades councillors have from time to time predicted outbreaks of violence.[7] In 2001, this took the form of warnings about the potential emergence of vigilante groups. In effect, the threat under discussion was often one of potential violence against Travellers that might transpire if Travellers were not excluded. The very presence of Travellers was portrayed as provoking anger.[8] In other words, Travellers constituted a danger to the social order because of the violence and hostility that they inspired in the dominant community.

MODERNISATION AND COLONISATION

A number of studies have emphasised the role of modernisation in the exclusion of Travellers.[9] In particular, accounts from an anthropological perspective emphasise their economic displacement from the rural economy from the 1950s and their transformation into urban poor.[10] This modernisation thesis draws upon accounts of, and justifications for, the displacement of less advanced societies by more advanced ones. In essence, it is a 'structuralist functionalist' thesis that posits that the social structures of societies converge as they become more advanced.[11] Convergence theorists imply that modern societies by virtue of their use of similar technologies will develop similar social structures and similar norms. In this context, social control and socialisation are understood as expressions of an underlying social consensus.

Deviance is understood in terms of distance from dominant norms. Groups out of step with or at a considerable 'social distance' from the dominant social consensus can be stigmatised as part of a process of social rationalisation. From this perspective, the expulsion of Travellers can be deemed reasonable.

MacLaughlin relates anti-Traveller racism to a hegemonic modernisation thesis that perceived a 'social-Darwinist' conception of social progress that hierarchically ranked societies according to their ways of utilising resources. Each 'stage' of the evolution of society was characterised by a different mode of production. The destruction of ineffective societies could be justified in the name of progress.[12] Specifically, he notes the institutionalisation of a form of social-Darwinist ideology in Irish society following the Famine that ideologically justified the displacement of the rural poor. Emigration can be understood as an aspect of the post-Famine rationalisation of Irish society. So too can the subsequent stigmatisation of 'out-groups' within the Irish nation such as Travellers. They did not become objects of state policies of assimilation until they had been displaced from the rural economy.

The general movement of Travellers to urban centres was part of broader demographic changes in Irish society. However, the urbanisation of Travellers rendered them extremely vulnerable to hostility from the dominant community as the spaces within Irish society for non-sedentary ways of life diminished.[13] In this context, Travellers were constructed as a social problem experienced by sedentary people. Assimilationist policies to address the Traveller problem emerged but, for the most part, assimilation was vigorously rejected. Residents' groups and local politicians vigorously sought to displace rather than settle Travellers.[14] This took the form of 'spontaneous and organised enmity' towards Travellers. As explained by Sienead Ni Shuinear:

> We need to look no further than our daily papers for examples of this: from the more dramatic manifestations like pickets, marches and mob attacks on Traveller camps, to the institutionalised harassment of evictions and the deliberate blocking off of and destruction of any and all possible camp sites by boulders (officially termed 'landscaping') to the *de facto* apartheid of barring Travellers from pubs, schools and dances on the (all too justified) grounds that their presence would lead to trouble.[15]

The terms of reference of the Commission on Itinerancy set up in 1960 were 'to promote their absorption into the general community' and 'pending such absorption, to reduce to a minimum the disadvantages to themselves and the community resulting from their itinerant habits'.[16] The problem was formulated as the problem of the existence of Travellers. Depictions of Travellers as a sub-culture of poverty predominated within official discourse until the 1990s when a degree of acceptance of their ethnic distinctiveness emerged alongside an emphasis on the role of discrimination in explaining intergenerational poverty amongst some Travellers.[17] By contrast with the modernisation convergence thesis, a conflict thesis of social order emphasises the exploitative nature of power relations. Dominant or hegemonic ideologies and norms are seen to maintain social inequalities.[18] From this perspective their displacement is explained in terms of class conflict and colonisation.

Present-day depictions of Travellers as an 'underclass', and a corresponding state emphasis on punitive policies of social control, strikingly resemble anti-Irish racism during the Victorian era, to the extent that racist discourses in both cases often seem interchangeable. Friedrich Engels, writing in 1844 in *The Condition of the Working Class in England*, described Irish immigration to Britain as the product of long centuries of colonial injustice. However, Engels also viewed the Irish firmly through the lens of colonial stereotypes. He depicted them as a danger to the English nation in viewing them as corruptors of the moral character of the English working classes. The Irish were 'rough, intemperate and improvident' and to blame for degrading the English working classes with their 'brutal habits'. For Engels, the solution was, where possible, to turn them into Englishmen:

> For work which requires long training or regular pertinacious application, the dissolute, unsteady drunken Irishman is on too low a place. To become a mechanic, a mill-hand, he would have to adopt the English civilisation, the English customs, become in the main, an Englishman . . . And even if the Irish, who have forced their way into other occupations, should become more civilised, enough of the old habits would cling to them to have a strong degrading influence on their English companions in toil, especially in view of the general effect of being surrounded by the Irish. For when, in almost every great city, a fifth or a quarter of the workers are Irish, or children of Irish parents, who have grown up amongst Irish filth, no one cannot wonder if the life, habits, intelligence, moral status – in short the whole character of the working-class – assimilates a great part of the Irish characteristics.[19]

A number of accounts of anti-Irish racism cite nineteenth-century depictions of the Irish as physically brutish and biologically inferior.[20] Engels, in common with Victorian 'race' thinking, oscillated between an environmental (and hence malleable) and a biological (and hence immutable) conception of the Irish character.[21] In the post-Famine era, the Irish in Britain were racialised as harbingers of crime and disorder. Such stereotypes predominantly drew on the poorest Irish immigrants absorbed into the urban 'underclass'. Irish 'ghettos' became a specific focus of police and media scrutiny and to some extent the Irish became over-represented in crime statistics and contemporary accounts of disorder.[22] These were also, to some extent, an aspect of a spatial politics of exclusion insofar as accommodation discrimination was frequent and remained common more than a century later.[23]

The social control of Travellers in modern Ireland can be seen to partly reflect an internalisation of colonial preoccupations with race and hygiene. Welfare and philanthropy debates in nineteenth-century Ireland were influenced by racialised stereotypes of the Irish poor. On the one hand, Irish philanthropy reflected determinist Victorian notions of the poor as a race apart. On the other hand, the social control of the Irish 'underclass' in Ireland was guided by dominant colonial ideals of social membership. Protestant and Catholic charities alike promoted the notion that the Irish poor were morally and intellectually inferior to such ideals.[24] Twentieth-century Catholic welfare institutions such as the Magdelene Laundries perpetuated mid-nineteenth-century Poor Law conceptions of the poor as immoral and indolent.[25]

MacLaughlin identifies two of the 'principal setbacks' encountered by displaced Travellers in Ireland in recent decades. Firstly he emphasises the rise of a virulent anti-Traveller racism characterised by violence and intimidation.[26] This is seen as a manifestation of their rejection by the dominant community. Generally this rejection is expressed in the use of stereotypes of Traveller deviance from contemporary social norms. One much-quoted 1996 article in the *Sunday Independent* erroneously claimed that Travellers were responsible for over 90 per cent of violent crimes against the rural elderly.[27] It employed stereotypes that evoked the most histrionic Victorian constructions of the poor as a 'race' apart:

> It is a life worse than the life of beasts, for beasts are at least guided by wholesome instinct. Traveller life is without the ennobling intellect of man and the steadying instinct of animals. This tinker 'culture' is without achievement, discipline, reason or intellectual ambition. It is a morass. And one of the surprising things about it is that not every individual bred in this swamp turns out bad. Some individuals amongst the tinkers find the will not to become evil.[28]

According to John O'Connell, anti-Traveller racism builds on 'fantasies related to dirt, danger, deviance and crime'. It invokes a pariah syndrome that is employed to legitimate prejudice and to deny that such prejudice is racism. Its central theme is a depiction of Traveller nomadism 'as an atavistic aberration which has to be eliminated by modernisation or failing that, coercion'.[29] Anti-Traveller racism can therefore be represented as the ideological expression of an increase in 'social distance' between the dominant community and Travellers over the last number of decades. Michael MacGreil concluded from attitudinal surveys undertaken in 1977 and 1988–89 that majority negative responses to questions about willingness to be friends with Travellers, to avoid them in social situations and to buy a house next door to Travellers, that Travellers had the status of a *lower caste* in Irish society. His findings indicated that a majority of Irish people were hostile to Travellers.[30] The findings of a 1999 survey indicate that this hostility has increased rather than diminished.[31]

Jim MacLaughlin argues that a second important set-back has been the gradual internalisation of feelings of social inferiority among Travellers themselves. 'Having been oppressed and demoralised for so long, a growing body of evidence suggests that many Travellers are beginning to internalise feelings of racial inferior[ity] and taking to alcohol abuse and petty crime as outlets for the frustration they experience in their day-to-day lives'.[32] Similar arguments have been made by other writers who seek to come to terms with the overwhelming negativity of stereotypes of Travellers:

> It is worth noting that settled perceptions of Travellers are so overpower-ingly negative that if the individual Traveller demonstrates that he or she clearly does not conform to the negative stereotypes, he or she is sud-denly redeemed from Traveller status: they become 'a former itinerant', a 'housed Traveller', 'a settled Traveller', 'of Traveller stock' or whatever.[33]

Frantz Fanon's argument that colonialism is predicated on the negation of the colonised subject, the notion that at every level the colonised subject is induced to reject his or her own culture and internalise the values of the colonial power, has previously been applied in analyses of anti-Irish racism.[34] According to this argument, colonisation is expressed through ideological stereotypes through which those experiencing colonisation recognise that; 's/he is an object of fear, an unpredictable and violent natural force, in the eyes of the colonist'.[35] Fanon's argument can similarly be applied to Travellers in Ireland. The choices for those experiencing colonisation are stark. They can opt for an identity created by the colonialist 'other' or internalise the pathological projections of the colonialist's fears and risk further alienation from their own experience.

FROM RACIST IDEOLOGIES TO VIOLENT ACTS

Stereotypes of the 'violent Irish' and the 'violent Traveller' have both served to ideologically justify assimilation and coercive social control measures. Assimilation implies an effort to subordinate groups perceived as deviant *within* the presumed civilisation of the dominant group. However, the coexis-tence of racism and xenophobia alongside assimilationist ideologies more often than not justifies the rejection and exclusion of groups deemed not to meet the criteria for admission into the dominant social order. In this context, the relationship between racist ideology and acts of coercion and violence needs to be explored.

The experiences of Travellers highlight a number of ways in which the rejection of outgroups can be attained. They have been the subject of acts of hate speech, acts of discrimination, acts of intimidation and acts of violence aimed at achieving spatial exclusion and a form of social 'apartheid'.[36] Gordon Allport identifies five categories of behaviour associated with the rejection of outgroups: (1) antilocution, or verbal rejection: the use of speech to articulate antagonism, (2) avoidance: withdrawal from the disliked, (3) discrimination: denial of treatment accorded to the dominant group, (4) physical attack: various forms of violence including intimidation, and (5) extermination. He argues that violence (the last two categories) is always the result of milder forms of rejection.[37] As he puts it; 'most barking (antilocution) does not lead to biting, yet there is never a bite without previous barking'.[38] According to Pierre-André Taguieff, this suggests that speech acts are always capable of engendering physical attack. Verbal rejection is not a substitute for violence but a potential cause of violence: 'the penchant for racist murder is present in each of us; the genocidal drive is natural in humanity, as it is already at work in prejudices (hate prejudices) which arise spontaneously in the world of humanity's common experience'.[39] The ever-present lure of violence then is something that must be consciously overcome. The question of the relationship between racism and violence has been central to academic debates on the causes of the Holocaust, of colonial genocide and, more recently, of ethnic cleansing.[40] Bauman, in the case of the former, offers a functionalist account of the relationship between racist ideology and racist violence that can be seen to explain the resort to violence in terms of a failure of actions within Allport's first three categories to achieve such ideological goals. If verbal rejection does not work, if withdrawal from the disliked is unfeasible and if discrimination does not secure their displacement then the lure of violence may beckon.

Travellers remain invisible in most academic histories of Ireland.[41] However, there are indications that a disproportionately high number of Travellers were murdered during the Irish civil war.[42] In 1940, the Minister of Justice noted that the *Gardai* (police) were under ongoing pressure at a community level to shift Travellers from their campsites.[43] Such intimidation has persisted to the present time. A history of anti-Traveller intimidation and violence in Clare can be identified from local media records. For example, there have been ongoing efforts by residents' groups and councillors to deprive Travellers of water and other basic amenities.[44] There have been some mob actions against Travellers. In 1985, a group of Travellers were surrounded by 'a crowd of about 100 drunk and aggressive locals chanting for blood'.[45] They attempted to burn a van containing six Travellers and then to push it into a river. A Traveller woman was chased by a group of twelve or thirteen people armed with sticks, planks and hurleys. She fell through a glass window, extracted herself from the glass and continued to flee. In 1986, a large crowd of about one hundred gathered outside the local authority house of a Traveller family chanting 'burn them out'.[46] Some councillors used the latter incident to argue that no local authority housing should be allocated to Travellers in future.[47]

The response of the *Gardai* in such cases was to arrest Travellers so as to placate mobs of settled people. The *Gardai* tended to view 'friction' between settled communities and Travellers as a problem to be addressed through the prosecution and criminalisation of Travellers.[48] In 1992, residents who lived near an unofficial halting site outside Shannon hired a mechanical digger to make it uninhabitable whilst many of its occupants were on a pilgrimage to Croagh Patrick. They physically prevented the Travellers from accessing the site on their return.[49]

Anti-Traveller racism was exploited by the main political parties in the run-up to the 2002 general election. One of the opposition parties, Fine Gael, introduced a Bill which sought to criminalise Travellers who halted on unofficial sites. This was endorsed by the government and became the Housing (Miscellaneous Provisions) Act (2002). It was passed with overwhelming cross-party majority. On 16 July 2002, the caravans of four Traveller families in Ennis were confiscated by the *Gardai*. Other seizures followed. Traveller families who lived on the roadsides in and around the town had been periodically brought to court by the local authorities. However, prior to the 2002 Act, prosecutions were generally overturned by the courts because the local authorities were deemed to have failed in their statutory obligations to provide accommodation under the Travellers (Housing Accommodation) Act (1997). The 2002 Act allowed Travellers to be evicted and to have their caravans seized even where their statutory accommodation entitlements had not been met. Objections to the 2002 Act by members of 'Citizen Traveller', a state-funded anti-racism body, led to the withdrawal of its government funding.[50] State intimidation arguably reflects political hostility towards Travellers.

At present, legal remedies to the politics of verbal rejection – what Allport describes as the use of speech to articulate antagonism – are weak. The Prohibition of Incitement to Hatred Act (1989) has had little or no impact on anti-Traveller racism. The Act made it an offence to incite hatred against any group of persons on account of their 'race, colour, nationality, religion, age, sexuality, ethnic or national origins, or membership of the Travelling Community'. Just one case relating to Travellers has been referred to the Director of Public Prosecutions (DPP). The case was acquitted. In September 2000, the Minister of Justice, Equality and Law Reform acknowledged that the Act was ineffective and stated that new legislation was necessary. The Act was ineffective, in part, because of the extensive burden of causal proof required to demonstrate that racist acts had been incited.[51]

Although the *Gardai* have begun to document allegations of racist assaults, they do not yet disaggregate these so that offences against Travellers are identifiable. There is some evidence that Travellers are subject to over-policing. Traveller and *Garda* respondents, in a recent study of the policing of Traveller wedding and funeral rituals, described the approach of the *Gardai* as 'heavy handed'. One Traveller respondent described how the *Gardai* 'establish roadblocks and prosecute a captive audience. They create an impression that everyone who is attending the funeral is a potential trouble maker'. Another described how *Gardai* used the occasion of rituals to 'target Travellers' vehicles for tax, insurance and tyre inspections and encouraged shop, café and pub owners to temporarily close their premises and as such endorse discrimination against Travellers'.[52] Indications of over-policing and undue criminalisation of Travellers, combined with an apparent lack of emphasis on them as potential victims of crime, suggests some commonalities to the forms of institutional bias revealed by the Macpherson inquiry into the London Metropolitan Police.[53] This identified the simultaneous criminalisation of black people and the under-protection of black communities from crime and racist violence. Again, some similarities with the past experiences of the criminalisation of the Irish in Britain can be noted.[54]

DISCRIMINATION AND VIOLENCE IN CLARE 2000–2002

In October 2001, a statement by an Ennis councillor, reported in the *Clare Champion* under the front page headline, 'Vigilante Uprising Against Travellers', provoked a degree of national controversy. As stated by the councillor:

> Vigilantes will be in this town in the near future. People out there are not prepared to put up with what is going on anymore. They are going to stand up. You are going to have people organising themselves against what is happening at the moment. They are going to get together to win back our town. They are going to fight back.[55]

To some extent the statement itself was typical of claims made by councillors in Ennis over the years that the presence of Travellers might provoke violence. The specific context of the statement was, as often before, a campaign to displace 'indigenous' Ennis Travellers with no access to an authorised site from an unauthorised one. The novel element here was the implied threat of vigilante action against Travellers. The vigilante claim was subsequently reiterated by the councillor in a media briefing organised to press for the removal of eight Traveller caravans from a housing estate in the town. On that occasion, a resident's spokesperson stated that 'we are law-abiding citizens but unless something happens soon we may be forced to take action'.[56] The threat emerged in a context where the courts and the *Gardai* were unable to evict the Travellers because the local authorities and local councillors had demonstrably failed to provide the Travellers with an alternative option.

The previous year, another councillor had claimed, again at an Urban District Council meeting, that vigilante groups could emerge in response to a growing drugs crisis in the county.[57] During the 1990s in some urban areas, there had been vigilante expulsions of suspected drugs dealers and users from their homes and a high-profile political debate on the issue. Populist protest against drugs users was, to a considerable extent, protest against perceived inaction by the *Gardai* and the government. Some forms of such anti-drug activism, such as punishment beatings, echoed paramilitary communitarianism against 'anti-social behaviour' in Northern Ireland and in themselves constituted a law-and-order problem. The response of the government was to instigate proactive police actions against suspected drugs dealers.[58] In May 2002, the Minister of Justice, Equality and Law Reform criticised the statements of the Ennis councillor about vigilantism and insisted that law and order is 'solely a matter for the *Gardai*'.[59] The vigilante discourse presented Travellers as perpetrators of anti-social behaviour which was not being addressed by the state. Typically anti-Traveller activists claimed that the *Gardai* 'did nothing'.[60] This behaviour was seen to legitimise a violent community response. Within the 'vigilante' discourse this violence could only be avoided if the government and the *Gardai* took action against Travellers. This generally took the form of prosecutions aimed at securing the eviction of Travellers from unauthorised halting sites. However, with the passing of the Travellers (Housing Accommodation) Act 1997, local authorities had a statutory duty to provide accommodation for Travellers and the courts were often unwilling to evict Travellers in the absence of designated halting sites or other accommodation options.[61]

In 2002, there were a total of 258 'indigenous' Travellers, including 101 children, living on unauthorised sites in Clare. These constituted over 40 per cent of the county's Traveller population. Clare had the joint highest proportion of unaccommodated Travellers in any county in the Republic of Ireland.[62] In April 2000, the High Court permitted the Gaelic Athletics Association (GAA) to evict a number of families who were halted outside the Cusack Park sports grounds in Ennis.[63] These families had been periodically displaced from one unauthorised site to another since 1997, when a large official halting site outside the town had been closed down. A number of these relocated, by necessity and as an act of protest, to two local authority office car parks. This time the courts rejected an application from the council to evict them 'because the council had no designated site'. An editorial in the *Clare Champion* noted that: 'nobody is likely to shed tears at the arrival of Traveller caravans outside the offices of Clare County Council in Ennis.' This, it noted, was an opportunity for councillors and officials to learn about the hardships experienced by Travellers : 'They can learn, for example, what it is like to sleep, eat, cook, wash and socialise in a confined space without running water or sanitary facilities . . . if they're really alert, they may even learn something important about human dignity from a group of human beings so marginalised that they are effectively ostracised from mainstream society.'[64]

The occupation had some impact on the accommodation crisis insofar as plans to identify official sites were stepped up.[65] One site for eight families was designated.[66] Contrary to the requests of Traveller representatives, these places were offered to incompatible families. Those selected were threatened with fines and imprisonment if they did not comply.[67] The council's response suggested that its principal aim was to respond to community demands that Travellers be moved. Many other families remained without access to legal accommodation in the town. The movement of some families onto a housing estate in the town precipitated the aforementioned threat of vigilante action. Other families moved onto the grounds of a school. These were described in a *Clare Champion* editorial as intimidating children.[68] An Ennis Chamber of Commerce statement referred to the 'deep anger and hurt that the settled people in Ennis feel'.[69] The school organised a protest march against the Travellers to the council offices.[70] Traveller representatives alleged that on one occasion a 'group of vigilantes' drove past the school and fired shots into the air and that on another there was a petrol bomb attack on a Traveller caravan elsewhere in the county.[71]

Anti-Traveller politics are by no means unique to Clare. A Dublin TD (member of parliament) with strong anti-Traveller credentials proposed what became the Housing (Miscellaneous Provisions) Act 2002.[72] The Act permitted local authorities to respond to political pressure from anti-Traveller groups insofar as evictions and other sanctions could be employed even when no official sites for Travellers were provided. Threats against law and order by settled people could be alleviated by the expulsion of Travellers. Following the first evictions in Ennis, the local Catholic Bishop allowed twelve caravans to relocate onto the grounds of his official residence. He described this as a response to the intimidation experienced by the Travellers. 'If somebody knocks at your door as someone did the other night – she has a child of two years old and is pregnant with another child and terrified that her caravan is going to be taken – one is put in a position where one has to respond in a Christian way.'[73] The Clare Traveller Support Group has argued that Travellers become vulnerable to violence because the unwillingness by local politicians to develop authorised sites exposed them to the hostility of residents' groups. It has also described an unwillingness by the local authorities to provide support for Travellers experiencing intimidation from neighbours.[74]

CONCLUSION

Intimidation and violence have historically played a central role in anti-Traveller racism in Ireland. It is argued that such racism is partly an ideological expression of an Irish nation-building project, dating from the late nineteenth century, that emerged, again partly, in opposition to colonialist constructions of the Irish as deviant, feckless and violent. Parallels have been identified between colonial anti-Irish racism and expressions of racism against black peoples.[75] Continuities can be seen between past anti-Irish racism and present day anti-Traveller racist discourse. Irish nation-building to some extent internalised colonial understandings of deviance and reflected a Victorian project of racial hygiene and social control that subjected Travellers to similar forms of racism to those experienced by Irish 'underclass' immigrants in nineteenth-century Britain. Both the Irish and Travellers were identified as dangerous uncivilised outgroups at odds with social modernisation, and were subjected to forms of colonisation and assimilation. Violence against Travellers in present-day Ireland and present-day versions of the 'violent Traveller' discourse are to some extent manifestations of the ideological modernisation of the dominant imagined community. This has resulted in racist politics grounded in a perceived irreconcilable social distance between both and in coercive state practices.

Present-day threats of violence against Travellers can be understood to some extent as part of a politics of exclusion aimed at expunging Traveller ways of life from Irish society. Traveller culture was constructed as increasingly at variance with dominant social norms as Irish society modernised. Since the 1960s, social policies have sought to achieve the assimilation of Travellers. These policies were problematic both in terms of meeting the needs of Travellers and in terms of political acceptability. A deepening hostility to unsettled Travellers over the last four decades has been accompanied by a growing unwillingness to designate sites for Travellers. Anti-Traveller politics have been predicated upon resistance to efforts to provide legal accommodation for Travellers and simultaneous efforts to displace Travellers with no access to such sites. The imposition of legislation in 1997 requiring local authorities to develop accommodation for Travellers and a resultant unwillingness of the courts to evict Travellers whose statutory entitlements were being ignored arguably deepened political hostility to Travellers. Similarly anti-discriminatory legislation introduced in 2000 also prompted anti-Traveller activism. In both cases this activism has been sufficient to undermine earlier progressive measures. The criminalisation of unofficial halting sites under the 2002 Act has, if anything, reduced the impetus to adhere to legislation requiring the development of Traveller accommodation. It has increased the vulnerability of Travellers to violence and harassment and has deepened the potential for institutional racism.

Allport viewed racist speech (verbal rejection) and discrimination as preconditions for racist violence and intimidation. In the case of Travellers, racist speech about violence (violent speech) is central to the articulation of prejudice and is central also to acts of intimidation. Violent speech functions, like any threat, as a negotiating tool. In this case what is sought is the expulsion of Travellers. Violence therefore serves modernisation goals of social rationalisation where assimilation and colonisation have failed. This points to the relevance of a functionalist thesis about the relationship between racism and violence. However, as Allport noted, prejudice fulfils both rational and irrational functions for its bearer.[76] So too do acts of violence and intimi-dation. Violence and intimidation need to be seen alongside discrimination and institutional racism as part of a larger repertoire of coercive mechanisms. Accusations of violence by Travellers, on the other hand, serve to legitimise goals of expulsion. The ideological stigmatisation and racialisation of out-groups is again part of the coercive repertoire. For these reasons, concerns about violence, as something to be consciously overcome, must be central to efforts to address racism in social policy.[77] This suggests the need for stronger legislation against incitement to hatred. However, such legislation does not in itself address the causes of such hatred or address the politics of exclusion perpetrated by it.

NOTES

1 Fianna Fail Councillor at a Waterford County Council meeting, *Sunday Independent*, 14 April 1996.
2 For example, headlines such as 'Patience Runs Thin When Uncivilised Travellers Spill Blood', *Sunday Independent*, 25 May 1997.
3 Notably the *Report of the Task Force on the Travelling People* (1995) which set the tone of an Irish state project of promoting the integration of Travellers into Irish society. The report was critical of past failed assimilationist policies. It made some 400 recommendations aimed at addressing inequalities and discrimination encountered by Travellers.
4 The campaign began in Westport County Mayo when publicans collectively decided to refuse to serve Travellers who had come to the area as tourists under-taking their annual pilgrimage to Croagh Patrick. It was endorsed by the Clare branch of the Vintner's Federation of Ireland. *Clare Champion*, 'Clare Publicans Defend Right to Refuse', 11 February 2000, p 3.
5 Fanning, Bryan, *Racism and Social Change in the Republic of Ireland*, 2002, pp 122–151, Manchester: Manchester University Press.
6 For example, allegations often focused on how elderly settled people or women at home during the day lived in 'a constant state of fear' of Travellers. These often combined with allegations that Travellers posed a threat to the health of settled people. Similarly allegations that Travellers deposited excrement on the doorsteps of vulnerable 'old people' were made from time to time. Fanning, Bryan, *op cit*, pp 131–132.
7 For example, *Clare Champion*, 12 November 1982 and 12 December 1997.
8 This could be seen in the headlines of *Clare Champion* newspaper articles. Examples include 'Fifteen Houses For Itinerants Amid Angry Objections by Residents', 'Itinerant Problem Heading for Explosive Situation', 'Outrage Over Plans for Halting Site' and 'Halting Site to Spark Residents' Revolt' illustrate the long-standing permissibility of hostility to Travellers in local politics. See *Clare Champion*, 14 July 1972, 26 June 1982, 1 March 1996 and 12 December 1997.
9 Gmelsh, George, *The Irish Tinkers: The Urbanisation of an Itinerant People*, 1985, Illinois: Waveland Press; MacLaughlin, Jim, 'Nation-building, Social Closure and Anti-Traveller Racism in Ireland', *Sociology*, 33.1 (1999), p 128.
10 Gmelsh, Sharon Bohn and Gmelsh, George, 'The Itinerant Settlement Movement: Its Policies and Effects on Irish Travellers', *Studies*, 63. 249 (1974), p 1.

11 Structural functionalist theories, derived from the sociology of Talcott Parsons, understand social order as the product of consensual social norms that serve a functional purpose. This implied that as society changed, the functional necessities for social order changed too. See Ritzer, George, *Sociological Theory*, New York: McGraw and Hill, 1992, pp 233–239, 271–274.

12 MacLaughlin, Jim, *Travellers and Ireland: Whose Country, Whose History?*, 1995, pp 24–25, Cork: Cork University Press,.

13 Fanning, *op cit*, p 51.

14 Fanning, *op cit*, p 117.

15 Ni Shuinear, Sinead, 'Irish Travellers, Ethnicity and the Origins Question' in McCann, May, Siochain, Seamus and Ruane, Joseph (eds) *Irish Travellers: Culture and Ethnicity Question*, 1994, p 50, Belfast: Institute of Irish Studies.

16 Commission on Itinerancy (1963) *Report of the Commission on Itinerancy*, Dublin: Official Publications.

17 McCarthy, Patricia (1994) 'The Sub-Culture of Poverty Reconsidered' in McCann, May, Siochain, Seamus and Ruane, Joseph (eds), *op cit*, p 122. Portrayals of Travellers as a sub-culture of poverty predominated in Irish academic literature until the 1980s. See for instance the main state policy document of that era, *The Report of the Travelling People Review Body*, 1983, Dublin: Official Publications.

18 Hall, Stuart, 'Gramsci's Relevance for the Study of Race and Ethnicity' *Journal of Communication Inquiry* (1986), 10 (2), pp 5–27.

19 Engels, Friedrich, *The Condition of the Working Class in England*, 1971 (first edition 1844), p 122, Oxford: Blackwell.

20 Perry, Curtis L., *Apes and Angels: the Irishman in Victorian Caricature*, 1971, p 21, Newton Abbot: David and Charles.

21 Howard, Kevin (2003) 'From Group to Category: The Emergence of the Irish in Britain as an Ethnic Minority', University College Dublin: Unpublished PhD Thesis, p 149.

22 Swift, Roger, 'The Irish in Britain' in O'Sullivan Patrick (ed.), *The Irish in the New Communities*, 1992, p 66, Leicester: Leicester University Press.

23 Hickman, Mary, *Religion, Class and Identity: The State, the Catholic Church and the Education of the Irish in Britain*, 1995, p 73, Aldershot: Avebury.

24 Preston, Margaret, 'Race and Class in the Language of Charity in Nineteenth Century Dublin' in Foley, Tadhg and Ryder, Seàn (eds) *Ideology and Ireland in the Nineteenth Century*, 1998, p 108, Dublin: Four Courts Press.

25 *Ibid*. As suggested by Preston; 'The training of women as laundresses might be considered as a metaphor for the spiritual and bodily cleansing of the poor'.

26 This he describes in the strongest possible terms; 'As a result of the emergence of what are little short of Ku-Klux-Klan-type delegations that are not adverse to employing the tactics of urban gangs, isolated Traveller families in many part of the country are now literally living in fear of their lives'. MacLaughlin, *Travellers and Ireland*, p 3.

27 See O'Connell John (2002), 'Travellers in Ireland: An Examination of Discrimination' in Lentin, Ronit and McVeigh, Robbie (eds) *Racism and Anti-Racism in Ireland*, p 54, Belfast: Beyond the Pale.

28 From an article entitled 'Time to Get Tough on Tinker Terror Culture' by Mary Ellen Synon, *Sunday Independent*, 28 January 1996.

29 O'Connell, *op cit*, p 58.

30 MacGreil Michael, *Prejudice and Tolerance Revisited*, 1996, pp 330, 447, Maynooth: Survey and Research Unit.

31 Citizen Traveller, *Information Pack*, 1999, Dublin: Citizen Traveller.

32 MacLaughlin, *op cit*, p 3.

33 Ni Shuinear, Sinead, *op cit*, p 50.
34 Fanon Frantz, *The Wretched of the Earth*, 1968 (*Les Damnés de la Terre*, 1961), p 42, New York: Grove Press; Greenslade, Liam, 'White Skin, White Masks' in O'Sullivan, Patrick (ed.), *The Irish in the New Communities*, 1992, p 213, Leicester: Leicester University Press.
35 Greenslade, Liam, *op cit*, pp 214–215.
36 Examples include segregation in the provision of social services, state benefits and segregation in schools. See National Consultative Committee on Racism and Interculturalism (2003) *Travellers in Ireland: An Examination of Discrimination and Racism*. www.nccri.com/travellr2.html.
37 Allport, Gordon W., *The Nature of Prejudice*, 1966, p 14, Cambridge, Mass: Addison-Wesley.
38 Allport, Gordon W., *op cit*, p 57.
39 Taguieff, Pierre André, *The Force of Prejudice: On Racism and Its Doubles*, 2001 (*La Force du préjugé*, 1988), p 327, Minnesota: University of Minnesota Press.
40 The functionalist school maintains that the 'final solution' of genocide emerged through a rational process of attempting and then discarding other means to exclude Jews from the Reich. Bauman describes Nazi efforts to get rid of the Jews in functionalist terms; whereby the 'final solution' emerged not as a considered choice made at the start by ideologically motivated leaders; 'It did, rather emerge, inch by inch, pointing at each stage to a different destination, shifting in response to ever-new crises, and pressed forward with a "we will cross that bridge once we come to it" philosophy'. See Bauman Zygmunt, *Modernity and the Holocaust*, 1989, p 15, New York: Cornell.
41 There is no mention of Travellers within published histories of Ireland save for mention, in a few cases, of the establishment of a *Commission on Itinerancy* in 1960.
42 Hart, in his study of violence in Cork between 1916 and 1923, found that disproportionately high numbers of Travellers and Protestants were murdered by the IRA. He confirmed that eight so-called 'tinkers or tramps' were killed as 'spies or informers' out of a total of 122 persons. He identified four further accounts of killings of tramps which could not be fully verified. The specific targeting of Protestant landowners and Travellers arguably suggests that a degree of ethnic cleansing occurred during the war of independence and the civil war. Hart, Peter, *The IRA and Its Enemies: Violence and Community in Cork 1916–1923*, 1998, p 304, Oxford: Oxford University Press.
43 Helleiner, Jane, *Irish Travellers: Racism and the Politics of Culture*, 2000, p 74, Toronto: University of Toronto Press.
44 See Fanning, Bryan, *op cit*, p133. By way of a recent example, on 16 June 2000 the *Clare Champion* published a letter from Travellers asking that the council provide temporary water, refuse collection facilities and temporary toilets 'which would ease many problems identified as concerns of residents'.
45 *Clare Champion*, 2 August 1985.
46 A *Garda* stated in court that he had begged and implored the crowd to go home. He asked one person in the crowd whom he knew to be a sensible man to get the people to go home. The man replied; 'no, let ye go home and we'll deal with them.' *Clare Champion*, 9 January 1987.
47 *Clare Champion*, 6 February 1987.
48 For example, *Clare Champion*, 13 November 1992.
49 *Clare Champion*, 13 November 1992.
50 An advertisement by *Citizen Traveller* described the 2002 Act as racist. The Minister of Justice, Equality and Law Reform announced an immediate review of the funding of the group which was subsequently disbanded.

51 Fanning, Bryan, *op cit*, p 188.
52 The views of Travellers about over-policing were endorsed by some senior *Garda* interviewees in the same study. O'Brien, F. (2002) 'What Are The Perspectives of Senior Police Managers and Members of the Traveller Community in the Context of Implementation of Traveller Rituals', Templemore: Garda Siochana College, unpublished.
53 MacPherson, William, *The Stephen Lawrence Inquiry: Report of an Inquiry by Sir William Macpherson of Cluny*, 1999, London: The Stationery Office.
54 A number of studies of nineteenth-century Britain discuss the targeting of the Irish by new police forces, disproportionate prosecutions and specific ordinances that criminalised the consumption of alcohol in Irish areas. See Hickman, Mary, *op cit*, p 78.
55 *Clare Champion*, 12 October 2001.
56 *Clare Champion*, 19 October 2001. 'Travellers Have Made Life Hell In Cloughleigh', 19 October 2001, p 1.
57 *Clare Champion*, 'Vigilante Threat For Clare Drug Dealers', 21 January 2001, p 1.
58 Notably operation Dochas. See statement by Minister of Justice, Equality and Law Reform, (21719/96) *Dail Eireann* vol 47.1.
59 *Clare Champion*, 'Minister Warns Against Vigilante Action', 5 February 2002.
60 *Clare Champion*, 'Traveller Accommodation Crisis Could Spark Racist Attacks', 10 March 2000, p 1.
61 *Clare Champion*, 'Judge Slams Council Over Traveller Accommodation', 22 September 2000, p 1.
62 *Clare Champion*, 'Council Rejects Traveller Accommodation Figures', 30 August 2002, p 1.
63 *Clare Champion*, 'High Court Moves in Traveller Accommodation Showdown', 7 April 2000.
64 *Clare Champion*, 'Travellers Move in on The Council', 14 April 2000.
65 *Clare Champion*, 'Council "Disgusted" by Presence of Travellers', 17 November 2000; *Clare Champion*, 'Travellers Force Councillors To Move', 21 April 2000; *Clare Champion* 'Council Unveil Emergency Halting Sites Behind Closed Doors', 28 April 2000.
66 *Clare Champion*, 'Breakthrough in Ennis Traveller Accommodation Crisis', 9 March 2001, p 1.
67 *Clare Champion*, 'Jail Threat Forces Traveller Movement', 1 March 2002, p 1.
68 *Clare Champion*, Editorial, 21 July 2001.
69 *Clare Champion*, 'Chamber Calls for Action on Halting Site', 21 September 2001.
70 *Clare Champion*, 'Children Protest Over School Halting Site', 19 October 2001.
71 *Clare Champion*, 'Petrol Bomb Attack on Travellers', 22 February 2002.
72 Fanning, Bryan, 'The Political Currency of Irish Racism: 1997–2002', *Studies*, 91, 364, (2002) pp 319–327, p 325.
73 *Clare Champion*, 'Bishop Calls For Action on Traveller Problem', 26 July 2002.
74 For instance, it cited the case of a family made homeless because of intimidation from neighbours being offered the same house that they had already vacated. They accused the council of ignoring allegations of intimidation. Now the family were 'staying in an inadequate leaking caravan outside Tesco's (supermarket) pending prosecution and eviction'. *Clare Champion*, 'Traveller Group Criticises Council', 9 June 2000.
75 Rolston, Bill, 'Bringing it all Back Home: Irish Emigration and Racism', *Race and Class*, 2003, vol. 45(2) 39–53, p 48.
76 Allport, *op cit*, p 12.
77 Taguieff, *op cit*, p 327.

Chapter 9

Hate speech made easy
The virtual demonisation of gays

Marguerite J. Moritz [1]

> *Rather than seeking to win adherence through superior reasoning, hate*
> *speech seeks to move an audience by creating a symbolic code for violence.*
> *Its goals are to inflame the emotions of followers, denigrate the designated*
> *out-class, inflict permanent and irreparable harm to the opposition, and*
> *ultimately conquer.* [2]

Prior to the advent of the Internet, anti-gay campaigns often focused on conventional delivery systems: newsletters, group mailings, church sermons and various other public relations efforts. As representations of gays and lesbians moved from the media margins to the mainstream, television became an important battleground. After decades of debates and struggle, gay characters are now regularly featured on American network and cable programming and gay issues are prominently covered in the news. To be sure, this remains a contentious issue, but mainstream American television in the twenty-first century is more respectful of gay people and their civil rights claims than it has ever been.

Archconservatives who want to deliver anti-gay rhetoric have an increasingly difficult time doing it even on cable television, where constraints are almost non-existent. The Reverend Jerry Falwell was widely denounced in 2001 when he used his television programme to accuse gays and lesbians (along with feminists and abortionists) of being at least partly responsible for the 9/11 terror attacks. [3] In 2003, NBC dismissed cable talk show host Michael Savage after the following exchange with a caller:

> Savage: You're one of those sodomites? Are you a sodomite? So you are one of the sodomites? You should only get AIDS and die you pig, how's that? (Exclamation by crew/camera people, who yell 'whoa') Why don't you see if you can sue me, you pig? You got nothing better than to put me down you piece of garbage? You got nothing to do today? Go eat a sausage and choke on it, get trichinosis. Do we have another nice caller who is busy and didn't have a nice night in the bathhouses and angry at

me today? Get me another one, put another sodomite on – I don't care about these bums, they mean nothing to me . . .

If speech as blatantly hateful as that is increasingly difficult to find on American television, it has not disappeared. Instead, efforts to demonise gays have found the more hospitable venue of the Internet. 'Hate groups use the Internet as a tool for self-organising and for recruiting new members. Debra Guzman, of the United States-based Human Rights Information Network, has said that the Internet is "a utopia for all kinds of hate groups, from new-Nazis to anarchists".'[4]

HATE SPEECH WEBSITES

The good news is that everything is on the Internet. The bad news is that everything is on the Internet.[5]

In the last decade, the Internet has emerged as a powerful new tool not only for spreading hate but also for mobilising a highly organised opposition movement. Indeed, the Internet provides a unique opportunity for linking huge numbers of individuals, for providing them with e-mail connections, contact information, prescribed protest letters and other resources, which are used to vilify gay people and fictionalised portrayals of them. Because the Internet in the United States is almost totally unregulated, it is also an easy place to publish without having to face legal restraints or the typical gatekeepers who oversee content in other mass mediated arenas.

The World Wide Web has allowed marginalised extremist groups with messages of hate to have a more visible and accessible public platform. Hate-based websites have grown dramatically in recent years. In 1995 at the time of the Oklahoma City bombing, there was only one hate site, but today the Simon Wiesenthal Center and the Anti-Defamation League have documented about 2,800 hate sites.[6]

The most prominent groups engaged in this activity are the Ku Klux Klan, the Nazis/neo-Nazis, Skinheads, and Christian Identity Movement. All are supremacist and target non-Whites, Jews, homosexuals, and the politically progressive. Many of these sites are directed explicitly at gays. They range in approach from extreme (godhatesfags.com, you'regoingtohell.com) to mainstream (American Family Association).

For example, as Katz and Rice note,

Hate groups also propagate their messages on the Internet. These include the Imperial Klans of America and stormfront.org [which] is apparently the first, and certainly the most popular, hate Web site. It boasts more than 5,000 daily visitors and several hundred daily visitors to its 'children's pages'.[7]

The Internet era has broadened the reach of hate speech with a whole array of technologies that were previously not readily available or not available at all, thus creating a world of unprecedented reach for messages that can be accomplished at relatively low costs. With equipment that is not only widely available but also easy to use, individuals and groups can become overnight publishers. And their materials are subject to very limited oversight.

The Internet's potential for harm has been addressed by Mary Robinson, the United Nations commissioner for human rights. At the 2001 International Forum on Combating Intolerance, she said that the Internet 'becomes, in the hands of some, a weapon of racism' disseminating 'messages of hate and prejudice' . . .[8]

According to Robinson, that such messages have the very potential to corrupt is something we must 'be alert to'.

REGULATION

The Internet networks provide global, free communication that becomes essential for everything. But the infrastructure of the networks can be owned, access to them can be controlled, and their uses can be biased, if not monopolized, by commercial, ideological, and political interests. As the Internet becomes the pervasive infrastructure of our lives, who owns and controls access to this infrastructure becomes an essential battle for freedom.[9]

Since the Internet came into prominence in the 1990s, there has been considerable debate in the United States over its regulation. In 1996, the US Congress passed the Communication Decency Act, which was aimed at barring indecent and obscene materials from distribution on the Internet. The federal courts, however, found portions of the law unconstitutional.[10] One critical point of disagreement was that Congress saw the Internet as being most like radio and television and thus, they argued, words and images on the Internet could be regulated, as courts allow broadcasting to be regulated. The courts, however, saw the Internet as another form of printed material and thus they called for full protection of Internet expression under the First Amendment to the US Constitution.[11]

Researchers Sharkey and Meyer point out that legally, 'Americans [have] the right to hate anyone, and to express their anger on the Internet and elsewhere – as long as it does not lead to criminal activity.' So-called fighting words, which could by their very expression incite immediate violence, are illegal.[12] But, since a 'listener at some remote computer terminal is not likely to be provoked into imminent lawlessness upon reception of a hate message, as opposed to a face-to-face confrontation', they argue that hate speech on the Internet 'cannot be silenced'.[13]

Because Internet messages cross national borders with ease, this legal position has put the USA in direct conflict with many other nations which typically do try to control hate speech in cyberspace. In France, Germany, Sweden and Canada, racist hate messages are considered crimes, and websites that engage in such expressions are shut down.

> . . . human rights activists worldwide argue that the United States should be bound by the International Convention on the Elimination of All Forms of Racial Discrimination, to which the United States is a signatory. ICEDR makes hate expression a crime under international law. For better or worse, American standards seem to determine what is internationally acceptable, as it is easy for anyone to post a Web page in the United States. By default America seems to set the 'civility' standard.[14]

By now, hate sites have become a common space for the expression of hostilities that cannot be easily advanced in more controlled cultural spaces. Additionally, they have become effective recruiting tools that attract neo-Nazis, skinheads, survivalists, armed militias, Ku Klux Klan, Holocaust deniers, and many others. While Constitutional protections have made this possible so far, the question is far from settled.

> Cyberhate regulation is an increasingly noticeable issue for the courts even though prevailing First Amendment dogma maintains that speech may not be penalised merely because its content is racist, sexist or basically abhorrent. Internet policy is a dynamic realm not completely integrated into the American regulatory and legal system. Consequently, many questions remain about how traditional law should apply to this new medium.[15]

DOUBLE STANDARDS

The use of visceral words and images to enhance the message of hate continues to be a powerful tool of expression that in some cases can be marketed and made palatable to a mainstream audience, and in others is relegated to a narrower group whose more radical views are bolstered by these aggressive messages of hate. The godhatesfags.com website is a prominent case in point. For six years, the Gay and Lesbian Alliance Against Defamation (GLAAD) has argued against what it calls the 'arbitrary and inconsistent policy toward the use of hate language in domain names.'[16]

When GLAAD's Interactive Media Director Loren Javier investigated the standards employed in its naming policies, he was initially told that the Internet Service Provider InterNIC makes no political judgments and engages in no censorship, other than screening names for the so-called 'seven dirty words' listed by the US Federal Communication Commission (FCC). To test the policy, a GLAAD member attempted to register the domain name nigger.com. InterNIC denied the request and issued the following statement: 'Network Solutions has a right founded in the First Amendment to the U.S. Constitution to refuse to register, and thereby publish on the Internet, registry of domain names [containing] words that it deems to be inappropriate.'[17]

By allowing a domain name that is as patently offensive as godhatesfags .com when clearly this name could be barred, InterNIC perpetuates on the Internet a double standard that has been noted repeatedly in a variety of mass media venues. While the public expression 'of blatantly derogatory language against minority groups in our newscasts, classrooms or places of worship rarely is tolerated, the minority groups in question often do not include gays'.[18] In other words, anti-gay commentary remains acceptable in public discourse. In a 1999 survey of newspaper treatment of gay issues, the American Society of Newspaper Editors concluded that anti-gay speech remains the 'last acceptable basis for discrimination among so-called acceptable Americans, including editors'.[19]

RHETORICAL STRATEGIES

Today, as was noted above in the Savage incident, such starkly derogatory language is increasingly seen as problematic. While the more spectacular incidents do command media attention, they can easily be dismissed as over the top and fanatical. The hate.com website argues that the mass media typically ignore the most blatant sites, even though the sites are playing a role in fomenting crimes such as the massacre at Columbine High School, the mid-west shooting spree of Benjamin Smith, and other murders, bombings and robberies. The established media have also largely ignored the threats and armed plans of the extreme right, openly advocated on the Internet, for a 'Holy War' against what they call the 'mud races' (hate.com website).

Sites that convey messages of hate and exclusion in more subtle ways have the advantage of being 'naturalised, credentialed and hidden in everyday discourse'.[20] Consequently, many anti-gay groups are wrapping their messages in more acceptable rhetorical packages, starting with their own names, which include The American Family Association, Concerned Women for America, Focus on the Family, The Family Research Council, and Traditional

Values Coalition. They have similarly unremarkable domain names such as AFA.net.

> As routine expressions of hate are pushed out of public discourse they reemerge in more subtle and less newsworthy ways. Yet their impact remains significant and common attitudes toward hate are complicit in a marginalisation of hate – in the United States and elsewhere.[21]

The rhetoric of hate speech has a relatively long history; the dominant rhetorical strategies used in anti-gay messages on the Internet have much in common with messages delivered in print, on radio and televised media. They include the use of so-called 'expert' testimony from individuals identified as doctors, authors, pastors and educators as well as the creation of seemingly credible think tanks and associations. But, as closer examination makes clear, these experts and associations have been widely discredited in other venues, despite the implied authority they project.

The positions espoused by the American Family Association, for example, have frequently been cited in print without any qualification or identification. For readers unfamiliar with the group, just the name itself carries a great deal of credibility, reminiscent as it is of a government entity or a major US corporation – examples such as the Federal Bureau of Investigation (FBI), the Federal Aviation Association (FAA), the American Broadcasting Company (ABC) or National Broadcasting Company (NBC) come to mind. Thus in its very name, the AFA seeks to position itself as credible and mainstream. Its rhetorical naming strategy is precisely the opposite of the blatant offensiveness found in godhatesfags.com.

AFA as an organisation and as a website is far more subtle and more well read. Its sophisticated messages serve as a reminder that 'hate can be cloaked in civility . . . language does not have to be visceral to inflict harm'.[22] If you knew nothing of the organisation and its causes, you might very likely expect it to be a think tank, perhaps governmentally funded, where professionals including psychologists, family therapists, and other researchers study and write on family issues. In addition, the writing on the AFA website is direct, clear and sounds authoritative. The AFA website does not quote hellfire and brimstone passages from the Bible, nor does it refer to homosexuals as fags. Their language choices are acceptable for public discourse and their writers often invoke 'scientific evidence' to support their claims.

A typical example of the AFA website message was posted in July 2003. It is a report (available in text and audio formats) written by Stephen Bennett, entitled 'CBS Television Markets Gay Marriage to America'. The website identifies Mr Bennett as an evangelist whose music is frequently heard on Christian radio stations. In the report, Mr Bennett describes being interviewed for the network's 'Sunday Morning' programme, which was producing a news report on gay marriage. Mr Bennett's writing combines the dual themes that the AFA has pushed for more than a decade: that reparative therapy can 'cure' homosexuality, and that the mass media are involved in a vast conspiracy to promote a pro-gay agenda.

Mr Bennett begins his report by identifying himself as a former gay, a person who successfully stopped being a homosexual and went on to have a happy marriage that is now in its tenth year.

> We told the interviewer how I lived the 'gay' lifestyle for over eleven years, sexually active with over 100 male partners – many of whom are dead today from AIDS. We shared how I walked away from it all in 1992 – never to return to my dysfunctional past again – and how I no longer struggle with homosexuality whatsoever . . . No one is born gay . . . [it's] a behavior that can and should be permanently changed. We appropriately compared the lifestyle to that of drug addiction and alcoholism.[23]

Mr Bennett goes on to say that when it aired, the CBS report was 'nothing more than an infomercial for gay marriage'. Instead of reporting that he had undergone a successful conversion, the story made reference to his Christian affiliations. The network 'tried to make people of faith who oppose homosexuality look like "religious bigots" and "homophobes" to suit their one-sided story.'[24]

Long before they took their messages to a website, AFA and a host of other fundamentalist Christian groups were arguing that mass media do not 'tell the public the truth about gay and lesbian life and politics.' Instead they are 'trying to put out a message that these are a group of loving, caring people.'[25]

The Bennett essay is very much in line with this theme, positioning CBS as part of the 'secular media', which routinely lie to the public about gays. Included in those lies is the notion that gays cannot change their sexual orientation through sheer willpower or through reparative therapy. The essay concludes with the e-mail address for the CBS program and urges readers to write to CBS with their complaints.

What the website does not provide is a full discussion of the reparative therapy debate and an accounting of the research data about it. Much of the research data that supports reparative therapy as useful and successful was generated by Joseph Nicolosi, who is typically identified as a PhD and author of 'Reparative Therapy of Male Homosexuals.' His long-standing connections to the far right are typically not mentioned. Nor is it pointed out that many of the studies Nicolosi conducted have been discredited for lack of scientific rigour. In fact, reparative therapy has been the subject of writing and research by a number of credentialled people and 'has been similarly discounted by the vast majority of psychologists and psychiatrists and officially rejected by the American Psychological Association' for years.[26]

DISTRIBUTION STRATEGIES

The Internet is a powerful forum of communication with its broad reach, interactivity and multi-media capability to disseminate information. The Web is providing an unprecedented vehicle for forging communities and making communication quicker, easier and cheaper.[27]

While anti-gay sites employ a range of rhetorical strategies to create their messages, they typically use the same technological strategies to disseminate them. Included in today's technological arsenal are audio and video capabilities, which permit the re-broadcast and re-distribution of moving and still images, speeches, interviews and recordings. Resistance Records, for example, 'contains graphics, downloadable white power music and a message from its founder describing the state of crisis in the White world' and is a prominent example of the technical sophistication many of these websites display.[28]

Once these resources are put on line, they can be accessed by journalists, researchers, writers, and producers – any of whom may be in a position to further the distribution process, and more importantly, to seemingly certify the validity of the information simply by appropriating it for incorporation into more mainstream discourse. This kind of re-distribution in anti-gay materials was problematic before the advent of the Internet and is even more so in the Internet era.

You have a lot of stuff getting into the paper and on TV from extremist bigots, and it goes unchallenged . . . Somebody will say, 'Eighty-five percent of homosexuals are pedophiles' and because this is a quote it gets in unchallenged, simply because the editor in charge has no idea whether that's real or not.[29]

Sites are used to promote events and solicit financial support. Online event ticketing is just one example of how this is being done. At the same time, list subscribers are solicited to picket events, boycott programmes, disrupt meetings, demean and defame anyone who is speaking on behalf of gay rights. The website godhatesfags.com, for example, has links to gay events around the country with instructions on how and why to picket them. It has excerpts from radio programmes where its founder, the Reverend Fred Phelps, has been interviewed. It links to a variety of Biblical quotations that ostensibly demonstrate that 'god hates fags'. It links to various statistics on AIDS at the Center for Disease Control. The Concerned Women of America website has an eleven-point programme of action it advises its readers to take, as well as links, phone numbers and mailing addresses for a variety of Christian ministries where financial donations can be made.

The development of what GLAAD calls 'one-click' activism is a common tool by now and in wide use by both anti-gay and pro-gay groups, as are message boards and chat rooms. Typically, a model letter is posted on a site and list recipients are called upon to send the letter to some person in power – the president, the mayor, the newspaper editor, the book publisher or the local pastor. With no more effort than it takes to hit the send key, these electronic protest letters can then be used as a pressure tactic and further cited as evidence of how the public at large is opposed to any number of gay rights issues. But, in addition, there are more graphic sites that go well beyond the bounds of being anti-gay: they advocate violence and they urge action that incites readers to physical retribution.

> The conditions that create a receptive audience for hate speech – ignorance, inequity and fear – comprise the problem. To address these is much more difficult than simply attempting to silence the voices that remind us, by example, that the problem exists. Suppressing hate speech is suppressing or masking the symptoms rather than treating the cause. Hate speech exists because people find it relevant; such speech is relevant: it articulates and typifies the felt condition of people's lives . . . it must be allowed and listened to and admitted as a form of public discourse. We should not try to expunge it but should instead ask why it exists and examine critically what is really being said and why. This is difficult and problematic and valuable.[30]

NOTES

1 Professor and UNESCO Chair in International Journalism Education in the School of Journalism and Mass Communication at the University of Colorado at Boulder. May Farrah, MA, formerly a doctoral candidate in the School of Journalism and Mass Communication, assisted in the research for this article.
2 R.K. Whillock, 'The Use of Hate as a Stratagem for Achieving Political and Social Goals', in R.K. Whillock and David Slayden eds, *Hate Speech*, 1995, p 32, Thousand Oaks: Sage Publications.
3 On 13 September 2001, the Rev. Jerry Falwell addressed the home audience of his television broadcast of The 700 Club, saying: 'I really believe that the pagans, and the abortionists, and the feminists, and the gays and lesbians who are actively trying to make that an alternative lifestyle, the ACLU, People for the American Way – all of them who have tried to secularize America – I point the finger in their face and say, "You helped this happen".' During a subsequent live interview on Good Morning America, host Diane Sawyer, replayed the 700 Club videotape and excoriated Falwell for the remarks. At first, he attempted to argue that his state-ment had been taken out of context. 'Tell me', she demanded, 'any conceivable context that would redeem those words.' As Falwell stumbled, the outraged Ms Sawyer said she wondered if he wanted to create an American Taliban, adding that his claim of being misread by the media 'defies credulity'. Similarly, the *New York Times* wondered if the so-called Culture Wars were one more thing that would never again be the same.
4 J.E. Katz and R.E. Rice, *Social Consequence of Internet Use: Access, Involvement,*

and Interaction, 2002, p 117, Cambridge: Massachusetts Institute of Technology Press.

5 R. Wachbroit, 'Reliance and Reliability: The Problem of Information on the Internet', in V. Gehring ed., *The Internet in Public Life*, 2004, p 29, Maryland: Rowman & Littlefield Publishers.

6 L. Leets, 'Responses to Internet Hate Sites: Is Speech Too Free in Cyberspace?', in *Communication Law and Policy* 6 (2001), 2, pp 287–8.

7 Katz and Rice, *op cit* p 313.

8 Katz and Rice, *op cit* p 314.

9 M. Castells, *The Internet Galaxy: Reflections on the Internet, Business, and Society*, 2001, p 277, Oxford: Oxford University Press.

10 *Reno v. ACLU*, 521 U.S. 844 (1997).

11 Leets, *op cit* p 295.

12 *Brandenburg v. Ohio*, 395 U.S. 444 (1969).

13 Stephen Sharkey and Howard Meyer, *The Proliferation of Hate Speech on the Internet* (1997). Online at: http://law.buffalo.edu/Academics/courses/629/computer _law_policy_articles/CompLawPapers/sharkey.htm.

14 Leets, *op cit* pp 295–6.

15 Leets, *op cit* pp 288–9.

16 Gay and Lesbian Alliance Against Defamation (GLAAD), News release, 18 April, 1997.

17 *Ibid*

18 R.K. Whillock and David Slayden eds, *Hate Speech*, 1995, p xi, Thousand Oaks: Sage Publications.

19 L.F. Aarons, 'Alternatives: Gays and Lesbians in the Newsroom', *Newspaper Research Journal*, 11 (1990) 40.

20 Whillock and Slayden, *op cit*, p xi.

21 *Ibid*

22 T.A. Van Dijk, 'Elite Discourse and the Reproduction of Racism', in Whillock and Slayden, *op cit*, p 2.

23 'CBS Television Markets Gay Marriage to America', http://www.afa.net/ homosexual_agenda/GetArticle.asp?id=96.

24 *Ibid*

25 M.J. Moritz, 'The Gay Agenda: Marketing Hate Speech to Mainstream Media,' in Whillock and Slayden, *op cit*, p 73.

26 *Ibid*

27 Leets, *op cit* p 288.

28 Sharkey and Mayer, *op cit* p 2.

29 P. Freiberg, 'Gays and the Media,' *Washington Blade*, 24 (1993), p 57.

30 Whillock and Slayden, *op cit* p xv.

Chapter 10

Challenging the offence and reclaiming the offensive

The gay and lesbian movement in the United States and online homophobic speech [1]

Guillaume Marche

INTRODUCTION

Not all countries deal with hate speech in the same way. In France for instance, an 1881 law on the freedom of the press makes it a crime to publicly use speech encouraging hatred against members of any specific racial group.[2] The European Union likewise issued in 1989 and amended in 1997 a directive entitled 'Television without Borders', which makes it mandatory for member states to 'ensure that broadcasts do not contain any incitement to hatred on grounds of race, sex, religion or nationality'.[3] The original directive was in turn enacted into French law.[4] In the United States on the contrary, victims of hate speech refrain from struggling to have it silenced. Lesbian, gay, bisexual and transgender (LGBT) organisations and leaders in particular almost unanimously consider that anti-homosexual hate speech is only to be opposed with more speech. This chapter purports to examine the causes and implications of this quasi-consensus from the angle of social movement analysis. Do the French and American approaches for instance differ mainly as a matter of cultural idiosyncrasies? Free speech indeed has dissimilar values in American and French cultures, while hate speech does not assume the same historical significance in either culture. Or does it point to something more significant in terms of the mobilisation of gay and lesbian identities in social movement – namely: is it a sign of weakness and submission to an unfavourable power dynamic, in which case it amounts to an expedient for lack of better political opportunities? Or does it on the contrary allow for a more offensive articulation of LGBT identity in public space? Online homophobic hate speech and gay and lesbian responses to it thus raise important questions about the definition of public and private spheres, and about individual and collective action in virtual space.

IDENTIFYING THE PROBLEM

Various types of homophobic hate speech are to be encountered on the Internet, the most blatant, though not the most frequent of which is on websites specifically dedicated to spreading anti-homosexual messages, such as http://www.godhatesfags.com, operated by Ben Phelps, the son of Reverend Fred Phelps of the ultra-conservative Westboro Baptist Church (WBC) in Kansas. The Internet also contains conservative – mainly religious – websites which condemn homosexuality as a part of their more general agenda. Such are the sites of the American Family Association (AFA) and of the Family Research Council (FRC), which characteristically represent homosexuality as a voluntary sin and the LGBT movement as a plot to destroy the American family.[5] In particular, LGBT activists are accused of provoking confused heterosexuals into bullying them, and of over-reporting homophobic hate crimes in order to gain 'special rights'[6] – which implies *they* are the real culprits of their own victimisation, while the actual perpetrators are presented as victims.[7]

The AFA and FRC's websites display less blatant occurrences of homophobic speech than WBC, but, because they are more subtle, they are in fact more likely to convince undecided Internet browsers: this is especially true of the FRC, which uses a rhetoric similar to that of the AFA but with a scientific angle to it. Whether this amounts to hate speech is debatable, as there are no explicit encouragements to assault homosexuals, for instance; but these sites do publish forged truths, which *is* hate speech insofar as they make a case against LGBT rights, based on such false premises as stereotypes, misconceptions, or outright lies.

The Internet is also replete with forums where individuals happen to express homophobic views: Web-ministry for instance is a religious forum whose webmasters launch topics to which people respond. The forum gives vent to a wide array of sentiments on homosexuality, from the critical but benevolent[8] to the most aggressive.[9] Many posters typically stigmatise the LGBT movement as being out to destroy American society in order to gain special rights for homosexuals,[10] while others preach hating the sin without hating the sinner and commit themselves to helping homosexuals 'revert' to the correct sexual orientation – which, they claim, is the only true way of loving homosexuals.[11] The discourse on this forum is less subtle than that of the FRC, even than the discourse of the AFA, since its moral condemnation of homosexuality is blunter and resorts to simplistic, repressive language, carefully avoided by the promoters of the AFA's site. It is the webmaster, and not even one of the most radical posters, who pens the following equation: 'Adultery = Child Molesters = Homosexuality = Bestiality'.[12] But the general agenda is the same, namely to marginalise the LGBT movement by claiming religious, moral and political legitimacy to articulate the public discourse about homosexuality.

But homophobic hate speech is also to be encountered on forums whose primary focus has nothing to do with religion or morality. Such examples may be found in a discussion thread from the Law discussion board of the Princeton Review forum, a student online forum operated out of Princeton University, on which students from all over the country post messages. While explicitly claiming not to be prejudiced, some posters for instance portray gay men as oversexed, and subsume homosexuality to such sexual acts as anal intercourse, which are frequently regarded as repulsive or abnormal – even as they are by no means characteristic of homosexuality, or even of male homo-sexuality.[13] Others either explicitly resort to offensive language,[14] or make ambiguous statements in which it is unclear whether they adhere to the wide-spread condemnations of homosexuality – for instance as 'abnormal and freakish' – which they cite.[15] Such statements certainly amount to an even subtler form of misrepresentation of homosexuality than even on the FRC's website, but they nonetheless portray homosexuality in an offensive and inaccurate way, which tends to deny LGBT people any legitimacy as full-fledged participants in American society. It also condones – if not sanctions – hostility toward them, and such rhetoric does participate in the perpetuation of their oppression.

ASSESSING THE PROBLEM'S SERIOUSNESS

Online hate speech is generally considered to be harmful insofar as it harasses stigmatised readers[16] and it is likely to generate actual violence in 'physical space' against the outsiders' group.[17] Some analysts argue that hate speech may be cathartic.[18] This may appear all the truer as online hate speech is generally anonymous. People assume fake identities so that they can get away with expressing hateful views and thus release aggressiveness which could otherwise result in actual violence. But the Internet is also a way for extremist groups to recruit[19] by offering such services as music and video-games, which are particularly appealing to youths.[20]

Nevertheless analysts' views as to whether online hate speech should be silenced are not merely a function of how serious a problem they consider it to be. There are three main types of stances on the issue. Free speech absolutists – also referred to as civil libertarians[21] – invoke John Stuart Mill to argue in favour of a 'free market of ideas', in which citizens should be able to engage in 'free trade of ideas', so that the generally accepted truth may emerge from competition between adverse views.[22] It should be noted that Mill's own view regarding freedom of speech is actually more subtle than free speech absolutists' claims, as his whole-hearted defence of freedom of opin-ion in *On Liberty* is followed with an at-length examination of the conditions under which freedom of action may be curbed: 'No one pretends that actions should be as free as opinions. On the contrary, even opinions lose their immunity, when the circumstances in which they are expressed are such as to constitute in their expression a positive instigation to some mischievous act.'[23] The champion of freedom of opinion thus considers speech and acts to be on a continuum, whereas free speech absolutists in the United States tend to regard the two categories as utterly distinct. The American Civil Liberties Union (ACLU), for example, resorts to legal action to defend free speech unconditionally, and famously once stood in favour of the right of a Nazi group to speak in public, arguing that one may not demand the silencing of Nazis while advocating the free expression of oppressed minorities.[24]

Civil rights adherents, such as philosophers Richard Delgado, Mari Matsuda, Charles Lawrence,[25] and the Anti-Defamation League (ADL),[26] hold a context-dependent, rather than universalistic, definition of rights: whereas free speech absolutists stand for the right of the minority to be free from the tyranny of the majority in expressing contentious views, *they* claim that the minority whose rights are in jeopardy nowadays are not hate groups, but the victims of hate speech.[27] This calls for focusing on the victim's point of view[28] and prohibiting hate speech because it does not express an opinion and is devoid of social merit or utility.

Accommodationists, such as philosophers David McGowan and Ragesh Tangri, Sean SeLeague, Kent Greenwalt, Thomas Grey,[29] and the American Library Association (ALA)[30] claim that – even within Mill's theory of a free market of ideas – there is room for *some* control of speech. Whereas in Mill's days limitations to free speech resulted from government tyranny, a utilitarian approach nowadays should also focus on the social harmfulness of hate speech: in other words, in the United States liberty is to be balanced against equality, and First Amendment protections against Fourteenth Amendment protections.[31] In their view, the ideal of free individual expression must be accommodated with the pragmatic requirement of dealing with potentially harmful situations, which under specific circumstances may validate content-based limitations to hate speech, a liberal – rather than libertarian – view in the Rawlsian sense.[32]

Nevertheless two main problems are raised by analysing the issue of online homophobic hate speech in these terms only. These three categories indeed do not quite subsume the extent of the issue from the point of view of social movement analysis, as they emphasise the institutional side of the question – whether or not to litigate, or legislate – rather than the necessity of mobilisation. The Gay and Lesbian Alliance Against Defamation (GLAAD), for instance, technically adheres to a civil libertarian philosophy and does not seek *government* control of online speech at all, but does take action to curb hate speech in cyberspace and elsewhere. GLAAD actively campaigned for three years to have Laura Schlessinger's 'Dr. Laura' television show removed from the air, as the host used her credentials to hold pseudo-scientific – in fact moralistic – rhetoric about homosexuality, and advocated the same kind of dangerous 'conversion therapy' as do the AFA and the FRC.[33] And when, in March 2001, the show was cancelled GLAAD applauded.[34]

Besides, a lot, if not most, of the online speech which is actually detrimental to individual gay lives or collective gay rights would not legally qualify as hate speech, since it does not consist in explicit calls to physical violence.[35] That does not mean however that the LGBT movement fails to consider it as a problem which needs to be addressed; and just because one decides not to seek government control of online speech does not mean that one unquestioningly subscribes to a 'free market of ideas' conception of public debate. The above-mentioned three categories therefore fail to account for alternative ways of dealing with hate speech, especially homophobic hate speech and especially online homophobic hate speech.

MOBILISING AGAINST HATE SPEECH

Generally speaking, LGBT movement organisations adhere to what in the United States is the mainstream response to hate speech, and fight it with 'more speech'. But they do so for two main reasons of their own, the first of which being that LGBT people's own freedom of expression is curtailed. Because '[t]he protests of *sex/gender outsiders* to [unfair treatment] are typically dismissed as ungrounded, self-serving, histrionic, insincere, flaunting or inflammatory',[36] Martha Zingo writes, they cannot afford to try to silence their opponents: as silencing is what *they* are threatened with, such a strategy would infallibly backfire,[37] so that 'even when it reaches, or intensifies to, the level of hateful, debilitating "spirit murder", [hate speech] cannot be prohibited for fear of the even greater risk of repression against lesbians, gay men, bisexuals and transgenderists.'[38]

The Internet is furthermore a locus where the availability of positive material about homosexuality is currently at stake. The Children's Internet Protection Act (CIPA) of 2000 requires federally subsidised libraries to adopt strict acceptable use policies (AUPs) and filtering software, whose overbroad screening of key-words disproportionately blocks sympathetic and neutral accounts of homosexuality.[39] Monitoring online speech restricts LGBT people's own expression in less obvious ways, too. In 1999, it was found out that America On Line (AOL), the largest Internet service provider (ISP) in the United States, denied service to its users whose individual profile included language which was deemed offensive – such as 'submissive bottom' – even as forums hosted by AOL were replete with anti-gay and racist epithets, and members whose profiles included homophobic slurs were not frowned at.[40] Several LGBT organisations, such as the ACLU, NationalGayLobby.org, and Hate Watch took action to protest against AOL, for instance by holding a demonstration in San Francisco, and to negotiate with the company so that the biased enforcement of its terms of service should be corrected.[41]

Negotiating with the companies which operate the Internet also involves getting search engines to adopt anti-hate speech policies.[42] For instance, this author's recent Yahoo and Google web searches with 'hate fags' or 'bash gays' as key words yielded predominantly anti-hate and anti-bashing results. Negotiating can also be more informal. Will Doherty is an executive director with the Online Policy Group, an organisation dedicated to promoting disenfranchised people's equal access to, and fair treatment on, the Internet. He once accidentally came across a skateboarding website with an advertisement for skateboarding equipment which used a famous skateboarder, Ed Templeton. It consisted in a video game where the sportsman was featured with a bubble above his head saying 'I'm a fag' and one was expected to shoot at him so that blood would squirt out of his body. Will Doherty sent the skateboarder an email asking him what he really thought about the homophobic implications of the animation. The latter responded that it was to be understood neither as a homophobic slur, nor as a vindication of his sexual orientation, but simply as a joke. He however did understand that it could offend people, so he would have it removed. When Will Doherty later realised that the author of the animation had it posted on another website, he reached Ed Templeton again to have the animation permanently removed from the other website.[43] This case may seem anecdotal, but a significant result was thereby achieved in that, not only was that particular animation removed, but Ed Templeton grew likely to be more alert to the implications of the use of his image in public discourse in the future, because he was made to see things from a perspective other than his own, which is tantamount to a process of recognition.[44]

The second reason why LGBT organisations generally agree to fighting hate speech with more speech is due to the specific nature of the online medium, as pointed out by the example above: the Internet differs from the mass media in that it allows for individualised response, hence it is not one-directional, like television in particular. The Internet does not broadcast, but *carries* messages so that the receiving end is a potential publisher of opposite views: it is not a 'one-to-many' medium, as Michael Jaffe puts it, like the traditional mass media, but a 'many-on-many' medium, hence a public medium.[45] This is a crucial distinction for LGBT activists who regard online homophobic discourse as a symptom – not a cause – of the real problem, and would therefore rather have it remain visible.[46] As Will Doherty points out,

> if you make [hate speech] illegal and tell people they're going to be arrested if they do it, that doesn't really create change. In fact what it usually does is it causes a movement to develop in support of the person who's being vilified by the laws; [whereas] when [people are] speaking freely on line we can keep track of who they are and where they are, and we can engage in a dialogue.[47]

These remarks are premised on the observation that, whereas it is difficult to compare the harmfulness of intentional homophobic online speech with that of involuntary speech, the frequency of the latter undeniably outweighs that of the former. As a result spontaneous, individual responses do contribute to challenging disparaging views of LGBT people. This is eloquently illustrated in the above-mentioned discussion thread from the Princeton Review forum, in which a prospective student at the University of Alabama law school who goes by the pseudonym 'another regular poster' asks for other posters' advice. He has found a male roommate via an online message board, but will not meet him until the day they sign the lease, and wonders whether he should let him know he is gay before they do. Answering the above-mentioned, rather prejudiced response by 'The Last Earl of Manigoat', which defines homosexuality exclusively in terms of sexual behaviour, a more sympathetic 'Mr. Futomaki' states: 'you can be a gay guy and have sex with women (e.g. if you're closeted or curious), or not have sex with anyone at all, and you're still gay.'[48] More significantly, as, in the course of the thread, 'another regular poster' expresses apprehension of being alienated as a gay man by his prospective roommate and fellow-students at the University of Alabama, several respondents post disheartening messages implying that *he* is to blame for his predicament, having applied to a presumably conservative law school and sought a roommate without first stating that he is gay. But a subsequent poster in the thread – whose pseudonym is 'x ekg x' – nevertheless reveals that the actual situation at the University of Alabama is not as severe as earlier respondents imply, exposes the fact that 'The Last Earl of Manigoat', who is the most vocal author of disheartening comments, is not even a student at that school, and refers 'another regular poster' to the websites of LGBT groups on the university campus and in the city of Montgomery.[49] Not only are prejudiced views of homosexuality thus exposed, but the very idea that 'another regular poster' should make amends for wanting to be out as a gay student in Alabama is thereby challenged.

Using the Internet to confront online homophobic hate speech with more speech nevertheless raises several problems. It firstly boils down to a defensive, rather than an offensive approach, since it consists in individuals committed to LGBT rights reacting to anti-LGBT speech – *not* taking the initiative to produce and promote positive speech about homosexuality. As LGBT advocates do not have the initiative, their merely reacting seems to amount to a confession of weakness – which is the last thing a social movement should aim at.[50] Perhaps more importantly, this form of action happens to be private and individual, which casts doubt upon its political significance in terms of social movement mobilisation. In fact, the reason why this form of action is neither collective, nor structured partly owes to the nature of the Internet, which simply cannot be systematically monitored. Activists who are intent on responding to any anti-LGBT online speech are therefore bound to an almost haphazard sort of action. Thirdly, the question is what the chances are that such informal, individual action should yield thorough, long-lasting results. One of the recurrent characteristics of anti-LGBT speech – online as elsewhere – is to label homosexuality as morally wrong because it is chosen, and this view happens to be by far more firmly established than the alternative view that homosexuality is legitimate, even if defined as a chosen identity.[51] One would expect the reversal of such a power imbalance to be dependent on more offensive action, rather than on individual, apparently random reaction.

RECLAIMING THE OFFENSIVE

It is our claim here that the key to answering these questions lies in the very reasons why LGBT groups support free speech, as the study of concrete examples will evince. In reacting to online hate speech, LGBT social actors indeed firstly develop creative forms of action. A Google search with the key words 'hate gays' for instance leads to a page entitled 'five reasons to hate gays', which lists five usual reasons for condemning homosexuality ('it's a sin'; 'it's unnatural'; 'it's non-productive'; 'it's socially harmful'; 'it's disgusting') only to debunk them on the basis of a religious argument.[52] Such a page title is likely to appeal to a homophobic browser, and the argument is in turn apt to get a religious reader to think again. Similarly, whereas Fred Phelps advertises on godhatesfags.com that he and his family and supporters will picket AIDS or homophobic violence victims' funerals, the supporters of a victim once cut out angel wings which they wore on their backs while standing in a row between the funeral and Fred Phelps's supporters; thus instead of confronting the picketers by yelling at them or trying to make them go away, they made them invisible behind a beautiful, dignified row of angel wings.[53] Both responses consist in meeting the challenge of a hate message, not with more hate, but with a message of an altogether different nature, which ultimately renders the former less visible and thus creates an alternative to it.

In another instance, when Fred Phelps once advertised that he was going to picket a gay bar in Ann Arbor, Michigan, a bar-owner decided to organise a fund-raising campaign for the local gay advocacy group and community centre, and asked people to pledge a money donation for every minute Phelps was going to actually stay in town. 'In this way . . . the longer Phelps stayed to spew hate, the more money he would raise for [the local organisation]', he explained.[54] As Fred Phelps stayed in town for 60 minutes, *he* finally helped raise more than $7,000 for his own opponents. Reacting to hate speech therefore does not necessarily imply a passive attitude, but can lead to defusing its harmfulness, or even to actually turning the damage of hate back against the hater.

Through informal action LGBT advocates may also develop innovative – hence offensive – articulations of LGBT identity, for instance by participating in forums to claim that homosexuality is a choice and that that does not undermine the legitimacy of the LGBT movement's claims. One poster on the above-quoted Princeton Review forum thread expounds the established view that if homosexuality were biological it might be condoned, but because it is chosen, it is morally reprehensible. Instead of comparing sexual orientation to race or ethnicity, which are imposed identities, one should therefore compare homosexuality to being 'a prostitute or a drug dealer, as both of these groups choose their behavior, even though it is not approved of by society at large', he claims.[55] But one poster, who identifies as 'commiegal', provocatively responds: 'perhaps a better comparison would be mothers – motherhood is in some ways rooted in biology, and it is also a choice.' In a later post, she elaborates on the notion that 'even if queerness is a choice, there is no reason to stigmatise', by arguing: 'I have absolutely no clue why anyone in their right mind would want to be a scientologist, and yet people choose it. And I dont [sic] believe that scientologists should be treated unequally.'[56] 'Commiegal' thereby challenges both the notion that homosexuality is wrong, and the widespread assumption – espoused even by many gay and lesbian rights' advocates – that it must be proved to be an involuntary condition before it can be legitimised. She thus confronts homophobia with an alternative to the arguably self-limiting strategy of the mainstream gay and lesbian movement, which consists in framing the gay and lesbian community as an ethnic minority,[57] and articulates what happens to be one of the most offensive strategies for the LGBT rights movement, for though it may grant American gays and lesbians fewer instrumental gains in the short run, it holds more rewarding promises of symbolical recognition in the long run.[58]

And the action is far from being devoid of efficiency as the prejudiced poster later acknowledges the validity of his challenger's argument, thus showing he has been made to approach the issue from a perspective different from his own.[59] In fact, such an individualised, cultural movement style may fall short of the traditionally political achievements of standard gay and lesbian mobilisation, but because it is oriented toward informal, rather than institutional forms of action it participates in a more general shift in the course of LGBT mobilisation, which is characteristic of what Doug McAdam names 'spin-off' – as opposed to 'initiator' – movements.[60] Rather than lobby or litigate to obtain new rights, this form of mobilisation indeed aims at generating interactions premised on a more balanced distribution of power – in other words on mutual respect and recognition. This implies that for a social movement to be significant, the locus of contention does not have to be the government, and that the private–public boundary may be renegotiated, which has historically been one of the key contributions of gay and lesbian mobilisation to American democracy.[61]

Besides, in the case of more antagonistic verbal exchanges when no resolution is found, responding at least generates empowerment through speech, especially through the public reappropriation of one's self-definition, which has also historically been a crucial aspect of gay and lesbian mobilisation.[62] On a discussion thread of the Web-ministry forum entitled 'God hates homosexuality', one poster thus bluntly states: 'If God doesn't like homo's [*sic*], why does he keep making them????'[63] On a British forum explicitly dedicated to posting offensive, graphic limericks about gay male sexuality, one response to a message whose sole content is its title – 'I hate fags' – reads: 'stop smoking, then'.[64] The tone is so flippant that the content may indeed seem politically insignificant, but on a *public* medium this interpersonal exchange between two individual posters is apt to trigger exhilaration in a reader otherwise disheartened by the vehemence of the anti-LGBT speech on the forum. The respondent thus at once frames the exchange as a struggle on equal terms with a clearly defined enemy, and fosters empowerment in his virtually supportive readers – two undeniable boons in the context of social movement conflict. Such use of speech is consistent with the means by which LGBT mobilisation has managed to counter stigmatisation, whereby labelling outsiders as deviant functions as a way to claim that being an insider makes one normal,[65] and this is the reason why free speech is so particularly crucial for this movement. Thus the performativity of language, which is the source of hate speech's harmfulness, is available for use in a liberating way.[66] In this case, adopting a confrontational, rather than a submissive, attitude creates an opportunity to engage in conflict over the cultural definition of sexual legitimacy, which is at the core of the LGBT movement's agenda.[67]

What appears from the study of these examples is that understanding the LGBT movement's approach to online homophobic speech is inseparable from the issue of speech. LGBT organisations and activists tend to advocate responding to online hate speech with more speech, because the availability of positive material about homosexuality on the Internet is at stake. Furthermore, LGBT oppression in the United States nowadays often consists in denials of First Amendment rights, for instance when gay or lesbian literature is seized by the US Customs as pornographic material, or when employees get fired for 'flaunting' their homosexuality – be it in the military or elsewhere.[68] LGBT rights therefore appear to be an issue of protection under the First Amendment as much as under the Fourteenth Amendment. As David Richards puts it, '[h]omosexuality is today essentially a form of political, social, and moral dissent.'[69] Seeking the recognition of homosexuality as a legitimate form of expression however remains marginal within the gay and lesbian movement, whose mainstream is intent on gaining equal protection of the law for a distinct category of people. But such discourse on homosexuality is more easily broadcast on the Internet than in the traditional, physical public sphere, due to the very characteristics of online communication which make online hate speech a particularly concerning problem: it is cheap and fast, and one need not negotiate the content to have access to the medium. Conversely, this means that offensive, challenging views of LGBT identity can be articulated online, whereas the agenda of LGBT rights in the traditional media tends to reflect the institutionalised, mainstream gay and lesbian movement.[70]

As it is a way for activists to do away with the mainstreaming constraints which characterise top-down organising, and to articulate LGBT identity with a view to authenticity,[71] online communication represents an invaluable resource for grassroots mobilisation. That is why the issue of the electronic divide is central to any discussion of online LGBT mobilisation against hate speech. One may be tempted to dismiss online homophobic speech as a less serious issue for the LGBT movement than homophobia in physical space, partly due to the fact that access to the Internet is far from universal. But those constituencies which are the most severely hit by the digital divide happen to be those most likely to articulate an alternative, innovative LGBT agenda – the economically disadvantaged, including the homeless, youths, and ethnic minorities.[72] Increasing their mobilisation is thus crucial for broadening the grassroots constituency of the LGBT movement, and they make up a social movement constituency for whom the Internet proves a well-suited tool: people in working-class jobs for example often cannot leave work to attend a demonstration or a meeting as easily as their middle-class counterparts; but they may well have access to the Internet at work, as computer use and Internet access in employment are becoming more and more widespread and less and less restricted to managerial positions. Likewise, homeless LGBT people are typically disenfranchised for both material and symbolical reasons, but online anonymity and Internet access in public libraries empowers them to speak out and become a constituency within the LGBT social movement.[73] That is why educating people to 'internet media literacy',[74] which is what such organisations as the Electronic Freedom Frontier (EFF) and People's Electronic Network (PEN) are doing,[75] is so crucial in order to generate empowerment thanks to the Internet.

CONCLUSION

Far from being primarily a tool of LGBT oppression, the Internet therefore appears to be a means of empowerment for those constituencies least represented in the mainstream gay and lesbian movement. The harmfulness of online homophobic speech is not to be denied, but the forms of action it requires – short of seeking to have it banned – display the characteristics of offensive, grassroots social movement. LGBT mobilisation against online hate speech indeed tends to articulate a political collective identity which is more seldom encountered in physical space, and which calls for a more challenging agenda than that of the mainstream gay and lesbian movement. The easiness of expression on the Internet is what makes online homophobic speech such a serious issue, but it is by the same token an opportunity for LGBT mobilisation to move beyond the mainstreaming of gay and lesbian rights.

NOTES

1 I wish to thank Jennifer Rakowski and Andy Wong of Community United Against Violence (CUAV) in San Francisco, and Will Doherty of the Online Policy Group in San Francisco for their time and their insightful help.
2 *Loi du 29 juillet 1881 relative à la liberté de la presse.*
3 Directive 97/36/EC of the European Parliament and of the Council of 30 June 1997 amending Council Directive 89/552/EEC on the coordination of certain provisions laid down by law, regulation or administrative action in Member States concerning the pursuit of television broadcasting activities, Article 22.1 <europa. eu.int/eur-lex/lex/Notice.do?val=218531:cs&lang=en&list=273587:cs,218531:cs, 149743:cs,&pos=2&page=1&nbl=3&pgs=10&hwords=3K~television~& checktexte=checkbox&visu=#texte> (9 December 2005). The date when a web page was last modified is indicated before the URL, when known. Unless otherwise specified in parentheses after the URL, web pages were last visited on 15 January 2004.
4 *Loi n°86–1067 du 30 septembre 1986 relative à la liberté de communication, Article 15* <www.legifrance.gouv.fr/texteconsolide/PCEAJ.htm> (9 December 2005).
5 Sprigg, Peter S, 'Defending the Family: Why We Resist Gay Activism' <www.frc.org/get.cfm?i=PD01L1>.
6 Farish, Leah, 'Hate Crimes: Beyond Virtual Reality' <www.frc.org/get.cfm?i= IS03K01>; Bennett, Stephen, 'The Deception and Desensitization of America's Youth', 20 February 2003 <www.afa.net/homosexual_agenda/GetArticle. asp?id=81> (9 April 2004).
7 Brown, Jim, 'Attorney Claims Homosexual Students Often Incite Reaction on Campus', 14 January 2004 <headlines.agapepress.org/archive/1/afa/142004d.asp>.
8 hari, 2 October 2003 <www.web-ministry.com/topic_threads.php?postID=928& parentid=801>.
9 Chris, 27 November 2002 <www.web-ministry.com/topic_threads.php?postID=201 &parentid=198>.
10 An Episcopalian, 15 August 2003 <www.web-ministry.com/topic_threads.php? postID=664>.
11 webmaster, 30 October 2002 <www.web-ministry.com/topic_threads.php?postID= 169&parentid=168>; Patsy, 17 November 2003 <www.web-ministry.com/topic_ threads.php?postID=1168&parentid=1152>.
12 webmaster, 20 July 2002 <www.web-ministry.com/topic_threads.php?postID= 20&parentid=16>.
13 The Last Earl of Manigoat, 11 August 2003 <discuss.princetonreview.com/forums/ Thread.cfm?CFApp=6&Thread_ID=534340&mc=118> (16 August 2003).
14 TalkCollegeonBolt, 11 August 2003, *Ibid.*
15 TalkCollegeonBolt, 11 August 2003, *Ibid.*
16 Delgado, Richard and Stefancic, Jean, 'Hate Speech Is a Hate Crime', in Espejo, Roman (ed.), *What Is a Hate Crime*, San Diego, CA: Greenhaven Press, 2002, pp 54–7.
17 Tsesis, Alexander, *Destructive Messages. How Hate Speech Paves the Way for Harmful Social Movements*, New York: NYU Press, 2002, pp 74–6.
18 Levendosky, Charles, 'Hate Speech on the Internet Should Not Be Restricted', in Roleff, Tamara (ed.), *Hate Crimes*, San Diego, CA: Greenhaven Press, 2001, pp 90–2.
19 Jaffe, Michael, 'Riding the Electronic Tiger: Censorship in Global, Distributed Networks', in Cohen-Almagor, Raphael (ed.), *Liberal Democracy and the Limits of Tolerance*, Ann Arbor, MI: University of Michigan Press, 2000, pp 282–3.

20 Ray, Beverly and Marsh, George E., 'Recruitment by Extremist Groups on the Internet', *First Monday*, (2001) 6/2, <firstmonday.org/issues/issue6_2/ray/index.html> (18 January 2004); Tsesis, Alexander, *Destructive Messages*, pp 70–1.

21 See for instance Smith, Stephen, 'There's Such a Thing as Free Speech: And It's a Good Thing, Too', in Whillock, Rita Kirk and Scayden, David (eds), *Hate Speech*, Thousand Oaks, CA: Sage Publications, 1995, pp 230–40; Bracken, Harry, *Freedom of Speech: Words Are Not Deeds*, Westport, CT: Praeger, 1994; Abel, Richard, *Speaking Respect, Respecting Speech*, Chicago: University of Chicago Press, 1998; Jacobs, James and Potter, Kimberly, 'Hate Speech Is Protected by the First Amendment', in Espejo, Roman (ed.), *What Is a Hate Crime*, pp 63–73. For a synthesis of the civil libertarian view see Zingo, Martha, *Sex/Gender Outsiders, Hate Speech and Freedom of Expression: Can They Say That about Me?*, Westport, CT: Praeger, 1998, pp 23–7.

22 Tsesis, Alexander, *Destructive Messages*, pp 130–7.

23 Mill, John Stuart, *On Liberty*, New York: Bantam Books, 1993 [1st edn 1859], p 64. I wish to thank Michel Prum for pointing this out.

24 Macavinta, Courtney, 'GLAAD fights for Net protections', *CNET News.com*, 25 May 1999, <news.com.com/2100-1023_3-226316.html?tag=st_rn> (22 January 2004); Kretchmer, Susan and Carveth, Rod, 'Challenging Boundaries for a Boundless Medium: Information Access, Libraries and Freedom of Expression in a Democratic Society', in Hensley, Thomas (ed.), *The Boundaries of Freedom of Expression and Orderly American Democracy*, Kent, Ohio: Kent State University Press, 2001, pp 189–94.

25 See Zingo, Martha, *Sex/Gender Outsiders*, pp 27–30; Heyman, Steven, 'Overview: A History of Hate Speech Laws', in Roleff, Tamara (ed.), *Hate Crimes*, pp 62–63.

26 ADL, *Combating Extremism in Cyberspace: The Legal Issues Affecting Internet Hate Speech*, 2000, available at <www.adl.org/Civil_Rights/newcyber.pdf>.

27 Sumner, L.W., 'Should Hate Speech Be Free Speech? John Stuart Mill and the Limits of Tolerance', in Cohen-Almagor, Raphael (ed.), *Liberal Democracy*, pp 143–5.

28 Zingo, Martha, *Sex/Gender Outsiders*, p 27; Tsesis, Alexander, *Destructive Messages*, pp 137–39.

29 Zingo, Martha, *Sex/Gender Outsiders*, pp 30–2.

30 Kretchmer, Susan and Carveth, Rod, 'Challenging Boundaries', pp 207–10; ALA, *Libraries and the Internet Toolkit*, 9 December 2003 available from <www.ala.org>.

31 Sumner, L. W., 'Should Hate Speech Be Free Speech?', pp 136–41; Tsesis, Alexander, *Destructive Messages*, chapter 11.

32 Tsesis, Alexander, *Destructive Messages*, pp 140–7.

33 PBS, 'Debating Dr. Laura', *Online News Hour Forum*, 15 June 2000, <www.pbs.org/newshour/forum/june00/drlaura.html>; GLAAD, 'GLAAD Launches New "Dr. Laura" Online Activism Program', 11 August 2000, <www.glaad.org/media/archive_detail.php?id=83&>.

34 GLAAD, 'GLAAD Applauds Cancellation of Dr. Laura', 20 March 2001 <www.glaad.org/media/archive_detail.php?id=3186&>.

35 Rakowski, Jennifer, personal interview with the author, San Francisco, 21 August 2003.

36 Zingo, Martha, *Sex/Gender Outsiders*, p 33 (emphasis in original).

37 McMasters, Paul, 'Hate Speech Should Not Be Restricted', in Roleff, Tamara (ed), *Hate Crimes*, pp 80–2.

38 Zingo, Martha, *Sex/Gender Outsiders*, p 177.

39 Macavinta, Courtney, 'GLAAD fights for Net protections'; Kretchmer, Susan and Carveth, Rod, 'Challenging Boundaries', pp 189–95.

40 GayToday, 'AOL Disks Burned in San Francisco by Angry Activists' <gaytoday. badpuppy.com/garchive/events/102799ev.htm>; Hu, Jim, 'Gay rights groups attack AOL speech policy', *CNET News.com*, 21 October 1999, <news.com.com/ 2100–1040_3–231759.html>; TSESIS, Alexander, *Destructive Messages*, p 72.

41 GayToday, 'AOL Disks Burned'; Hu, Jim, 'Gay rights groups attack AOL speech policy'; AOL in particular was targeted because it is the largest ISP in the United States and it has at the same time very strict anti-homophobic hate speech terms of service and a record of dubious treatment of LGBT users: most notably, an AOL agent in 1998 inadvertently released to Navy personnel one Navy officer's confidential information, thus disclosing the officer's homosexuality (he had entered 'gay' as his marital status in his profile), which nearly resulted in his discharge – see: Kornblum, Janet, 'Navy Retreats – Gets Sued over Sailor's AOL Profile', *Badpuppy Gay Today*, 16 January 1998, <gaytoday.badpuppy.com/ garchive/events/011698ev.htm>.

42 Rakowski, Jennifer, interview.

43 Doherty, Will, interview, San Francisco, 19 August 2003; GLAAD, ' "Kill Ed Templeton": A Dangerous Game', 27 February 2001, <www.glaad.org/action/ al_archive_detail.php?id=1482> (19 August 2003).

44 Taylor, Charles, 'The Politics of Recognition', in Gutman, Amy (ed), *Multiculturalism: Examining the Politics of Recognition*, Princeton, NJ: Princeton University Press, 1994, pp 37–44.

45 Jaffe, Michael, 'Riding the Electronic Tiger', pp 282–4.

46 Zingo, Martha, *Sex/Gender Outsiders*, pp 179–81; Smith, Stephen, 'There's Such a Thing as Free Speech', pp 259–62.

47 Doherty, Will, interview.

48 Mr Futomaki, 11 August 2003, <discuss.princetonreview.com/forums/Thread.cfm? CFApp=6&Thread_ID=534340&mc=118> (16 August 2003).

49 x ekg x, three posts (11 August 2003; 12 August 2003; 12 August 2003), *Ibid.*

50 Levendosky, Charles, 'Hate Speech on the Internet', pp 90–2.

51 Moritz, Margaret, 'The Gay Agenda', in Whillock, Rita Kirk and Scayden, David (eds), *Hate Speech*, Thousand Oaks, CA: Sage Publications, 1995, pp 74–77.

52 Gayvolution, 'Five Reasons to Hate Gays', <www.geocities.com/WestHollywood/ Heights/1847/reasons.htm> (18 January 2004).

53 Doherty, Will, interview.

54 Stiles, John, 'Homophobe Contributes to Gay Group in Spite of Himself', *The Normal Heart: Newsletter of the Lesbian and Gay Community of Southern New Mexico and West Texas*, April 2001 <www.zianet.com/tnh/april01/story17.htm> (18 January 2004).

55 Leiter, Myron, 12 August 2003 <discuss.princetonreview.com/forums/Thread.cfm? CFApp=6&Thread_ID=534340&mc=118> (16 August 2003).

56 commiegal, 12 August 2003, *Ibid.*

57 Marche, Guillaume, 'Homosexualité et ethnicité: rupture et recomposition d'un modèle identitaire', in Prum, Michel (ed.), *La Peau de l'autre*, Paris: Syllepse, 2001, pp 118–24; Brookey, Robert A., *Reinventing the Male Homosexual. The Rhetoric and Power of the Gay Gene*, Bloomington: Indiana University Press, 2002, pp 1–23.

58 Whisman, Vera, *Queer by Choice. Lesbians, Gay Men, and the Politics of Identity*, New York: Routledge, 1996, pp 11–36; Marche, Guillaume (2000), 'Identités privées et identités politiques dans les dynamiques de mouvement social gai et lesbien aux Etats-Unis depuis 1980', unpublished PhD thesis, Université

Paris 7, pp 220–31; Brookey, Robert A., *Reinventing the Male Homosexual*, pp 118–48.

59 Leiter, Myron, two posts (12 August 2003), <discuss.princetonreview.com/forums/Thread.cfm?CFApp=6&Thread_ID=534340&mc=118> (16 August 2003).

60 Marche, Guillaume, 'Les familles homosexuelles aux Etats-Unis: dissolution d'un mouvement social ou redéfinition de sa portée politique?', *Revue Française d'Etudes Américaines*, (2003) 97, pp 110–13; McAdam, Doug, ' "Initiator" and "Spin-off" Movements: Diffusion Processes in Protest Cycles', in Traugott, Mark (ed.), *Repertoires and Cycles of Collective Action*, Durham, NC: Duke University Press, 1995, pp 223–6.

61 D'Emilio, John, *Sexual Politics, Sexual Communities. The Making of a Homosexual Minority in the United States: 1940–1970*, Chicago: University of Chicago Press, 1998, pp 223–39; Jennes, Valerie, 'Coming Out: Lesbian Identities and the Categorization Problem', in Plummer, Kenneth (ed.), *Modern Homosexualities: Fragments of Lesbian and Gay Experience*, New York: Routledge, 1992, pp 65–74; Blasius, Mark, 'An Ethos of Lesbian and Gay Existence', *Political Theory*, (1992) 20/4, pp 642–71.

62 Chauncey, George, *Gay New York. Gender, Urban Culture and the Making of a Gay Male World (1890–1940)*, New York: Basic Books, 1995, pp 17–23; Young, Allen, 'Out of the Closets, Into the Streets', in Jay, Karla and Young, Allen (eds), *Out of the Closets: Voices of Gay Liberation*, London: Gay Men's Press, 1992, pp 6–31; Shelley, Martha, 'Gay Is Good', *Ibid.*, pp 31–34; Sollors, Werner, *Beyond Ethnicity: Consent and Descent in American Culture*, Oxford: Oxford University Press, 1986, pp 191–95.

63 Kevster, 29 April 2003. <www.web-ministry.com/topic_threads.php?postID=454&parentid=16>.

64 KingFox, 22 November 2002, <www.lcsa.org.uk/wwwboard/messages/1969.html> (18 January 2004).

65 Moritz, Margaret, 'The Gay Agenda', pp 65–9.

66 Butler, Judith, *Excitable Speech. A Politics of the Performative*, New York: Routledge, 1997, pp 1–41.

67 Jaffe, Michael, 'Riding the Electronic Tiger', pp 289–92.

68 Zingo, Martha, *Sex/Gender Outsiders*, pp 39–42.

69 Richards, David quoted by Zingo, Martha, *Sex/Gender Outsiders*, p 38.

70 Marche, Guillaume, 'Somewhere Inside the Rainbow: The Use of Marginality in the Lesbian and Gay Movement in the United States', *Groupe de Recherches Anglo-Américaines de Tours (GRAAT)*, (2000) 22, pp 183–90; Vaid, Urvashi, *Virtual Equality: The Mainstreaming of Gay and Lesbian Liberation*, New York: Doubleday, 1995, pp 106–47.

71 Taylor, Charles, 'The Politics of Recognition', pp 28–38.

72 Badget, M. V. Lee, 'Beyond Biased Samples. Challenging the Myths on the Economic Status of Lesbians and Gay Men', in Gluckman, Amy and Reed, Betsy (eds), *Homo Economics: Capitalism, Community, and Lesbian and Gay Life*, New York: Routledge, 1997, pp 65–71; Hussain, Pat, 'Class Action: Bringing Economic Diversity to the Gay and Lesbian Movement', *Ibid*, pp 241–8.

73 Rakowski, Jennifer, interview; Wylie, Margie, 'Homeless People Homestead in Cyberspace', *Saint Louis Post*, 24 February 1999, available at Homeless People's Network, <aspin.asu.edu/hpn/archives/Feb99/0243.html> (1 January 2004); About.com, 'Bridging the Digital Divide: Closing the Gap between the Haves and the Have-nots', *Race Relations Newsletter*, <racerelations.about.com/library/weekly/aa121399a.htm> (14 September 2004); likewise people who are not out of

their environment may find it difficult to participate in LGBT mobilisation in physical space, but may find it easier in cyberspace.

74 Jaffe, Michael, 'Riding the Electronic Tiger', p 288, Kretchmer, Susan and Carveth, Rod, 'Challenging Boundaries', pp 202–04.
75 Jaffe, Michael, 'Riding the Electronic Tiger', pp 287–88.

Chapter 11

The impact of interdependence on racial hostility

The American experience

Jack Levin and Gordana Rabrenovic

THE IMPACT OF INTER-GROUP CONTACT ON PREJUDICE

Social psychologists have long suggested that prejudice was largely a result of ignorance – a lack of knowledge about another group of people.[1] From this standpoint, the members of hostile groups need to engage together in activities that allow them to gain mutual understanding. This explanation became commonly known as the *contact theory of prejudice*, whereby increased interaction between the members of different groups is expected to decrease the antagonism between them.

We realise, of course, that not every form of contact leads to improved inter-group relations. Indeed, there are numerous examples that support the opposite conclusion: that physical proximity can lead to an escalation of conflict and violence. This was made abundantly clear in the escalation of hostility between black and Jewish residents of the Crown Heights neighbourhood of New York City. In August 1991, following a long history of mutual resentment, a seven-year-old black child, Gavin Cato, was killed in an accident involving an Orthodox Jewish motorist, whose car had jumped the curb.[2] To retaliate, black youngsters ran through the streets of Crown Heights, shouting anti-Semitic epithets and threats. Shortly thereafter, a twenty-nine-year-old rabbinical student from Australia who was totally unrelated to the accident was stabbed to death. For almost a week, Blacks and Jews exchanged insults, broke windows in homes and cars, and threw bottles and rocks at one another. Before the violent confrontation finally ended, dozens more were injured.[3]

In Crown Heights, mistrust and suspicion were palpable on both sides. Many black residents were convinced that the motorist who hit the black child would be completely exonerated, because of the perception that Jewish residents had an unfair advantage in the way they were treated by city officials. At the same time, the Jewish residents of Crown Heights were equally certain that the black mayor of New York City would never bring the murderer of the Australian rabbinical student to justice.

Another example of the ineffectiveness of contact to bring groups together occurred during the 1970s, when black and white children in Boston were bussed to schools outside of their own neighbourhoods to comply with a court-ordered desegregation plan that was widely opposed by white parents. Because youngsters had previously been assigned to schools based on where they resided, schools in primarily white areas of the city such as South Boston and Charlestown had a mostly white student population. Schools in black areas such as Roxbury and Dorchester remained overwhelmingly black. In the original desegregation plan, much attention was given to how these youngsters would get to school – on yellow school buses; little attention was paid to what they would do together when they reached the classroom.

Some white parents in South Boston expressed their resentment by congregating in front of the newly integrated high school. Many of them hurled eggs and rotten tomatoes, shouted epithets, and threw stones at the windows of the buses carrying the black youngsters. Nine black students were wounded.[4] The resentment of white parents to the desegregation plan was transferred to their children; they were given almost no guidance in getting along with their new classmates, who were different in both racial and social class terms. The contact between black and white students only supported and encouraged their bigotry. For too many, stereotyped thinking prevailed. At South Boston High School, a black student stabbed his white classmate.[5] At Charlestown High School, a dozen white boys heaved stones at the buses carrying black students home.[6] At both schools, black and white students confronted one another in the hallways. In classes, the black students sat on one side of the room; the white students sat on the other.

Neither in the Boston bussing episodes nor in Crown Heights was contact effective in reducing the hostility between groups. In Boston, black and white students occupied seats in the same classrooms and ate lunch in the same cafeteria; but their negative inter-group attitudes remained intact. In Crown Heights, black and white residents lived side by side. Yet identity seemed primarily to be based on race ('the black community'), religion ('the Jewish community'), or a shared sense of being part of the much larger New York City population. In this regard, sharing the Crown Heights neighbourhood was almost irrelevant to the members of either group.

THE EFFECT OF INTERDEPENDENCE ON RACIAL CONFLICT

It is clear that only certain kinds of interaction are likely to reduce the hostility between groups. In particular, getting individuals to become interdependent; that is, to put aside their differences and work together toward the satisfaction of their common objectives, has long been demonstrated to be an effective strategy for inoculating a community against inter-group hate and violence.

Interdependence has two distinct yet overlapping forms. On the one hand, *instrumental* interdependence occurs in the context of formal organisations – civic associations, workplaces, and schools – where the members of different groups come to rely on one another in order to achieve their shared goals.[7] On the other hand, interdependence also has an *affective* version, in which individuals from diverse backgrounds become emotionally reliant on one another. In friendship and neighbourliness, individuals are mutually dependent with respect to emotional support and encouragement, rather than for the satisfaction of their instrumental objectives. The interaction is informal and personalised so that it breaks through the stereotyped thinking and forms the basis for a common bond.

Locating positive examples of America's racial or religious groups coming together in a spirit of cooperation or friendship is possible, albeit difficult. In the aftermath of the vicious 1998 murder of James Byrd in Jasper, Texas, for example, the community's reactions were surprisingly conciliatory and remorseful. The three white supremacists who were eventually convicted of Byrd's murder – John King, Lawrence Brewer, and Shawn Berry – had beaten the African-American hitchhiker until he was unconscious, had chained him to their pick-up truck, and then had dragged him down the road for more than two miles to his death. Investigators discovered a Ku Klux Klan manual among the possessions carried by one of the assailants; and two of them wore white supremacist body tattoos depicting the Confederate Knights of America. The killers were definitely ardent admirers of the Klan who used white supremacist propaganda and proudly identified themselves with white supremacy symbols of power.

Given the cultural tradition of racism in the Deep South, it might seem that the brutal murder of a black resident in a small and impoverished southern town would precipitate a melee or a riot. Yet, rather than divide the community on racial grounds, the murder of James Byrd actually served to bring the black and white residents of Jasper together. In the aftermath of the slaying, townspeople reportedly went out of their way to cross racial lines in greeting residents and felt a new street-level friendliness toward members of the other race.[8]

As in many other southern communities, Blacks and Whites in Jasper had not always been friendly toward one another.[9] The legacy of Jim Crow segregation continued to colour the informal relations between Blacks and Whites, keeping them separated in their daily lives. One issue which had long symbolised the community's struggle with race relations was the town's cemetery, where a fence down the middle kept Whites buried on one side from Blacks buried on the other. After Byrd's murder, however, the town came to an agreement to integrate its cemetery. Many residents of Jasper, black and white, joined together to pull out the posts and tear down the fence.[10]

The political leaders in Jasper enjoyed strong credibility with both its black and its white residents. Local government had long been racially integrated. Indeed, black residents, who comprised 45 per cent of the town's population, occupied the position of mayor, two of the five city council positions, and the directorship of the Deep East Texas Council of Governments. In addition, school principals and the administrator of the largest hospital were black. Even in the almost total absence of inter-racial friendships, Blacks and Whites in Jasper had developed a tradition of cooperating at the formal level.

The leadership in Jasper inspired new areas of reconciliation and non-violence. The community's white sheriff went out of his way to encourage confidence among black residents in the aftermath of Byrd's slaying. Within 24 hours, he had arrested two suspects and then immediately requested the assistance of the FBI. Moreover, the local radio station kept residents informed in an even-handed way about developments related to the murder and the trials, ensuring that racially dangerous rumours and anxieties never had an opportunity to spread.[11]

Jasper, Texas, represented a source of community pride for black and white residents alike; all of them felt a common bond to the town, that transcended racial differences. Even extremists on both sides of the racial ledger were genuinely embarrassed by the cruelty and sadism of James Byrd's murder. They seemed to unite across racial lines against the very strong stigma imposed on their community by members of the outside world. Inter-race unity was possible because many of the town's formal organisations had already brought together representatives of both groups, who were accustomed to working together.[12]

In divided communities where inter-group violence can tear apart the fabric of social relations, it is difficult to maintain ties of friendship between the members of different racial or ethnic groups. Even inter-group marriages may not survive in places with extreme hostility, because of the absence of support from either side. To protect themselves from the violence, people often choose to live in segregated circumstances. The avoidance of the members of other groups decreases the contact between them and consequently the possibility for conflict to develop. Thus, in many places, walls make good neighbours.

The historic divisions between Blacks and Whites in Jasper, Texas all but eliminated any chance that its residents would, in the short term, establish friendships across racial lines. The 'glue' that held together the community consisted of instrumental interdependence – a sharing of formal leadership functions that made residents, regardless of their racial background, feel a sense of identification with Jasper rather than with only the white or only the black segment of the town. Thus, a precedent for inter-racial cooperation had long existed. It served to immunise the community against an outbreak of collective violence in the aftermath of Byrd's murder.

Another example of the effectiveness of instrumental interdependence can be found in America's treatment of its citizens of Japanese descent during World War II. In the aftermath of Japan's December 1941 attack on

Pearl Harbor, the American government introduced several policies, on the federal level, that were discriminatory toward Japanese Americans. Executive Order 9066 became a legal foundation for this approach. Many Japanese Americans were forced to give up their jobs and live by a 6 am to 6 pm curfew. They were also restricted to travelling within five miles of their homes.

Then, in 1942, most Japanese Americans were forced into internment camps. It is important to note that more than two-thirds of Japanese Americans were not immigrants, but American citizens who were nevertheless regarded as a security risk based solely on their Japanese ancestry. Also, there was virtually no evidence of Japanese disloyalty to the US. The rationale for this policy was the fact that the US was at war with Japan and according to the federal government, simply could not afford to permit disloyal Americans of Japanese descent to sabotage the American war effort.

It can be argued that cultural bigotry was behind this approach. However, there were other reasons that contributed to it. Because they would be gone for a period of time, many Japanese Americans were also forced to sell their houses and personal property in a few days, for next to nothing. Real estate agents eagerly bought up the land left by farmers of Japanese descent. A few white Americans helped their Japanese-American neighbours by assisting them in renting their homes; the majority, however, did not interfere. Though many white Americans recognised the injustice of forcibly moving an entire group of people, only a small number had the courage to speak out against government policy.[13]

Although discrimination against Japanese Americans was widespread on mainland America, Japanese Americans in Hawaii were treated in a much more humane way. First of all, there was a good deal of tolerance in Hawaii's collective background. Their multi-racial, multi-cultural population had accumulated a history of respect for differences between groups. Second, many of their leaders did not see a political benefit in removing their Japanese-American neighbours. In addition, Hawaiians of Japanese descent were not widely regarded as posing a threat. And most importantly, perhaps, Japanese Americans were widely seen as providing an important economic function that would have been sorely missed in their absence.

From the beginning of the war, the local military commander, the business community, the mass media, and ordinary long-term Hawaii residents refused to label their fellow Americans of Japanese descent as a danger to the security of Hawaii. In that way they were charting a policy that was very different from the official government view championed by Navy Secretary Frank Knox, who saw Japanese American residents of Hawaii as a potential 'fifth column' in assisting the enemy in attacks on American soil. Even though investigations both by naval intelligence and the FBI found no evidence to support his claim, Navy Secretary Knox recommended on 19 December that all Japanese aliens from the islands be interned on the mainland.[14]

General Delos Emmons, who was the military governor of Hawaii, decided not to obey the order. Instead he went on radio and gave an address in which he declared, 'No person, be he citizen or alien, need worry, provided he is not connected with a subversive element.'[15] What happened next is an example of how leadership can make a difference in how we respond to crisis. General Emmons was a man of integrity. He had a good grasp of local conditions and was aware of Japanese Americans' loyalty to the United States. As an argument against the deportation, he used the actual behaviour of Japanese Americans, instead of relying on unsupported anti-Japanese feelings. For example, during the attack on Pearl Harbor, Japanese Americans were active in civil defence and gave blood for the wounded. Some two thousand Japanese Americans fought enemy planes as part of the US Army forces stationed on the island.[16] When in January of 1942, the War Department requested the evacuation of Japanese Americans from Hawaii, General Emmons contested the order as dangerous and impractical. 'How can you evacuate 100,000 people without straining military resources which were needed to protect the islands?' he argued. 'And if the islands are in danger, we should first evacuate more than 20,000 white civilian women and children who live there.'[17]

On the grounds that Japanese labour was 'absolutely essential' for the rebuilding of the military base, Emmons also fought the War Department order from 9 February 1942 to dismiss all Japanese workers employed by the army. In the end, a compromise was reached whereby General Emmons ordered the internment of 1,444 Japanese out of a population of 158,000. This proportionally small number contrasted sharply with the size of the Japanese American population from other Pacific Ocean states such as California, Washington, and Oregon, where more than 100,000 Japanese Americans were sent to internment camps.[18]

General Emmons's leadership clearly made a difference. However, he was also helped by the fact that other important leaders on the Hawaiian Islands supported his actions. For example, the president of the Honolulu Chamber of Commerce called for just treatment of Japanese residents. He suggested, 'there are 160,000 of these people who want to live here because they like the country and like the American way of life . . . The citizens of Japanese blood would fight as loyally for America as any other citizen. I have read or heard nothing in statements given out by the military, local police or FBI since December 7 to change my opinion. And I have gone out of my way to ask for the facts.'[19] In addition, local newspapers and radio stations refuted rumours about Japanese disloyalty and criticised federal government policies against Japanese Americans. Police Captain John A. Burns and the head of the FBI in Hawaii, Robert L. Shivers, also spoke publicly in defence of the loyalty of Japanese-American residents.

It is no exaggeration to attribute Hawaii's approach to Japanese Americans to the Island's self-serving economic interests. Hawaii's 158,000 Japanese represented 37 per cent of Hawaii's population, as compared to California's

94,000 Japanese Americans, representing 1 per cent of the population of the state.[20] The economic life and military defence of Hawaii would have been seriously threatened if its Japanese population had been removed. But the Japanese were also well integrated into the life of the island, and not only in an economic sense. They had a long history of peaceful coexistence and cooperation with Hawaii's other ethnic groups.

INTERDEPENDENCE AND HATE CRIMES

If interdependence contributes to a reduction in racial conflict, then its presence might also reduce the likelihood of hate or bias crimes being committed on a racial basis. In the American legal system, a hate crime is regarded as an offence committed against an individual because he or she is different with respect to race, religion, sexual orientation, ethnicity, or disability status. The motivations for hate crimes have been categorised as thrill, defensive, and mission.[21]

Most of the hate crimes in the United States are committed by dabblers who, on a part-time basis, are looking to have a thrill at the expense of their victim, or to defend their way of life from outsiders. Only about 5 per cent of all hate attacks in the United States involve the members of an organised hate group whose mission involves the elimination or removal of all Blacks, Latinos, Asians, Whites, Jews, or Muslims.

More than half of the hate crimes in the United States are committed for the thrill or the excitement, frequently by two or more teenagers or young adults against a single victim. Idle and bored, the perpetrators of a thrill hate attack are usually willing to travel by foot, public transportation, or car to another neighbourhood, where they expect to locate a vulnerable victim. Bashing someone who is different gives them bragging rights with their friends. The fact that they are so much influenced by their peers suggests, however, that their previous relationships with the members of another racial group – whether cooperative or antagonistic – will have relatively little influence. Indeed, the particular racial characteristics of the victims of thrill hate attacks may be all but irrelevant. Perpetrators of thrill hate crimes usually do not specialise. They will attack anyone who has been defined by their culture as weak, inferior, and vulnerable. Thus, if a group of adolescents cannot locate a victim who is black or Asian, they will look for someone who is gay or Jewish or Muslim.

Defensive hate crimes are quite different in this respect and, as a result, can be reduced to the extent that formal interdependence in a community is strengthened. The perpetrators have firmly in mind the removal of certain members of a particular group and are motivated by a threatening incident – the first black family to move into a previously all-white neighbourhood, the first Latino student in a college dormitory, a competitive co-worker who happens to be Asian, or an Islamic immigrant who is regarded as a terrorist threat. Moreover, the perpetrators of a defensive hate attack tend to be somewhat older and less likely to operate in a group than their counterparts who commit a thrill attack. Under such circumstances, friendship or more formal cooperation has a chance to reduce the perception of threat from someone who is racially different. Moreover, unlike the perpetrators of thrill hate attacks who frequently travel to an area where members of a vulnerable group are known to congregate, defensive hate crime offenders usually share territory – a neighbourhood, classroom, dormitory, or workplace – with their victims. As a result, the informal ties that unite people of diverse background can protect those who are racially different from being victimised with impunity. Inter-group friendship sends an important message. To the victim, it suggests the presence of neighbours of goodwill and civility who support and encourage the sharing of the community with those who are racially divergent; to would-be perpetrators, friendship indicates that intolerance will not be tolerated.

CONCLUSIONS AND LIMITATIONS

Where inter-group relations operate in a positive direction, there is almost always a large degree of interdependence. In some cases, members of different groups cooperate formally in political leadership and organisational memberships. In other cases, members of different groups become close friends and neighbours. Either way, they find that people who are different from one another need one another. They cooperate, collaborate, encourage and assist. Rather than treat one another as the enemy, they depend on each other as allies and friends.

Few researchers continue to assert that the substance of formal education represents a powerful instrument for the reduction of hate and hostility between groups. In an early study in the United States, sociologists Gertrude Selznick and Stephen Steinberg[22] found an inverse relationship between anti-Semitism and amount of education, a relationship that could not be explained by differences in social class. Yet results claiming to show the impact of education on hate are extremely difficult to interpret and may demonstrate only that the educated members of our society have learned to express their prejudices publicly in subtle, more sophisticated ways – especially on the paper-and-pencil questionnaires generally employed by social science researchers to measure changes in attitudes. Another limitation is the way we measure education – usually as an individual's or a society's educational attainment such as the number of years of formal schooling. By this measure, the residents of Nazi Germany, for example, represented one of the best educated populations in the history of the world, yet bigotry and violence prevailed. By contrast, the citizens of Bulgaria, an ally of the Nazis during World War II, were far less educated as a people; yet not one of the 50,000 Bulgarian Jews went to a death camp.

The two nations differed in more characteristics than just education. In Nazi Germany, Jews and Christians lived side by side but rarely formed friendships. In Bulgaria, Jews and Christians were close friends. In Nazi Germany, Jews were widely regarded as an economic threat. In Bulgaria, Jews were almost indistinguishable from Christian members of society and considered just like everyone else. In Germany, anti-Semitism was a long-standing tradition. In Bulgaria, there was a tradition of tolerance. In Nazi Germany, Hitler benefited politically by placing the blame for the nation's economic woes on Jewish residents. In Bulgaria, political, professional, and religious leaders refused to carry out Hitler's order to round up all Jewish residents and put them on trains to the death camps.

Rather than examine the content of education in relation to bigotry, our analysis suggests instead that it may be useful to consider the structure of schooling. Behavioural scientists have long recognised that the structure of American education depends on strategies that reinforce academic and athletic performance: students tend to be encouraged to exceed the achievement levels of classmates and friends. Competition is emphasised, while personal improvement tends to be ignored. Being the best you can be is less important than doing better that the rest of the class. High schools in the United States give each student a number as his or her placement standing. Learning that competitive skills are highly valued, they have their competitive edge for interpersonal comparisons (for example, 'grading on the curve' and percentile scoring). But it is not only academic achievement that pits one student against another. At the high school level and again in college, there is also intense competition for popularity, status, financial assistance, organisational budgets, internships, jobs and acceptance by the more prestigious colleges. Thus, in order to properly examine the role of education we should also study structural characteristics of education.

So far, there is relatively little compelling evidence in the literature to indicate that individuals who interact cooperatively with some members of a group will generalise their positive attitudes to other members of that group or to the group as a whole.[23] Thus, interdependence cannot be counted on to reduce racial prejudice in general, even if it contributes to affection developing between individuals. We believe that we need to do more research in this area in order to understand how we can benefit from inter-group cooperation.

Another interpretation of friendship as a basis for assisting a vulnerable group to avert disaster, can be that it can only protect those within an individual's small circle of friends and neighbours, but not generate policies that affect every member of the vulnerable group. On the other hand, formal interdependence may be motivated by a desire to protect successful relationships across groups; however, the political consequences necessary to defend such relationships also assist those not involved in formal inter-group relations.

Interdependence appears to have a powerful impact on the quality of inter-group relations, but it also has its limitations. Because communities are limited by their local cultural, political and economic context, ethnic peace is almost always fragile. It tends to flourish in societies that nurture civic culture and democratic political institutions. Indeed, in the presence of autocratic rule, strong formal and informal relationships between groups may be all but irrelevant.

Moreover in times of economic instability, structural change, or political turmoil, the members of the majority group often react to a real or perceived threat to their position in society by turning against the members of minority groups in their midst. Operating under a zero-sum definition of the situation, members of the dominant group may try to limit the minority's civil rights and access to their country's economic resources. The perception that the members of a group constitute a threat to survival, economic well-being, or cultural values can prevent interdependence from ever developing or from working to reduce prejudice if it does develop.

We should not forget that certain individuals may benefit in an economic sense from hate and bigotry. In societies where ethnic or racial groups have unequal power, prejudice justifies one's position of power over the other and allows members of that group to claim more resources for themselves. Also in some multi-racial societies such as Brazil, residents can easily interact across racial lines with each other and even show genuine human warmth toward each other. Still, institutional racism makes it hard for black residents to enjoy the same political, social, and economic opportunities as Whites have.[24] Similarly, in Northern Ireland, some Protestants are not eager to give up their advantaged economic position, even when they claim Catholics among their friends. More importantly, community leaders are not likely to promote areas of cooperation between groups if they benefit from the continuation of inter-group hostility. For this reason, interdependence at the formal level may be a more powerful force for peace than its informal counterpart.

NOTES

1 Allport, Gordon W., *The Nature of Prejudice*, 1954, Reading, MA: Addison-Wesley.
2 Levin, Jack and Rabrenovic, Gordana, 'Hate Crimes and Ethnic Conflict: An Introduction', (2001) Vol 4 *American Behavioral Scientist* 45, pp 574–587.
3 Levin, Jack and McDevitt, Jack, *Hate Crimes Revisited: America's War on Those who are Different*, 2002, Boulder CO: Westview Press.
4 Formisano, Ronald P., *Boston Against Busing*, 1991, Chapel Hill: University of North Carolina Press; Lukas, J. Anthony, *Common Ground*, 1986, New York: Vintage Paperback.
5 Formisano, Ronald P., *op cit.*

6 Lukas, J. Anthony, *op cit.*
7 Allport, Gordon W., *op cit*; Lee, Y. T., Jussim, Lee J. and McCauley, Clark R., *Stereotype Accuracy: Toward Appreciating Group Differences*, 1995, Washington DC: American Psychological Association.
8 Shlachter, Barry, 'Jasper breathes a sigh of relief', 27 February 1999, *Fort Worth Star-Telegram.*
9 Temple-Raston, Dina, *A Death in Texas*, 2002, New York: Henry Holt.
10 Labalme, Jenny, 'Discussion Focuses on Hate Crimes', *Indianapolis Star* 17 November 1999, p B1.
11 Shlachter, Barry, *op cit.*
12 Levin, Jack and Rabrenovic, Gordana, 'Hate Crimes and Ethnic Conflict: An Introduction', (2001) 4 *American Behavioral Scientist* 45, pp 574–587.
13 Kochiyama, Yuri, 'Then Came the War', in Ferrante, Joan and Brown, Prince (ed.), *The Social Construction of Race and Ethnicity in the United States*, 2nd edn, 2001, Upper Saddle River, NJ: Prentice Hall.
14 Wilson, Robert and Hosokawa, Bill, *East to America: A History of the Japanese in the United States*, 1980, p 154, cited from Takaki, Ronald, *Strangers from a Different Shore: A History of Asian Americans*, 1989, p 380, Boston: Little, Brown and Company.
15 Commission on Wartime Relocation and Internment of Civilians, Personal Justice Denied: Report of the Commission on Wartime Relocation and Internment of Civilians, Washington, D.C., 1982 p 264 cited from Takaki, Ronald, *Strangers from a Different Shore, op cit*, p 380.
16 Lind, Andrew W., *Hawaii's Japanese: An Experiment in Democracy*, 1946, p 64, Princeton, cited from Takaki, Ronald, *op cit*, p 384.
17 Takaki, *op cit*, p 381.
18 Takaki, *op cit*, p 379.
19 Takaki, *op cit*, p 382.
20 Takaki, *op cit*, p 379.
21 Levin, Jack and McDevitt, Jack, *op cit.*
22 Selznick, Gertrude J. and Steinberg, Stephen, *The Tenacity of Prejudice*, 1969, New York: Harper Torchbooks.
23 Aronson, Elliot and Gonzalez, Alex, 'Desegregation, Jigsaw, and the Mexican-American Experience', in Katz, Phyllis A. and Taylor, Dalmas A. (ed.), *Eliminating Racism: Profiles in Controversy*, 1988, New York: Plenum Publishing; Aronson, Elliot and Patnoe, Shelly, *The Jigsaw Classroom*. 1997, New York: Longman; Miller, N., 'Personalization and the Promise of Contact Theory', (2002) 2 *Journal of Social Issues*, 58 pp 387–410.
24 Ribeiro, Darcy, *The Brazilian People: The Formation and Meaning of Brazil*, 2000, University Press of Florida.

Index